Read this book online today:

With SAP PRESS BooksOnline we offer you online access to knowledge from the leading SAP experts. Whether you use it as a beneficial supplement or as an alternative to the printed book, with SAP PRESS BooksOnline you can:

• Access your book anywhere, at any time. All you need is an Internet connection.
• Perform full text searches on your book and on the entire SAP PRESS library.
• Build your own personalized SAP library.

The SAP PRESS customer advantage:

Register this book today at *www.sap-press.com* and obtain exclusive free trial access to its online version. If you like it (and we think you will), you can choose to purchase permanent, unrestricted access to the online edition at a very special price!

Here's how to get started:

1. Visit *www.sap-press.com*.
2. Click on the link for SAP PRESS BooksOnline and login (or create an account).
3. Enter your free trial license key, shown below in the corner of the page.
4. Try out your online book with full, unrestricted access for a limited time!

Your personal free trial **license key** for this online book is:

63jp-2kin-7qey-vgtf

Optimizing Reverse Logistics with SAP® ERP

Dear Geoff and Serge

Enjoy reading

 PRESS

SAP® Essentials

Expert SAP knowledge for your day-to-day work

Whether you wish to expand your SAP knowledge, deepen it, or master a use case, SAP Essentials provide you with targeted expert knowledge that helps support you in your day-to-day work. To the point, detailed, and ready to use.

SAP PRESS is a joint initiative of SAP and Galileo Press. The know-how offered by SAP specialists combined with the expertise of the Galileo Press publishing house offers the reader expert books in the field. SAP PRESS features first-hand information and expert advice, and provides useful skills for professional decision-making.

SAP PRESS offers a variety of books on technical and business related topics for the SAP user. For further information, please visit our website: *www.sap-press.com.*

Martin Murray
Discover Logistics with SAP ERP
2009, 385 pp.
978-1-59229-230-1

Rajen Iyer
Effective SAP SD
2007, 365 pp.
978-1-59229-101-4

Martin Murray
SAP Warehouse Management: Functionality and Technical Configuration
2008, 504 pp.
978-1-59229-133-5

Martin Murray
Maximize Your Warehouse Operations with SAP ERP
2010, 300 pp.
978-1-59229-309-4

Srivathsan Narayanan

Optimizing Reverse Logistics with SAP® ERP

Galileo Press

Bonn • Boston

Galileo Press is named after the Italian physicist, mathematician and philosopher Galileo Galilei (1564–1642). He is known as one of the founders of modern science and an advocate of our contemporary, heliocentric worldview. His words *Eppur se muove* (And yet it moves) have become legendary. The Galileo Press logo depicts Jupiter orbited by the four Galilean moons, which were discovered by Galileo in 1610.

Editor Meg Dunkerley
Technical Editor Rajen Iyer
Copyeditor Julie McNamee
Cover Design Jill Winitzer
Photo Credit Image Copyright jokerpro. Used under license from Shutterstock.com.
Layout Design Vera Brauner
Production Editor Kelly O'Callaghan
Assistant Production Editor Graham Geary
Typesetting Publishers' Design and Production Services, Inc.
Printed and bound in Canada

ISBN 978-1-59229-325-4
© 2010 by Galileo Press Inc., Boston (MA)
1st Edition 2010

Library of Congress Cataloging-in-Publication Data
Narayanan, Srivathsan.
    Optimizing reverse logistics with SAP ERP / Srivathsan Narayanan. — 1st ed.
        p. cm.
    Includes bibliographical references and index.
    ISBN-13: 978-1-59229-325-4 (alk. paper)
    ISBN-10: 1-59229-325-5 (alk. paper)
    1. Business logistics.   2. Production management.   3. SAP ERP.   I. Title.
    HD38.5.N37 2010
    658.70285'53 — dc22

                                    2010005043

To my family and friends who have always supported and encouraged me along my journey of knowledge. Thank you for the inspiration and support in helping me give back in the form of this book.

Contents

Preface

In writing this book, I addressed the fundamental need for a good reverse logistics book that provides a strong foundation for understanding the basics of reverse logistics and explains the SAP ERP solutions.

Reverse logistics is a fairly complex business process that can deliver many benefits for companies that implement solutions to make this process effective. This book isn't a training document to perform transactions in SAP ERP, but it's more of a resource that describes the basic SAP tools, objects, and solutions, and teaches you how to configure the software, enabling you to set up a good baseline reverse logistics solution for your company.

Who This Book Is For

This book is for anyone interested in SAP ERP solutions for reverse logistics. Although this book may not provide training on every transaction that can be performed in reverse logistics, it certainly provides an overview of the reverse logistics process and the SAP solution for the process. This book serves as a guide for all supply chain managers or analysts who work in the logistics area and focus on reverse logistics. Whether you've already implemented SAP ERP or are thinking about implementing it, this book provides you with the knowledge to help you make the right decisions regarding how the SAP ERP system needs to be set up to enable effective reverse logistics for your company.

This book is also for SAP ERP functional and technical consultants who can use this book to gain knowledge about topics such as warranty claim processing and validation/substitution rules (VSRs) that are very powerful tools provided by SAP ERP.

As we move toward more automation, we're always looking for tools that can help us achieve the goal of doing fewer transactions and avoiding duplicate data entries to make system processes more efficient. This book was written with the goal of providing you with the first step toward a completely automated reverse logistics solution. This solution provides users with a frontend featuring a series of questions. If they are answered, the system provides the user shipping documentation to ship the products to a company-preferred location for repair, recycle, or scrap.

Organization of This Book

This book is designed to teach you about the reverse logistics solutions in SAP ERP. Although other core applications are mentioned in this book, the focus is primarily on SAP ERP and the functionalities within this application. The book is divided into eight chapters to explain the different subprocesses of reverse logistics and also the interfaces with the finance organization. Let's take a look at each chapter in detail.

Chapter 1 – Reverse Logistics

In this chapter, we discuss the definition of reverse logistics and how the process spans across several organizations in a company. All of these organizations perform key functions that are chained together to provide the overall reverse logistics value to the company. This chapter explains the functions of all of these organizations in detail and provides a good platform for the subsequent chapters in describing the reverse logistics business process and subprocesses in detail.

Chapter 2 – Returns

This chapter describes the returns process in detail and covers both internal and external returns. In internal returns, we'll review products returned by either a quality engineer or service engineer, and walk through the SAP ERP processing of this return from the engineer back into the company's network. External returns deal with the returns from an outside customer and provide details about performing this process in SAP ERP. In addition, the chapter provides details about configuring objects in SAP ERP such as order types, delivery types, and item categories.

Chapter 3 – Refurbishment

Refurbishment is the process of accepting the return of a defective product and repairing it so it can be be sold again as a refurbished or new product. In this chapter, we'll discuss refurbishment with repair done in-house as well as through a subcontractor. SAP capabilities, such as production orders and subcontracting purchase orders, are discussed in detail.

Chapter 4 – Customer Paid Repair

One of the very powerful SAP solutions provided in reverse logistics is the repair order and its interface with service management and finance. In this chapter, we'll discuss customer paid repair and the SAP solution provided for this purpose. The solution covers repairing the product in-house and subcontracting the repair, as well as how to roll up the costs from the service back into the repair order to bill the customer.

Chapter 5 – Warranty Claim Processing

Entitlement validation with both customers and vendors is very important to ensure that the overall goal of recapturing value is met. In this chapter, we'll discuss warranty claim processing in SAP ERP, which provides entitlement validation for customers as well as vendors. We'll also look into using the validation/substitution rules (VSRs) to define rules for solving complex validation requirements.

Chapter 6 – Serial Number Management in Reverse Logistics

Serialization is another standard SAP ERP functionality that provides a variety of benefits for reverse logistics. Even though this functionality provides benefits, it requires some complex configuration and process compliance that we'll look into in this chapter. Along with serialization, we'll also cover batch management, which is another useful tool for reverse logistics.

Chapter 7 – Finance in Reverse Logistics

Accounting, costing, and valuation are very important to enable that you are recapturing value properly via reverse logistics. In this chapter, we'll discuss different SAP objects that enable proper financial postings and valuation.

Chapter 8 – Conclusion

Finally, we'll recap all of the data in the previous chapters and discuss some enhancement options available for reverse logistics that will create user-friendly SAP ERP reverse logistics solutions.

Introduction

SAP software contains many components that are designed to provide system solutions to complex business requirements. In this introduction, we'll examine the different functionalities in SAP ERP that can be used to handle the business requirements for the reverse logistics business process.

Generally speaking, reverse logistics is defined as "the process of planning, implementing, and controlling the efficient, cost-effective flow of raw materials, in-process inventory, finished goods, and related information from the point of consumption to the point of origin for the purpose of recapturing or proper disposal."

As you notice, the reverse logistics process involves materials that are in different stages of the lifecycle and different organizations in the company. The complexity of reverse logistics arises from the fact that there are various organizations involved and a lot of processes that need to be completed to achieve the goal of recapturing value.

SAP is a leading provider of business software, and by using SAP solutions, companies of all sizes, including small businesses and midsize companies, can reduce costs, optimize performance, and gain the insight and agility needed to close the gap between strategy and execution. The SAP Business Suite contains the following core applications: SAP CRM (SAP Customer Relationship Management), SAP ERP, SAP PLM (SAP Product Lifecycle Management), SAP SCM (SAP Supply Chain Management), and SAP SRM (SAP Supplier Relationship Management). Most of the logistics and reverse logistics functions are provided in SAP ERP, and a few functions are also available in SAP SCM.

SAP provides the following capabilities that can be used in a reverse logistics context by using the service parts management software:

- Warranty management
- Claims processing
- Entitlement management
- Returns logistics
- In-house and outsourced repair

- Remanufacturing and refurbishment
- Scrap and recycling management

Clearly, SAP software provides capabilities to handle almost every company's logistics and reverse logistics processes. While SAP software provides the best practices available for reverse logistics, it still needs to be configured according to the requirements to enable effective reverse logistics.

Companies focus more on sales and forward logistics because that is the goal of almost every department in each company: sell and make money. This concept is adapted in almost every company invariably, even though each product is different: consumer goods, high-tech products, and even services. Reverse logistics is an afterthought in most of the companies because reverse logistics impacts revenue *after* the product is returned, inspected, repaired, and then sold to make revenue or profit for the company. But reverse logistics provides value in terms of monitoring the quality of the products sold and allows the companies to provide customer paid repair service, which provides companies an additional revenue stream for the company.

In addition, reverse logistics allows companies to validate customer entitlement and in turn provides customers excellent service by honoring the warranty. Vendor-provided warranty recovery is also contained in reverse logistics, which ensures that defective products from the vendors are returned for credit or replacement.

As we mentioned, SAP software provides solutions for reverse logistics based on best practices in different industries. Remember, however, that the software needs to be configured, customized, and, in certain cases, enhanced to meet the requirements of every company. To understand the configuration available in SAP ERP and also build enhancements, you need a good understanding of the functionality available in the standard SAP ERP system, and an excellent basic business process understanding of reverse logistics.

This book provides you with a good basic understanding of reverse logistics processes, as well as the SAP ERP system solution available. Enhancement points in certain cases are also discussed. The goal of this book is to provide you with the basic knowledge of the reverse logistics business processes and the SAP configuration and tools.

Let's get down to understanding, improving, and optimizing the reverse logistics process in your company using SAP ERP.

Reverse logistics provides several benefits to companies. Throughout this chapter, we'll discuss how to get the maximum return via reverse logistics and what that entails for all business processes within a company.

1 Reverse Logistics

Reverse logistics is an important process or collection of functions in your company's supply chain. If the business processes involved work as you've designed them, then reverse logistics creates an alternate source of supply, provides repair and refurbishment services to the customers, and increases the profitability of the company. In addition to this, reverse logistics protects the company's intellectual property by controlling the return and destruction of the products in a controlled manner. Reverse logistics provides the company with insight into quality issues that helps improve the quality of the products and reduces returns, thus improving the company's profits. Customers in every industry expect companies to provide an easy and seamless returns process. So, reverse logistics is an important requirement for providing excellent customer service and satisfaction, and it helps achieve several corporate goals such as reduced inventory, better quality, and increased customer satisfaction. Reverse logistics is also required in almost all types of industries, including but not limited to high tech, manufacturing, and consumer products.

The first step in optimizing reverse logistics in your company is to understand what reverse logistics is and how all business processes in your company interact to enable reverse logistics.

1.1 Definition of Reverse Logistics

The Reverse Logistics Association defines reverse logistics as follows:

> All activity associated with a product/service after the point of sale, the ultimate goal to optimize or make more efficient aftermarket activity, thus saving money and environmental resources.

Reverse logistics refers to the processes that control how products are returned and also the processing of the returns to either restock or refurbish the products.

Returning certain products and scrapping them in a controlled manner is very important in situations where the company's intellectual property needs to be protected. The reverse logistics process also protects the warranty entitlement provided to the customer so that the products under warranty can be returned for a customer replacement or credit. After the product is returned to the company, the product could also be returned to the vendor, if the product is under the vendor's warranty.

Reverse logistics is also the process that provides inspection requirements to be able to classify the products as return to stock, refurbish, or scrap. Reverse logistics also tracks returns to provide input into the product quality, vendor quality, and product performance.

SAP provides an end-to-end solution for managing reverse logistics, including customer returns, entitlement management, hazardous materials management, repair, and refurbishment. Understanding what SAP ERP provides and configuring the SAP ERP system to meet the company's requirements will ensure maximization of the reverse logistics capabilities for the company. This book provides more insight into SAP ERP capabilities and how to configure them. Let's move on to review the reverse logistics processes in SAP.

1.2 Business Processes in Reverse Logistics and SAP

Different departments/organizations within a company are responsible for executing the business processes that enable reverse logistics, as shown in Figure 1.1.

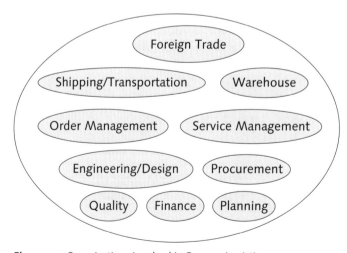

Figure 1.1 Organizations Involved in Reverse Logistics

The organizations in Figure 1.1 execute business processes in reverse logistics. These processes are displayed in Figure 1.2.

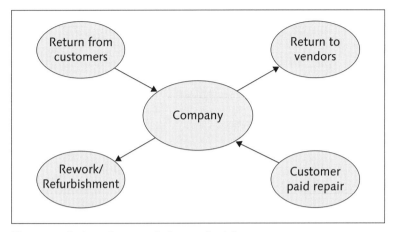

Figure 1.2 Business Processes in Reverse Logistics

We'll now look into the organizations and the business processes they execute in detail for reverse logistics. We'll also cover the system requirements and SAP solutions for these business processes.

1.2.1 Engineering/Design

The engineering and design team in a company makes one of the most important decisions for reverse logistics. This team determines how a material that is returned, refurbished, and repaired is represented in the system and the role of the other business processes in the reverse logistics processes.

Companies use different mechanisms both inside and outside the system to identify materials that are in a condition other than "new." The material number used to identify the material in new condition is called a base part number or a base material number. In this book, we'll refer to this material as the base material number, which means the material is in original or new condition.

Some companies use material attributes in the system, such as the material group, to identify that a material is broken, under warranty, or refurbished. Some companies use different material numbers or the base material number with suffixes to identify the other conditions of the material. For example, if the base material number was 00010, 00010-B is the material number for the material that is broken, and 00010-R for the material that has been refurbished.

Table 1.1 spells out some of the pros and cons of using a different material number or a suffix to identify the condition of the material.

Pro	Con
Different material numbers for materials with different physical conditions help warehouse users to store and identify parts easily. The material number and description are printed in the material identifier tag or label to help users with the identification.	Data maintenance in the SAP ERP system increases substantially. Every base material number needs to have a subsequent broken, refurbished, and repair material created in the system. Every attribute for every material number needs to be maintained. This increases the load on the system resources and also the human effort needed to maintain these materials in sync. If any change needs to be done to the new material number, that change also needs to be checked against all of the other material numbers to make sure those part numbers are also updated.
Prevents the physical mix up of broken and original parts.	Because material attributes aren't available in all SAP ERP programs, custom coding might be needed to use this field effectively in reverse logistics programs.
The costing of broken material can be different from the original material. This allows inventory value to be less for the broken and refurbished material compared to the base material in new condition.	Planning tasks need to differentiate material numbers to not include broken parts during replenishment planning and safety stock calculations.
Credit can be provided to the customer based on the material number that is being entered in the sales order or when received in the warehouse after inspection during receipt.	Serial number maintenance becomes an issue because every time a material needs to be changed to a different material number because the condition of the material changed, the serial number record needs to be updated in the system to reflect this change. Because the new material number and broken material number are unique material numbers, the serial number records could also exist uniquely for these material numbers even though in reality the broken material and the new material/serial number combination are the same piece of material but at different points of the lifecycle. So the serial number record should be updated with the correct material number instead of creating a new serial number record for every material number when the material number changes because of the change of the material's physical condition. The serial number update for the material number will need custom programs in the SAP system.

Table 1.1 Pros and Cons of Using Different Material Numbers or Suffixes to Differentiate Material Condition in Reverse Logistics

Pro	Con
When pricing materials to the customer, a refurbished material can be sold for a different price based on the material number because condition records can be maintained by material numbers.	Pricing record maintenance is a huge effort because the material numbers for new and refurbished material are different, so the pricing record needs to be maintained separately for these two part numbers.
Checking availability of the materials for substitution is easy because the refurbished materials have a different part number.	

Table 1.1 Pros and Cons of Using Different Material Numbers or Suffixes to Differentiate Material Condition in Reverse Logistics (Cont.)

In general, the engineering team consults with the other departments and then decides how to represent the different conditions of the material in the system.

The following section describes the system requirements for the engineering team to support reverse logistics processes.

System Requirements

As mentioned previously, the engineering team decides how to identify the material based on condition, so the team requires the SAP ERP system to be able to identify the material based on the decision made for the company. The decision could be a different material number, a different material attribute, or a different material number with a suffix to identify the condition.

All of the subsequent processes such as planning, logistics, order management, and finance, should also have a system design that is capable of handling the engineering team's decision for material identification. The SAP system provides configuration and objects that can handle these requirements, as described in the next section.

System Capability and Objects

You can handle the material identification requirement by using a material master record and the attributes available in the system, such as the material group.

> **Note**
>
> Custom programs may be needed to handle subsequent process requirements if the system needs to execute decisions based on the material number being returned. When SAP ERP is being implemented and during the analysis phase, the implementation team analyzes the requirements for custom programs due to this decision. So all of the company's teams should work with the implementation team to provide the program requirements based on this decision (material number with suffix, new material number, or any other identification).

For example, if a material being returned as a broken material is identified with a "B" suffix, the system needs to be capable of changing the serial number record of the new material to indicate it's now a broken material with a material number that contains a B suffix. Failure to do so will result in two serial number records: one for the base material and the other for the broken material. This will result in losing the history of the material number and the record of the different material movements that the material went through that are captured in the serial number history.

> **Example**
>
> In an automobile manufacturing company, material number M001 refers to a motor, and material number M001B refers to the defected motor and is considered unusable without rework. Because material number M001 is serialized, all of the material movements from the point of receipt of the material into inventory are tracked in SAP. So when a customer returns the broken motor with serial number 001, the serial number record for material number M001 and serial number 001 should be changed or updated to indicate that serial number 001 now refers to material M001B instead of M001. Failure to do this will result in two serial number records: one for M001 and serial number record 001 and the other for M001B and serial number record 001. This will also mean all of the history of material M001 and the serial number isn't tracked after return of the broken material. This is an issue for the quality department that needs the complete history of the material and the transitions from one material number to another because of the change in the physical condition. This data is used to track the complete lifecycle of the material from the receipt to the scrapping of the material.

The engineering team also provides drawings and standards for the quality department to use for defining the inspection characteristics. The characteristics are used to inspect the material and failure to meet the inspection tests during receipt of the material will result in the material being returned to the vendor.

1.2.2 Order Management

Order management is another important business process in reverse logistics. It refers to the process of collecting the required information from a customer and creating a sales order/quotation in the system. Customer Service Representatives (CSRs) typically perform this duty when they receive a call or email from customers with the order requirements.

The CSR creates the sales order by entering all of the data provided by the customer in the SAP ERP system and provides the customer with the information needed to return the product if the order is being created for returns. When an order is created to return a product, it's generally referred to as a *return order*.

When return orders are created, the company needs the following information from the customer to accept and process a return:

- Forward/original order number for reference
- Condition of the material being returned
- Serial number of the material
- Batch number of the material
- Return-from location (customer location)
- Customer contact information

After this information is provided by the customer, the CSR creates the return order and provides the following information to the customer:

- Return order number
- Delivery number (if applicable)
- Return-to location
- Return label with carrier information (if company is responsible for shipping cost to ship the product back to the company)

In certain cases, especially in the consumer goods industry, the return label is provided in the box in which the customer initially receives the material. The customer uses this label to return the material to the company. For other industries, such as semi-conductor, the company determines the return-to location based on the data provided by the customer. For example, if the material returned is contaminated, then the company moves the material to a location that can follow special handling procedures to decontaminate the material. Also in certain cases, the company might want to repair the material by sending it to a vendor. Depending on the vendor's location, the company requests the customer to ship the product to a location closest to the vendor to minimize handling within the company. Some companies also drop ship the material from the customer directly to the vendor provided there is an agreement with the customer and vendor to protect the company's interests.

Also if the material returned is under warranty with the vendor from whom the company purchased the material, then the company might ship the material to the vendor to get a replacement material or credit from the vendor. The company verifies the vendor warranty information based on the serial number of the product being returned or the forward order reference.

The replacement sales order is created if the material provided is under warranty to the customer and the customer requires a replacement material. If the customer doesn't want replacement material and instead requests credit, then it's provided to the customer via a credit memo that is also created by the CSR in SAP ERP. Typically, the actual credit is provided only after the material is returned, and the condition of the part is verified and inspected by the company.

To perform all of the activities described so far, the order management team needs the SAP ERP system to meet the following requirements.

System Requirements

Order management process requires the system capability to allow the following:

▶ **Easy entry of data into the sales order**
Most of the data in the return sales order should be automatically determined based on the customer and material information that is stored in the SAP ERP system in the customer master and material master. This includes the product's source location for return and the material's pricing based on the condition. Additional data such as contamination details and destination location can be entered during order creation manually or using custom coding in SAP ERP. The reason for rejection or return is also identified at the item level in the return sales order.

Automatic pricing calculations should be made based on the condition of the material being returned, and the customer should be provided credit for the returned material. This should be done immediately upon the creation of the return order or the return delivery or after the goods receipt of the part. The company determines the timing of the credit, and the SAP ERP system should be configured accordingly.

▶ **Workflow requirements**

Some returns need to be approved by the order entry supervisors and the finance department before the customer is credited for the return. This becomes an important requirement in companies where the credit is provided before the material is inspected in the warehouse upon goods receipt.

▶ **Different order types for the variations in the type of return**

If a material is being returned because it failed during the warranty period provided by the company, the replacement sales order should be created as a free of cost order. In the SAP ERP system, the replacement order should be triggered automatically based on the customer's request for a replacement material instead of credit.

Some products are shipped back to the company for repair or refurbishment. This process can be considered a return because the material that is being returned isn't in new condition. However, from a company's perspective, this is a service provided to the customer, and paid for by the customer, so it's considered a service, not a return. This process also should be handled by SAP using a different order to indicate repair and not return. In addition to this, the system should allow the company to bill the customer for the repair and capture all of the costs associated with the repair so that the company can bill the customer properly.

▶ **Reports to show return and repair order information**

The order management team will need reports to show the statistics of return orders created and other information regarding different types of returns. The reports also should show information about the repairs performed by the company with details about the customer, material, and costs associated with the repair.

▶ **Outputs**

When customers ship a material back to the company, they should reference the return order/return delivery information in the documentation accompanying the shipment. This will ensure smooth receipt and further processing of the material in the company's warehouse. Most often the company provides the customer with the return delivery document, a return packing list, or a return packing label to attach with the returned material. This output needs to be configured in SAP ERP so that this can be generated at the time of order/delivery creation and can be sent to the customer via an email or regular mail. This return document should contain all information about the product being returned, including the material number, condition of the part, contamination information, serial number, and batch number.

Figure 1.3 shows the data requested from the customer for creating a return order in SAP ERP and also, after the creation of the return order, the data being sent to the customer either in an email or by output of the return delivery or a label.

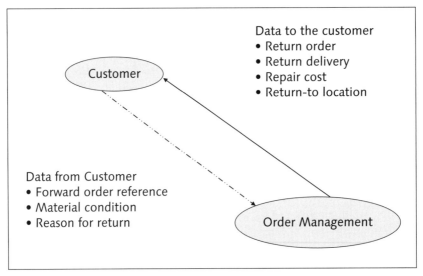

Figure 1.3 Data Requested from the Customer and Data Provided to the Customer by Order Management in SAP ERP

System Capability and Objects

SAP ERP is capable of handling all of these requirements for the order management team using standard configuration and some custom development. The following are some of the objects that enable you to handle these requirements using SAP ERP.

▶ **Sales order**
This object captures all of the data entered by the CSR and is the starting point for handling customer returns. SAP ERP provides order types that can be configured for returns that are different from the forward order types. The configuration of the return order type drives several subsequent actions and activities in the system, such as movement type determination, cost center, and accounting, which differentiate forward movements to the return movements. Figure 1.4 shows the display of a return sales order in SAP ERP. To display a return sales order use Transaction VA03 in SAP ERP. In Transaction VA03, if you enter the sales order number, the sales order details are displayed as shown in Figure 1.4.

Notice in Figure 1.4 the return sales order has a header that contains data relevant for all of the items in the order, as well as items that contain data specific to the item. Header data includes sold to party information, ship to party information, and the order reason. For return orders, you can specify "Returns" as the reason for the order. You can also use reasons such as poor quality, damaged in transit, and so on. The order reason in the header applies to all of the items in the order as mentioned before. The net price of the return sales order is also displayed in the header.

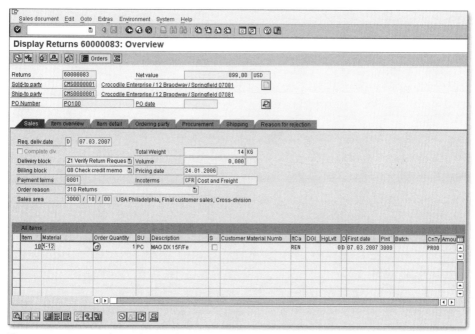

Figure 1.4 Return Sales Order Display in SAP ERP

Figure 1.5 displays the line item details of a return sales order. You can display the item details by selecting the item and double-clicking on the item or by selecting the item and selecting the item details icon below the items in the return sales order. The line item contains a lot of data, including the material number that is being returned, quantity of the material being returned, reason for rejection, and the pricing elements that indicate the net price of the item. To display the pricing details of the item, you need to select the item and then select the Conditions tab of the sales order line item. The reason for rejection at the item level is exclusively used to explain rejection by the customer for that line item. If a customer sends multiple line items back in a single returns sales order, this field at the line item level describes the reason for every line item.

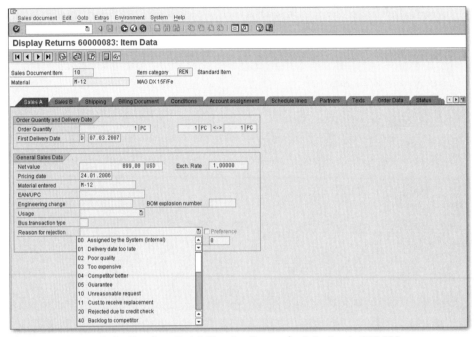

Figure 1.5 Return Order Line Item Detail Showing Reason for Rejection in SAP ERP

▶ **Credit memo**
   SAP ERP provides standard capability to create a credit memo to the customers if the customer expects credit instead of a replacement material. Credit memo is also another type of sales order provided in the standard SAP ERP system. The order type used for a credit memo is "CR" in the standard SAP ERP system.

▶ **Quotation**
   SAP ERP enables you to create a quotation that can be used for repair process. The customer is provided a quote, and if the quote is accepted, the company creates an order for the repair service. The repair order can then be created with reference to the quotation.

▶ **Repair order**
   Repair order is another type of sales order that is used for customer paid repairs. Repair orders drive repair processes, including internal and external repair. SAP ERP allows the company to create the repair order and create external purchase orders (POs) and internal service orders with reference to the repair order. This

allows the cost of the PO and the service order to be included in the repair order, enabling the company to easily bill the customer for the complete repair.

▶ **Pricing**

Using standard condition techniques, pricing can be determined during any type of order creation. Using pricing determination procedures, the pricing can be modified according to the type of the order: forward, return, or repair. In addition to this, the cost of the material can be included in the pricing based on the material attributes or the material number. Discount information can also be maintained in pricing conditions and can be configured to be used only for certain customers and certain types of orders. Figure 1.6 shows the pricing calculations of an item in the return sales order. As you can see, there are different pricing conditions such as PR00 – Net price, RC00 – Quantity discount, and VPRS – cost. The pricing procedures are defined in the configuration that determines which pricing conditions are applicable in every order. Different criteria can be used to determine pricing procedures such as sales organization, customer, and order type.

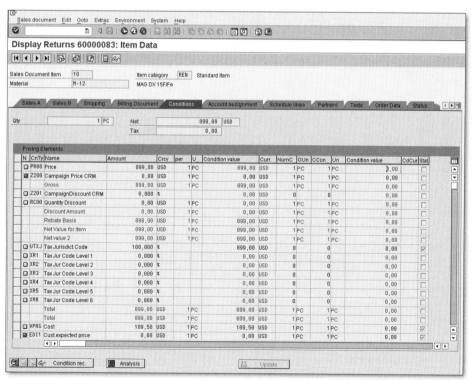

Figure 1.6 Return Order Line Item Detail Showing Pricing Calculation in an Order

▶ **Workflow**

SAP ERP provides workflow capability that enables approvals for returns or for credit. The workflow can be set up to include multiple levels of approvals based on the value of the credit/return and also based on the customer type. Workflow is also used to process a customer complaint order that could result in a credit or a debit memo request, a returns order, or a delivery to the customer free of charge. SAP ERP provides a standard business object that can be configured in the SAP ERP workflow to process the customer complaint order. Figure 1.7 shows the details of the SAP ERP business object BUS2033, which represents the customer complaint order. To display the details of the business object, you can use Transaction SW01; if you enter the business object number BUS2033, SAP ERP will display the details as shown in Figure 1.7. To configure the workflow process for BUS2033 used for customer complaint orders or to activate workflow for approvals of the returns order, contact your company's workflow administrator.

Figure 1.7 Business Object BUS2033 in SAP ERP Used for Customer Complaint Order Workflow Process

Let's now proceed to the planning organization requirements and processes.

1.2.3 Planning

The planning department plays an important role in making decisions regarding reverse logistics flow within the company. Planning decides if a product needs to be brought back into the supply chain for reuse, refurbishment, or repair. The planning team considers the material's condition, the material's version to see if it's worth refurbishing, and the material's forecast to determine whether to bring the material back into inventory based on the available inventory. To make this decision, the planning organization considers the following factors:

▶ What kind of products need to be included in materials requirement planning (e.g., broken parts shouldn't be included in planning because they can't be used as is).

▶ If a product is needed to be brought back to the network to destroy it in a controlled manner due to intellectual property control.

▶ Which plant should the return material be shipped to if they are usable based on the current inventory in all plants in the network.

The planning team also provides input on the available refurbished material inventory to the order management and customer service team to be able to substitute or sell those products at a discount to customers. The planning team is also responsible for redistributing inventory to the different network locations and also determines where the viable return stock should be sent. This determination is done based on the location of the return and the proximity to the nearest stocking location. For internal repairs, the planning department also considers the requirements of components needed for repair or kitting, and plans for acquiring or producing the inventory of components.

Because the planning department performs important functions for your company, it also requires the system to support important requirements.

System Requirements

The planning team has system requirements that need to be met to control the level of inventory and the product return decision. The following are the system requirements for planning:

▶ Planning needs to know the condition of the material to determine whether the material needs to be included in replenishment planning or whether to order additional quantities of the material from external vendors. The material condition can be identified either by material number or by a different material attribute in the material master in SAP ERP.

▶ When returned materials are brought back into the warehouse that manages both base parts and broken parts, the inventory of the broken parts needs to be eliminated from materials requirement planning.

▶ When a material is sent out for rework, the process needs to capture the inventory of the expected refurbished parts after rework to include it in planning for materials that are in inventory for sale or for internal use. The refurbished parts are generally used by the company when performing a service to a customer for whom the service contract is not based on the material used but instead is based on maintaining a service level only, or the material is sold to customers with a lesser price with an extended warranty.

▶ System capability is also needed to identify the return-to location for both internal and external returns to reduce the handling and transportation costs.

▶ Internal stock transport orders and intercompany order capability also need to be set up to move the returns and repair material within and outside of a company code. This includes shipping products across borders.

▶ Materials requirement planning should be set up in the SAP ERP system to consider materials in good and refurbished condition and also avoid materials that are broken and waiting to be scrapped.

▶ For purge or quality recall either due to internal quality reasons or for an external vendor, global recall planning requires the system to provide inventory visibility for the parts across the network and also with the customer information. In addition, the system should be able to return these parts to the centralized location from where the parts are returned to the vendor or scrapped.

▶ Planning also needs the consumption information for both external and internal customers to be able to forecast and plan for materials requirements.

Figure 1.8 provides the details of the communication that the planning organization has with other teams in the company. The figure provides the data to and from the planning organization to the order management team for reverse logistics purposes. During the return order creation, the order management team provides the details of the material condition along with the other information described in the figure and receives the return or scrap decision along with the return-to location information from the planning organization.

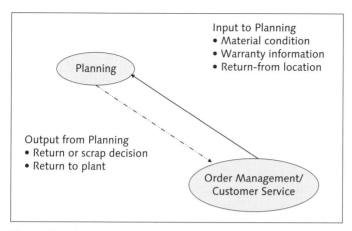

Figure 1.8 Planning in Reverse Logistics

System Capability and Objects

SAP ERP includes the following system capabilities to support the preceding planning requirements:

▸ **Materials requirement planning**
SAP ERP provides this capability to plan for materials based on consumption and forecast. Based on the setup of the material master, you can eliminate materials or include materials in materials requirement planning. In addition to this, you can also define what incoming documents, such as POs, can be considered for planning. Also planning can be done at different organization levels, thus ensuring that storage locations containing broken material inventory can be excluded when planning for that plant.

▸ **Inventory reporting**
SAP ERP provides extensive reporting on the inventory of materials in the company. Reports can be expanded to provide more details about specific materials and material groups as well. Planning organization uses these reports to plan for materials based on the forecast and the inventory.

▸ **Transport orders**
Stock transport and intercompany transport orders are available to be configured in the system. This setup allows materials to be moved within the network within or outside of a company code. This is needed in reverse logistics because materials need to be moved from the return location to the returns/repair plant that consolidates these materials to be sent to either the vendor or to the scrap

plant. If it's being returned to stock, the part can be transported to the centralized warehouse location where it can be stocked.

1.2.4 Procurement/Purchasing

Procurement plays a vital role in reverse logistics. If a material that is returned to the supply chain due to a defect is still under warranty with the OEM vendor, the material can be returned to the vendor for either a replacement or for credit. In general, to return a material to the vendor, the PO that was used for buying the material from the vendor needs to be referenced. In addition, if the material is serialized or batch managed, this data needs to be provided to the vendor to obtain a replacement or credit. In some cases, the material can be returned to the vendor so that they can refurbish the material and provide it back to the company free of charge and with additional warranty. This warranty data needs to be tracked by material number/serial number combination. The importance of serial number management in reverse logistics will be discussed later in Chapter 6, Serial Number Management in Reverse Logistics.

When the company performs a service to repair materials that belong to a customer, the company could be performing the service either using internal facilities or using an external vendor. The planning team compares the cost of performing this service internally versus externally and makes a determination on where the service should be performed. To do this, the planning team contacts the procurement team to get a quote from the vendor, and then the planning team compares it to the internal costs and makes the final determination to repair internally or externally. To get a quote, the procurement team needs to provide the vendor with the materials' condition, version (if the part is version managed), and contamination status so the vendor can provide an estimated cost to repair the material.

For customer paid repair processes, where customers send materials that they own to be repaired by the company, the procurement team gets a quote from the vendor and provides that information to the order management team to use for quoting the repair price to the customer. If the price is agreed upon, the procurement team creates either an expense PO or a subcontracting PO to get the material repaired. This PO is created as a part of the customer paid repair process, which uses a repair sales order to capture all of the costs for the repair, including the associated material costs.

The procurement team is also responsible for establishing contracts with the vendor in situations where the vendor is expected to repair a certain number of materials or perform repair for a total amount mentioned in the value contract. This is done either by a materials-based contract or a value-based contract.

When a repair is being performed, the vendor might determine that the part isn't repairable. In that case, the procurement team works with the quality and planning teams to determine the best method to get the product either scrapped or destroyed in a controlled manner. The vendor charges for the service by providing an invoice against the PO that was created for the repair. In some cases, the customer can ask the company to perform analysis on the part to identify the reasons for failure, and the company performs this either internally or by using a vendor and bills the customer for this service. This process is typically called failure analysis.

To perform the functions in this section, the procurement team needs the system to support the processes. In the next section, we'll discuss the requirements for these processes.

System Requirements

The system requirements from the procurement team are as follows:

▶ The procurement team needs the capability to create a request for quotation (RFQ), a purchase requisition, and a PO to handle reverse logistics situations.

▶ Easy data entry for purchase requisition, PO, and RFC. Most of the data should be defaulted, such as the material and vendor information, so that the manual data entry is limited.

▶ A release strategy to release subcontracting POs and expense POs. A release strategy is the list of approvers that the order needs to be passed through before it's considered released for procurement.

▶ Invoice setup for accepting invoices from vendors. The accounts payable team configuration and sets up this process.

▶ Workflow to approve/reject POs based on customers' acceptance/rejection of the repair based on the price quoted to them.

▶ Return to vendor capability in the system. Generally, this is triggered by the result of the quality inspection of the received material from the vendor.

▶ If a material returned by either a customer or an engineer is under vendor warranty, then the procurement team needs to be able to return it to the vendor with all relevant documentation referencing the original PO.

▶ Warranty tracking for materials sourced from the vendor. When a material is bought into the network from a vendor, certain details about the material, such as the serial number, need to be captured in the company's system. This enables communication with the vendor regarding any failure of the material and the recovery of the warranty.

▶ The history of failure of materials procured from a vendor is needed to evaluate the vendor's capability and also to monitor the quality of the materials supplied by the vendor.

Figure 1.9 describes the communication among the vendors, the procurement team, and the order management team. The order management team provides data such as the material's condition and serial number to the procurement team, and the procurement team in turn sends information regarding warranty (if applicable). For repairs, the procurement team provides material information such as material number, material version, and condition of the material to the vendor. The vendor then provides the quote for repair or provides the return material authorization number if a product under warranty needs to be returned to the vendor.

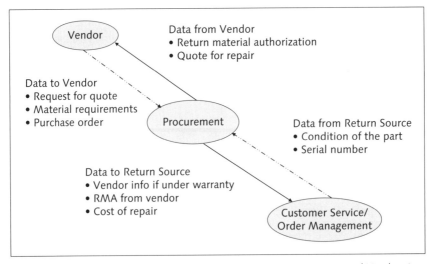

Figure 1.9 Data Transferred Among Procurement, Order Management, and Vendors in Reverse Logistics

System Capability and Objects

SAP ERP provides processes and system objects to handle the procurement requirements described in the previous section. They include the following:

▶ **RFQs, purchase requisitions, and POs:** These are all standard documents available in the standard SAP ERP system. These are documents that can be configured to meet the requirements of the procurement team.

The vendors submit invoices with reference to the PO for subcontracting. The accounts payable team can validate the invoice with the services provided by the vendor and also the receipt of the refurbished material or service. The invoice can also be accessed via the PO history of the PO line item.

▶ **Release strategy:** These strategies can be configured to allow approvals of documents by different managers in the company before the document is considered approved.

▶ **Return to Vendor:** SAP ERP provides return-to-vendor capability either with or without reference to the original PO. The return-to-vendor process can also be integrated into the quality processes to be able to reject an inspection lot and initiate the return to vendor based on the decision of the inspection process.

▶ **Vendor evaluation:** All quality issues and returns can be recorded in the system to provide details about the performance and quality of the vendors. SAP ERP provides standard configuration and reports to capture and report vendor performance based on quality, delivery time, and cost.

▶ **Warranty provided by vendor:** The serial number management functionality allows the vendor's warranty data to be captured in the serial number record. This data can be captured at the time of receipt from the vendor, and the end warranty date can be updated in the serial number record based on the length of warranty provided by the vendor.

▶ **Workflow requirements:** Workflow can be enabled to allow approvals by purchasing managers and other departments for accepting any changes proposed by the vendor with regards to the cost of the repair or additional materials needed to perform the repair.

1.2.5 Warehousing

Warehousing is a process within the logistics framework that deals with stocking the materials within the warehouse. This also includes receiving the products from the vendor and putting them away into the warehouse. The warehouse also deals with receiving returns from the customer and from the service engineers performing service on customers' machines.

The warehouse processes that are relevant for reverse logistics include the following:

- **Receiving returned products:** This receipt can be against a return sales order/returns delivery from a customer or a receipt against an internal return done in the system using a stock transport order or an intercompany transport order.

- **Identifying the returned part:** The returned parts need to be clearly identified using a label or any other form of identifier to prevent a mix up of regular inventory and broken parts inventory.

- **Storing the returned part:** The returned parts need to be stored in a location that is clearly identified for that purpose to ensure that the returned material isn't mixed with the base material until the inspection is completed and a decision has been made to either reuse or scrap the material.

- **Performing quality inspection:** Upon receipt of the broken parts inventory, the warehouse personnel perform quality inspection to determine the level of credit to be provided to the customer. For internal returns, the inspection determines if the product qualifies for a refurbishment or repair to be done by the vendor.

- **Shipping and transportation:** The warehouse personnel prepare the products to be shipped to the vendor for repair/refurbishment and also to ship the repaired product back to the customer.

- **Returning to vendor processing:** The warehousing team works with the quality and the procurement team to obtain a return material authorization (RMA) from the vendor so that a defective material under warranty can be shipped to the vendor for a replacement or credit.

- **Third-party logistics providers:** Companies often use third-party logistics providers (3PLs) to manage their warehousing needs and request the 3PL to use the company's SAP ERP system to process the transactions. In these scenarios, in addition to the company's needs for reports, the 3PL/company will need reports to monitor the 3PL efficiency and the 3PL performance in processing the returns and repairs.

Warehousing is a complex business process, and the SAP ERP system supporting needs to meet complex warehousing requirements as described in the next section.

System Requirements

Warehousing has several system requirements to store and process returns and repairs properly. The requirements include the following:

▶ Capability to receive broken parts and store them separately in the warehouse. The segregation of parts needs to be handled at different levels, for example, a floor area where the broken parts are stored or a set of bins within the warehouse marked for storing broken parts only.

▶ Producing appropriate identification tags or labels to indicate the condition of the material. The tag should contain information about the material's condition, the serial number, and the batch number.

▶ Manage shelf life expiration of parts that are shelf life managed.

▶ Manage contaminated parts and also hazardous materials. The system needs to be configured to store these materials in a separate storage area and also ensure that these materials are handled and shipped on their own, not mixed with other materials.

▶ Produce appropriate documentation to store, inspect, and ship materials. The documentation includes delivery, shipment, quality notification, pick lists, material identification label, and export documentation if materials need to be exported.

▶ Bin-level inventory maintenance to store materials at a bin level to facilitate easy putaway and picking.

▶ Reports to provide inventory data and material statuses.

System Capability and Objects

SAP provides the following processes or objects to facilitate warehousing:

▶ **Capability to store material at two levels — inventory management and warehouse management:** Depending on the amount of inventory and the need for bin-level stock management, the company can decide to manage at either level and at different company locations. Warehouse management provides the bin-level inventory management capability in SAP ERP.

▶ **Storage based on stock status:** Warehousing strategies are available to store hazardous materials in their own storage type. The same is possible with returns stock. This will ensure that these materials aren't mixed with other materials.

▶ **Material identification tag:** Company-specific forms and labels can be produced in SAP ERP to identify the materials so that they can be segregated based on either the material number or the material attribute.

▶ **Shelf-life management:** For parts, this can be achieved in the SAP system using batch management activation at the client level or at the plant level by material.

▸ **Reporting:** SAP provides standard warehouse reports for bin data, inventory data, and material status.

▸ **External warehouse interface:** SAP also provides the capability to allow interfaces with an external warehouse system. This becomes a very important requirement in situations where a 3PL is used to manage returns and repairs for the company, and the 3PL uses its own system to manage inventory.

▸ **Quality:** Warehouse management and inventory management functionalities in SAP ERP interface with the quality management functionality in SAP ERP to provide quality information related to the inventory stored in the warehouse. Quality objects such as quality notification and quality inspection lots provide information about the plant, storage location, and the warehouse information that shows accurately where the inspection lot material is stored.

Now that you have a good overview of the warehousing aspect of reverse logistics, let's move on to shipping and transportation.

1.2.6 Shipping and Transportation

Shipping and transportation is an integral part of reverse logistics as the parts move through the process chain. The shipping and the transportation departments are involved in making key decisions in reverse logistics, including the following:

▸ The responsible party — the company, customer, or vendor — for shipping the product back to the company

▸ The mode of transportation that should be used to ship the product back

▸ Which carrier should be used to ship the product back

▸ What documentation will need to accompany the product

▸ How the materials will be shipped to the vendor for repair

▸ How the materials will be packed to be shipped

▸ Whether the materials can be drop shipped from a customer to a vendor or vice versa

▸ Whether a 3PL should be used to do shipping and transportation

Depending on the type of industry, shipping and transportation could be simple with minimum system requirements or complex involving system enhancements. In the next section, we'll discuss the systems requirements for shipping and transportation to be able to support reverse logistics.

System Requirements

The following are the system requirements from a shipping and transportation perspective for reverse logistics:

▶ Automatic route determination to determine the optimum way of transporting a material back to the company and to the vendor

▶ Carrier determination, which is tied to the route determination, to ensure the company-preferred carrier is used to transport materials

▶ Freight cost determination, depending on the company's agreement with the customer

▶ Contaminated/hazardous material to be shipped separately

▶ Minimum handling between different points of the supply chain network

▶ All trade documentation printed correctly for exports

▶ Consolidated materials for transportation to save on transportation costs

System Capability and Objects

SAP ERP capabilities for shipping and transportation are widespread. The following list includes some of the capabilities:

▶ Deliveries, shipments, and picklists are all standard SAP documents provided for both forward and return shipping.

▶ Batch determination is available to activate for shelf life management.

▶ Route determination is set up for country combinations for all allowed service levels between the two locations.

▶ Carriers are assigned to the routes to be determined at the time of delivery and shipment creation.

▶ Shipping is segregated for hazardous and contaminated parts shipping. Typically these parts will be shipped on their own shipping point that allows defaulting special carriers and prints special handling instructions at the time of picking and shipment processing.

▶ Packing is performed at the shipment, and the materials are packed in handling units under shipment in SAP ERP.

▶ Using the SAP BusinessObjects Global Trade Services interface proper, ECCN (Export Control Classification Number), HTS (Harmonized Tariff System), and other foreign trade data is obtained and printed in all trade documentation.

Now that you understand the shipping and transportation's role in reverse logistics, let's move on to discuss the quality organization and processes.

1.2.7 Quality

The quality department provides key input in determining the disposition of the returned parts, including the following:

- Inspection requirements to determine whether the part is repairable
- If a returned part is good to be put back in stock
- Tests to check the quality of the product
- Inspection characteristics for incoming inspection
- List of parts to be activated for quality management for parts that fail often
- Global recall/global purge requirements
- Vendor quality based on amount of returns
- Failure analysis requirements and process
- Usage cycle of a part, which refers to the number of times a part is used and repaired and used again

To perform all of these functions accurately, there are specific SAP ERP system requirements.

System Requirements

The following are the system requirements for quality management for reverse logistics:

- Inspection activation for materials to be able to inspect for certain processes
- Notification process requirement so that the notification can be used to communicate between different teams
- Characteristics to be defined for quality inspection
- Pass/fail criteria to be defined in the system so that the inspectors can use this criteria to pass or fail inspection
- Purge/recall capability to bring products back to the processing location from existing inventory locations, including customer locations
- Definition and monitoring of criteria to manage vendor quality and provide feedback via reports to vendors

▶ Failure analysis capability to provide this service to customers

▶ Lifecycle management of parts to calculate usage of part

Let's move on to discuss the system capabilities and objects.

System Capability and Objects

In the quality management functionality in SAP ERP, there are the following objects and capabilities to meet the business requirements:

▶ Quality notification, quality inspection lots, and inspection characteristics can be managed at the material level.

▶ Inspection types in the material master, which can be activated for certain processes only, so that inspection is done only on the relevant processes for the material.

▶ Along with the definition of the inspection types for the material, the inspection characteristics can also be defined at the material master level.

▶ Usage decision/stock determination based on the usage decision can also be set up in the SAP system.

▶ Standard reports are available for quality data regarding the material and vendor.

This concludes the review of the role of the quality management functionality in SAP ERP in reverse logistics, so let's move on to finance.

1.2.8   Finance

The finance team provides input and performs several actions in the reverse logistics chain. The finance team consists of the accounts payable team that interacts with the vendors to ensure vendors get paid for subcontracting services. The finance team also is responsible for management of revenue from repairs, ensuring the accounting is done correctly for both forward and return material movements, providing credits to the customer for products returned, and obtaining credits from the vendors for products returned to the vendor. The input from finance to reverse logistics includes the following:

▶ They decide how to value the returns and repaired parts. In addition to this, they determine how the value needs to be posted to the correct accounts.

▶ They determine what type of accounting is used for different reverse logistics processes, for example, the use of cost centers for repair, refurbish, or using the

SAP General Ledger account to directly post the cost. They are responsible to ensure all of the cost is accounted for when responding to a quote for repair.

► In the case of internal repair, the finance department ensures the right amount of credit is issued to the customer service engineer's department when parts are returned based on the condition, and the department ensures that the right amount is credited/debited to the contract if the repair/return is done against a contract with a customer.

► Finally, the finance department provides input to the pricing determination for returns, repairs, and intracompany/intercompany movements of returned and repair parts.

The SAP system needs to be configured and enhanced to meet the financial department's requirements, without which reverse logistics can't be implemented or supported properly. So, it's not only important but also mandatory that the following system requirements are met.

System Requirements

As mentioned previously, the system requirements for the finance department are very important. These requirements include the following:

► Capability to review the returns value separately

► Reporting capability to isolate repair revenue

► Capability to display cost of returns and repair

► Costing broken, refurbished, and repair parts differently from a new part

► Pricing for warranty parts at a discount to customers

► Credit/debit memo capability to provide credit to the customers

► Credit based on the condition of the part after inspection at the time of receipt

► Capturing cost of repair provided by the vendor and rolling the cost up to the repair order to provide an accurate invoice/price to the customer

Now that you understand the requirements, let's move on to discuss the system capability and objects for the financial department.

System Capability and Objects

Concerning finance, the following objects and capabilities are needed to meet the business requirements:

- SAP standard account determination helps in determining the right accounts where the cost and value of parts are assigned based on the movement type.

- Standard cost of the parts can be maintained in the material master to indicate the lower cost/value of the broken/refurbished part.

- Pricing conditions and pricing procedures allow customer pricing to be done based on the part being sold.

- Pricing conditions can also be used to apply discounts to customers to buy refurbished parts.

Now that you understand how finance fits into the picture, let's move on to discuss foreign trade's role in reverse logistics.

1.2.9   Foreign Trade

Foreign trade is involved when returns, refurbishes, and repair parts are exported/imported within the network and outside when shipped to vendors for subcontracting services.

Because your company needs to comply with government regulations to import and export, it's important that the following requirements are met by the system.

System Requirements

Foreign trade requires compliance by customs in both the exporting and importing countries. In the system, the following capabilities are expected:

- The ECCN (Export Control Classification Number) and HTS (Harmonized Tariff Schedule) data of all of the items in the shipment needs to be available and printed in the export and import documents.

- The consignee or the importer of the record needs to be clearly identified and printed in all documents.

- When shipping products to vendors, the ship-to party needs to be verified to ensure that the ship-to party isn't on a sanctioned party list.

- If there are missing data, such as license information, then the logistics process needs to be notified and stopped ahead of time to avoid delays at the end of the logistics process.

- Any interface with the 3PL should be capable of passing the foreign trade data described previously.

Now that you understand the requirements, let's move on to discuss the system capability and objects for foreign trade.

System Capability and Objects

To meet the requirements of the foreign trade processes, SAP offers the following:

▶ SAP BusinessObjects Global Trade Services contains all of the standard checks and the data needed for foreign trade.

▶ SAP BusinessObjects Global Trade Services has the capability to check documents such as POs and deliveries during their creation. If a particular foreign trade object is missing, such as license information, then the creation or processing of these documents can be stopped.

▶ SAP BusinessObjects Global Trade Services is capable of producing commercial invoices, shipper export declarations, and all other foreign trade document with the necessary information, such as ECCN and HTS.

Now let's move on to service management.

1.2.10   Service Management

Service management deals with the services provided to customers and is also responsible for returning products from the field for new, unused, and broken parts from the machines that the company is servicing. Typically a service engineer or a customer engineer who is on site supporting the machines enters most of the data in service management. The engineer confirms the consumption of the parts used against the service order and the returns from the service order. The value of the broken part is typically credited to the service order if the part is repairable and can be refurbished. The customer engineer provides the condition of the part and the contamination information during the return confirmation, which is used to determine the destination location by the system.

Capturing details of the parts consumed and returned is critical to ensure the value of the service is calculated correctly. This becomes an important requirement for the finance team, and the system should be set up to capture and report all material movements, including consumptions and returns.

Parts returned from a service order are also sent to different locations based on criteria such as the condition of the part, the closest processing center, and the closest scrap plant.

Returned parts are generally inspected by the quality department and amount to be credited back to the service order is determined. In certain cases, the credit is given to the service order during the return, based on the contract with the customer.

The serial number capture is also an important requirement to ensure the machine information database is updated with the correct material/serial number information. This information is used to calculate the lifecycle of parts and to identify any quality issues that cause the breakdown of certain parts in a machine, which eventually affects machine efficiency and performance.

When parts are returned from service, data regarding the warranty information of the parts need to be provided so that the receiving entity can process the parts accordingly. This is important when the part is still under warranty to ensure the receiving entity sends the material back to the vendor to claim warranty.

Next we'll look at the system requirements for service management.

System Requirements

The service management process requires the system design to support easy data entry and automatic decision-making capability based on the data entered by the engineer. The following capabilities are also expected:

▸ The data entry process needs to be easy for the engineer, and the return input data should be available for the engineer to choose the item that is being returned.

▸ Based on the data entered, the system should create the follow-on documents, such as stock transport or the intercompany transport order to ship the products back to the return center.

▸ Serial number information needs to be captured for all material movements for parts that are serialized, and this information also needs to be updated in the equipment master of the machine from where the parts are pulled.

▸ Batch number of the parts need to be captured when batch-managed parts are returned as a part of the internal return process.

▸ All necessary outputs needed to ship a part need to be provided by the system. Examples of outputs are return delivery notes, return shipments, and material identifier tags to indicate the type of return and condition of the part.

▸ Carrier interface is another requirement to enable automatic carrier label printing to ship the part via a preferred carrier to the returns processing center.

System Capability and Objects

The SAP system has a robust Service Management module that supports all of these requirements:

▶ **Service Management module:** This module provides the following objects that help in achieving the goals of supporting internal returns and repair.

▶ **Service order:** As you can see in Figure 1.10, a service order allows a customer or engineer to process the requirements to perform a service and allows the engineer to return the used/unused stock.

Figure 1.10 shows the service order display. To display a service order in SAP ERP, use Transaction IW33. The service order contains the details of the different operations performed against the service order as displayed in the figure. Figure 1.11 shows the components used in a service order to perform the service. In addition to that, the plant where the maintenance is performed is also displayed in the service order line item.

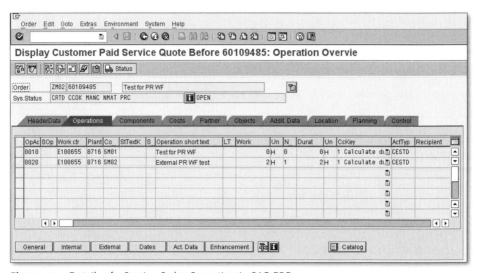

Figure 1.10 Details of a Service Order Operation in SAP ERP

▶ **Material movements:** Material movements are linked to a service order and allow engineers to trigger the required movements directly from the service order.

SAP also provides the capability to enhance the standard functionality to produce custom outputs and automatically create follow-on documents such as the stock transport orders. The details of this will be discussed in a subsequent chapter.

Material movements are referenced in a service order at the item level, providing visibility of the materials used and their consumption and return.

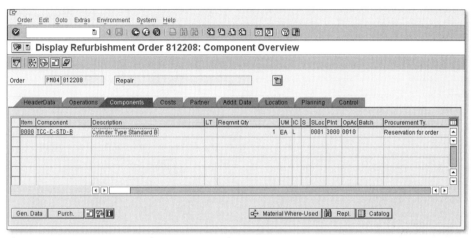

Figure 1.11   Components Listed in a Service Order in SAP ERP

1.3   Summary

In this chapter, we reviewed why reverse logistics is important to virtually every company and how it enables users to maximize efficiency, profitability, and quality. Several functional teams/business processes need to work together effectively to achieve a good reverse logistics model for the company. This chapter provided insight into the different processes in a company and the actions those processes perform, as well as the system requirements for every process team that need to be implemented to achieve the goal of reverse logistics success for the company.

In the next chapter, we'll discuss the returns process in detail, including internal and external returns, and how this process is handled in SAP. We'll also review configuration details that will enable you to use the SAP system to support your company's reverse logistics capability.

One of the critical components of reverse logistics is processing returns both from external and internal customers. In this chapter, we'll discuss the SAP tools and processes available to enable a streamlined returns process.

2   Returns

Returns refer to all materials returned as a part of a sales agreement or a service agreement. Returns can be done for many reasons, including part quality, wrong material number ordered, over shipment, or DOA (dead on arrival). There are typically two sources for returns to be made to a company. The first is from an end customer who bought the part against a sales order. The other is a service engineer who works for the company and returns a part used in the service provided to the customer. These returns are processed in SAP using a service order, so it's important to set up the SAP system to handle both of these returns with the correct configuration.

> **Example of Returns**
>
> A copier manufacturing company sells copiers to individuals and companies as a product and also leases copiers to companies. A customer who bought the product may return a defective copier, in which case the return is considered an external return. A leased defective copier may also be returned from the field by a service engineer who was trying to fix the machine at a customer location. In this case, the return of the copier or the copier components is considered an internal return because the copier is still owned by the manufacturer, and the customer pays only for the lease service.

Throughout this chapter, we'll use the example of the copier return or the component of the copier being returned and the copier manufacturing company to explain returns in SAP ERP. In this chapter, we'll review the configuration and objects available for returns in SAP ERP.

2.1   Internal Returns

Internal returns refer to the materials that are being returned (e.g., copier or copier component returned by the service engineer) because they were either found defective or ordered in excess by the service engineer during a preventive or corrective maintenance event. A service engineer usually carries components and supplies needed to perform preventive or corrective maintenance on machines leased to the customer or machines bought by the customer.

For preventive maintenance, the service engineer carries materials that he expects to change in regular intervals or materials that have shelf-life expiry and will need to be changed as part of the maintenance exercise. Typical examples of these materials include oil, washers, screws, nuts, and bolts.

For corrective maintenance, the customer engineer takes materials that he expects to replace as a part of the fix for the machine that broke down.

Now let's look at the objects and setup needed in the SAP ERP system to allow you to order, pick up, and service a tool, as well as return the used and unused materials.

2.1.1   Service Notification and Service Orders

Most of the internal returns in SAP are done with a reference to a service order. A *service order* is an object used to capture the materials and labor used for performing a service to a customer. In general, service orders are created with reference to a contract or service agreement but can also be created as a standalone order to perform the service in SAP ERP. A service agreement/contract specifies the agreement to perform a service for a customer and includes information about the type of service performed and whether it's a value-based or a quantity-based contract. You can view the contracts in SAP by using Transaction VA43. You can also display the contract by using the following menu: LOGISTICS • SALES AND DISTRIBUTION • SALES • CONTRACT • DISPLAY. Figure 2.1 illustrates a value-based contract.

As you can see in Figure 2.1, the target value is specified at the item level for value-based contracts. Additional data regarding the contract, such as service levels, are maintained in the characteristic values of the contract that can be accessed by selecting the item and selecting the item details configuration button at the bottom of the screen. The characteristic values are displayed in Figure 2.2.

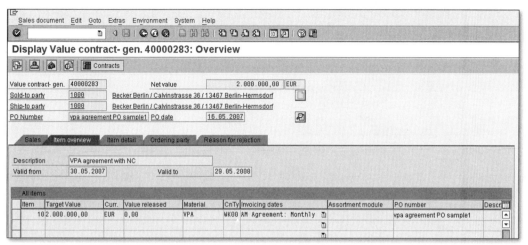

Figure 2.1 The Details of a Value-Based Contract

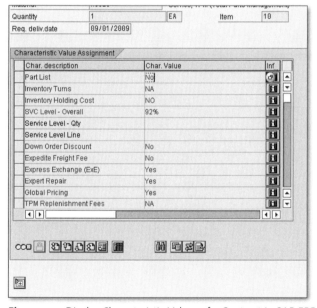

Figure 2.2 Display Characteristic Values of a Contract in SAP ERP

In addition, you can also specify whether or not you want to include repair/recycling and rebuild parts as a part of the contract. This is also specified in the display of characteristic values, as shown in Figure 2.3.

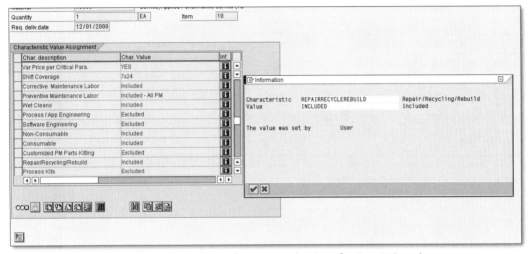

Figure 2.3 Characteristics Display of a Contract That Specifies Repair, Recycle, or Rebuild Inclusion

The contract contains data regarding all items in the contract at the header of a contract. In addition to the type of contract and the item details, the contract contains information about what is included and excluded. A contract serves as a starting point for most of the preventive maintenance activities in most companies.

A service order document provides more details about the actual service performed on the tool. This document contains the details of the materials used, as well the time and labor data used for the service. In SAP ERP, you can display a service order using Transaction IW33. Transaction IW33 can also be accessed using the menu LOGISTICS • CUSTOMER SERVICE • SERVICE PROCESSING • ORDER • SERVICE ORDER • DISPLAY.

The header of the service order shows the type of service order that is created — whether it's a contract-based service order or a standalone service order — as shown in Figure 2.4.

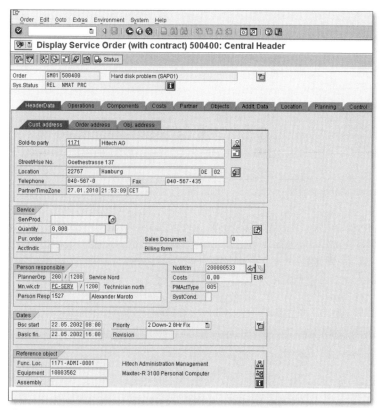

Figure 2.4 Display of a Contract-Based Service Order Header

In the service order, the materials that are required to complete the service are maintained in the Components tab, as shown in Figure 2.5, where the following data are maintained:

▸ Component or material

▸ Description

▸ Requirement quantity

▸ Plant

▸ Storage location

▸ Batch

▸ Item category

The plant and storage location are where the material stock needs to be to complete the service.

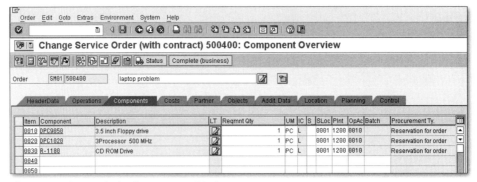

Figure 2.5 Service Order Components Display

The service engineer typically creates the service order, specifying the contract that the service order is created against, as well as the plant that will store the materials to be used in the service. This plant is called the maintenance plant associated with the main work center. The work center for the service order is stored in the header of the service order, as shown in Figure 2.6.

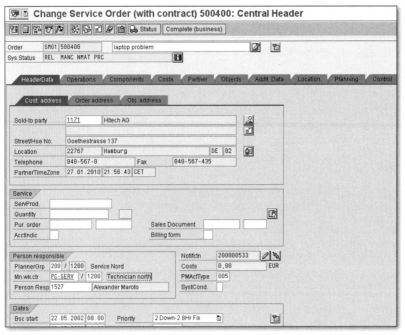

Figure 2.6 Header of the Service Order with the Work Center and the Plant Associated with the Order

From here, you can add the component in the service order and order the part from the company's plant network. You can do this by selecting the components and clicking on the Advance Shipment icon in the component screen of the service order, as shown in Figure 2.7.

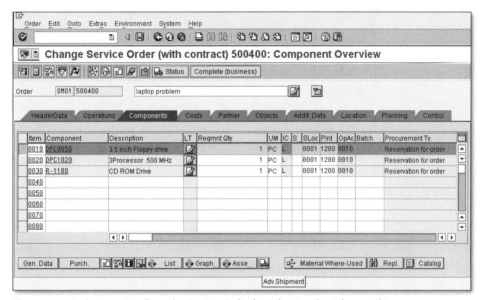

Figure 2.7 Ordering a Part from the Service Order by Selecting the Advance Shipment Notice Button

When the service engineer orders the material, a pop-up window appears where the user can enter the sales document type, sales organization, distribution channel, division, sales group, sales office, shipping condition, and account indicator as shown in Figure 2.8.

The parameters are important, so let's discuss the options in detail:

▸ **Sales Doc. Type**
The order type determines how accounting of the parts are handled in this service situation. In some companies, the materials aren't charged to the service order until the parts are used. This is handled by using order type for Consignment Fill Up (CF), which issues the stock to the customer consignment stock and doesn't charge the service order until consumption. In situations where the stock is used for corrective maintenance and the customer is charged for both materials and labor, the order type used will be the standard order type for customer sales. This ensures that the customer will be billed immediately upon delivery of the product to the customer location.

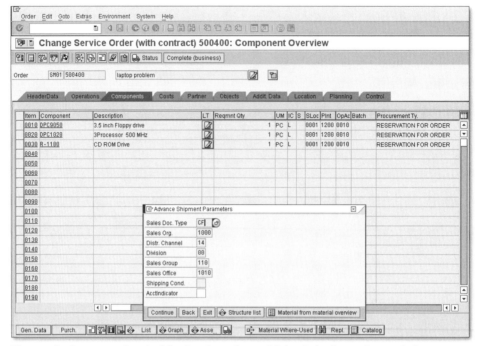

Figure 2.8 Parameters Required for Creating a Forward Sales Order from a Service Order

▶ **Material**
Material in the service order in the overview screen in the component field (i.e., DPC9050, DPC1020, and R-1180 as shown in Figures 2.7 and 2.8) denotes the materials needed to perform the service. The Materials Needed and Quantity Needed are entered in the component screen by the service engineer. The material master needs to be extended to the work center plant. This is a prerequisite for the material to be ordered and delivered to the work center plant.

▶ **Sales Org., Distr. Channel, and Division**
Depending on your SAP ERP configuration, the details of the sales organization, distribution channel, and division need to be entered so you can order the material. The accuracy of this information is important to make sure the accounting of materials and labor are posted to the correct accounts. Pricing of materials is also based on these parameters.

▶ **Shipping Cond.**
The shipping condition drives the service level, route, and carrier that will be used to deliver the product to the work center plant. Typically, the shipping condition determines if the part is needed for preventive or corrective maintenance

by the service level needed for the delivery. For preventive maintenance, the part is ordered in the normal service level; for corrective maintenance because the tool is down, the service level required is very high and needs express service to ensure the product is delivered as soon as possible to the work center plant.

After you've entered these parameters, the system does an Available to Promise (ATP) check to determine the location of the available part, as shown in Figure 2.9.

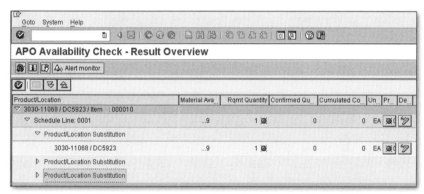

Figure 2.9 Available to Promise Results as Part of a Forward Order Creation

After the ATP proposal is accepted, the order creation screen is displayed with the details of the material and source plant. The sales order is then completed to order the product from the source plant.

> **Note**
>
> Note that when the item is returned, it may not be returned to the same location it was ordered from because the returns process typically doesn't use an ATP sequence to determine the returns plant.

For returns, you need to create a returns sales order to return parts used or unused. To create a return sales order, the forward order is referenced. Most of the data is copied from the forward sales order to the return sales order. Depending on the forward order type, you should use a corresponding return order type. For example, if the forward movement is created with an order type OR, then the return should also be done using order type RE, which is the standard SAP ERP order type for returns. If the forward movement is created using an order type that places the stock in customer consignment, then the return movement should remove the stock from customer consignment and return it to unrestricted stock.

The forward and return order proposals are configured in SAP ERP under copy control, which can be accessed via Transaction VTAA, as shown in Figure 2.10. Transaction VTAA can also be accessed using the following menu in the configuration SALES AND DISTRIBUTION • SALES • MAINTAIN COPY CONTROL FOR SALES DOCUMENTS.

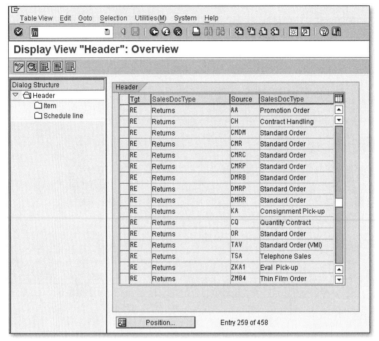

Figure 2.10   Copy Control to Link Forward and Return Order Types

Copy controls define the data transfer between two documents, for example, data that needs to be transferred from a forward sales order to a return order and transfers between subsequent documents such as a sales order to a delivery.

Within the configuration of copy controls, the individual fields and the data in the fields are defined in addition to the logic that is used to transfer the data between the fields and the documents associated with them. ABAP/4 code is written within copy control to define the logic and parameters of transfer, as shown in Figures 2.11 and 2.12.

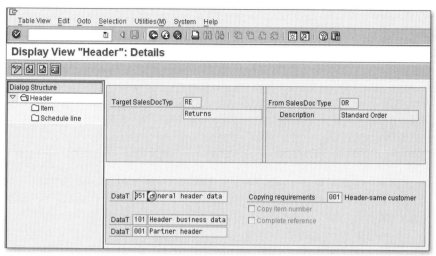

Figure 2.11 Copy Routines Within Copy Control Configuration from Forward Sales Order to Return Sales Order

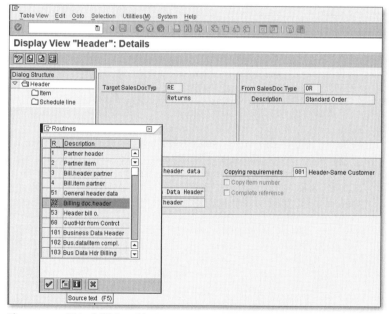

Figure 2.12 List of All Possible Routines to Use Between Sales Documents

To access the details of the data within copy controls, you need to select the Target document type (RE) and source document type (OR) (refer to Figure 2.10), and double-click the line item that shows the link between the two documents of the configuration screen. Figure 2.11 shows the details of the header level copy control between the sales order types RE and OR. In reverse logistics, copy controls play an important part in defining what data gets copied from forward sales orders to return sales orders, and also what forward order types need to be referenced to create a return sales order.

Within the definition of copy controls, like the example shown in Figure 2.11, there are data transfer routines such as 051, 101, and 001 that have code embedded within them to describe the data transfer. Each routine is defined for data transfer for different sets of fields. To display all of the possible copy routines available, you can use the pull down menu, as shown in Figure 2.12, which shows the list of all data routines.

To display the code within the data routines, you need to select the routine and the source text button at the bottom of the pop-up screen for displaying the data routine as shown in Figure 2.12.

The system displays the code that shows the data transfer logic and fields for the combination of documents. In addition to defining the data to be transferred, you can also code data such as selecting pick-up dates, as shown in Figure 2.13.

Example of the Use of a Copy Routine in a Return Order

In the copier sales example used in this chapter, when the copier is sold, certain information — such as the location that can receive the returns and also the instructions to open and inspect the components of the copier — is included in the text of the forward sales order in SAP ERP. The company wants this information to be copied from the forward sales order text to the text information in the return sales order when the return order is created with reference to the forward sales order automatically. This information is subsequently carried over to the return delivery. This requirement can be handled in SAP ERP by using copy routines at the header level of the sales document. Also if the product is returned after the first 10 days of the sale, the company can charge a 10% restocking fee and doesn't have to include the sales promotion discount provided at the time of sale. The price and discounts used in the forward sales order can be transferred to the return order using the copy routines. Then the necessary calculations can be applied to the return order to charge the 10% restocking fee and also the discount provided to the customer during the sale.

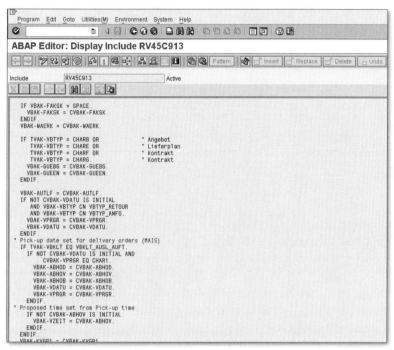

Figure 2.13 Code Defined Within the Data Transfer Routine to Set the Pick-up Date

For reverse logistics data, copy routines can be used to do the following:

▶ Control the return order types creation so that they are properly referenced to allowed forward order types.

▶ Either copy or use the forward order pricing to calculate pricing on the return orders.

▶ Determine shipping details such as shipping condition and delivery priority.

▶ Return a product against a service order by creating a return order (either KA order type or RE order type in standard SAP ERP depending on the company's business policies). The order type or the goods movement used to return a product against a service order is based on the forward order or goods movement used by the company in SAP ERP to fulfill the service order requirements. If a sales order was used to supply components to a service order, then a return sales order is used to return the material; if a goods movement transaction was used to supply materials to the service order, then a reverse goods movement is done to return the material in SAP ERP.

To create a return order, use Transaction VA01, and enter the return order type. Transaction VA01 can also be accessed in SAP ERP by using the menu path LOGISTICS • SALES AND DISTRIBUTION • SALES • ORDER • DISPLAY. Based on the configuration of the return order type, you'll need to enter the forward order reference, as shown in Figure 2.14.

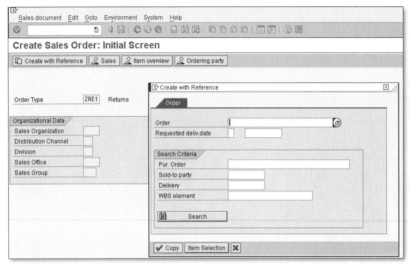

Figure 2.14   Return Order Creation Is Based on the Forward Order Reference

We'll get more details about the definition of the return orders through the configuration of the order type in the next section on return orders.

2.2   External Returns

External returns refer to the process of a customer returning a product before or after use. The return could be for one of many reasons such as a broken part that is under warranty, a wrong part received, a part that is DOA, or a part with bad quality.

In SAP ERP, the external returns are processed using return sales orders, just like the internal returns. The major difference between external and internal returns is the timing of the credit provided to the customer. For external returns, the company may decide to provide the credit only after the receipt and inspection of the returned material.

For external returns, the process starts with the customer contacting the company and providing the following key information needed for the return:

- Material being returned
- Quantity being returned
- Condition of the part
- Serial number of the part being returned
- Forward sales order
- Reason for return

All of this information can be configured as mandatory when creating a returns sales order. This is done in the configuration of the sales order type by choosing SALES AND DISTRIBUTION • SALES • SALES DOCUMENTS • SALES DOCUMENT HEADER • DEFINE SALES DOCUMENT TYPE.

At this configuration level, you can define the characteristics of all order types. The key information for defining the order type for a returns order as shown in Figure 2.15 includes the following:

- **SD Document Categ.:** The standard SAP-provided value for returns is H. The document category determines how the system stores and keeps track of document data.

- **Screen Sequence Grp:** The standard SAP-provided value for screen sequence group for returns order type is RE. The screen sequence group determines the screens and the sequence of screens for the order type.

- **Transaction Group:** The standard SAP provided value for returns order is 0, which refers to an order. The transaction group controls the types of sales documents you can process with certain systems transactions in sales processing.

- **Doc. Pric. Procedure:** This key provides the pricing procedure that will be used in determining the price for the return order type. For returns, there are several options to choose from depending on the type of return, such as A – Standard, C – Free of Charge, R – Repairs, or any custom pricing procedure.

- **Delivery Type:** This critical configuration element controls the type of delivery used as a baseline document for subsequent logistics processes. For returns, SAP ERP provides the standard delivery type LR, which is the returns delivery type. Deliveries are the source document for all logistics processes, and documents, such as shipment, picklist, and materials movements, are created with reference to a delivery. The receipt from the returns is processed in the receiving warehouse and is also done with reference to the delivery.

▶ **Delivery Relevant Billing Type:** This field controls whether or not the delivery is returned for credit or free of charge. Entry in this field means the return is for credit. The standard SAP value for returns for credit is RE.

▶ **Order Relevant Billing Type:** This field controls whether the service is returned for credit or free of charge. This field is applied when the product returned isn't material but a service or labor.

▶ **Intercompany Billing Type:** This field is relevant if the transaction happens between two entities in the same company code or is an intercompany transaction. For these transactions, the system uses the billing type provided here to calculate pricing information.

Figure 2.15 shows these fields with values for the configuration of the return order type RE.

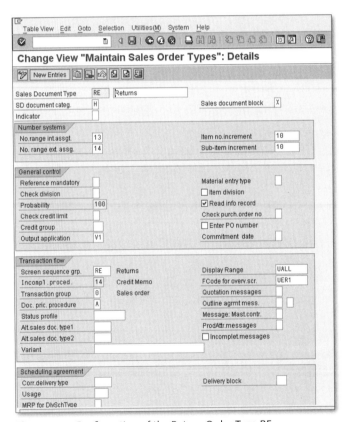

Figure 2.15 Configuration of the Return Order Type RE

A few other configuration options are available for return orders in addition to the order type relevant for reverse logistics, such as Define Order Reasons, which is discussed in the next section.

2.2.1 Define Order Reasons

Predefined order reasons are applied in the order header and copied into all items of an order. This is an effective tool in reverse logistics to help users understand the reason why a return order was created. Order reasons are configured using the following menu path in configuration: SALES AND DISTRIBUTION • SALES • SALES DOCUMENTS • SALES DOCUMENT HEADER • DEFINE ORDER REASONS. SAP ERP provides you with standard order reasons, as shown in Figure 2.16; in addition, you can define custom order reasons for your company.

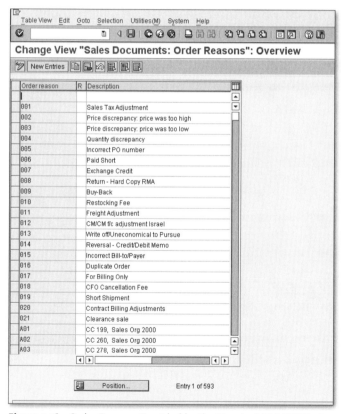

Figure 2.16 Order Reasons Provided by the Standard SAP ERP System

To add a new order reason, select the New Entries button, and enter the order reason code and the description. During the creation of a return sales order, you can select the order reason at the header level, which is used in many reverse logistics reports to help you understand the reasons for returns and take the necessary action to limit the returns. For example, if you find the order reason, Overshipment/Undershipment, used in many of the return orders, then it's an indication that the shipping department needs to inspect the quantities being shipped to improve accuracy.

During the return order creation using Transaction VA01 as described before, the order reason is available at the header level, as show in Figure 2.17.

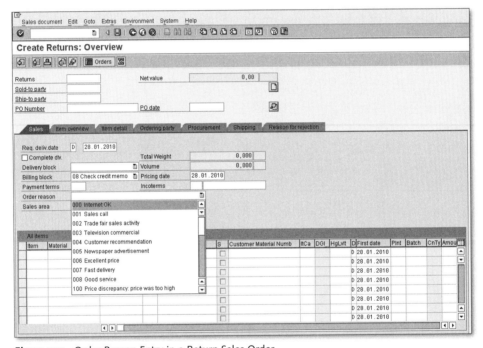

Figure 2.17 Order Reason Entry in a Return Sales Order

The order type and order reason are configurations that impact reverse logistics at the header level of the return sales order.

In the next section, we'll look into configuration at the item level that can impact reverse logistics.

2.2.2 Item Category

The item category defines how the system processes a sales order item for certain activities, such as delivery processing, billing, and pricing. All of these are important activities for reverse logistics. You define an item category in the configuration by choosing SALES AND DISTRIBUTION • SALES • SALES DOCUMENTS • DEFINE ITEM CATEGORIES.

SAP ERP offers a set of standard item categories that fit the needs of most companies. If you need to create a new item category, you can copy the existing SAP item categories to your new category, which is recommended because many of the SAP ERP programs in the background are linked to the item category definition. When an existing item category is copied into a new one, SAP ERP copies all of the associated data, such as the item category assignments, to the sales document types.

SAP ERP provides standard item categories that are specific to returns and are used mostly in reverse logistics, such as REN. The configuration of the item category has fields that indicate the relevance of the item category to returns. There is a field called Returns in the configuration or definition of the item category that indicates whether the item being returned with an item category is a returns item or not. Configuring the item category correctly is important for reverse logistics because this controls the subsequent configuration elements such as the schedule line category and delivery item categories.

In addition to defining whether an item in the order is a returns item, item categories also determine the billing type relevance, whether the item is relevant for order-related billing or delivery-related billing, and whether the item uses standard pricing or pricing for free goods (100% discount). Details of the item category definition are shown in Figure 2.18. This configuration is available by choosing SALES AND DISTRIBUTION • SALES • SALES DOCUMENTS • SALES DOCUMENT ITEM • DEFINE ITEM CATEGORIES.

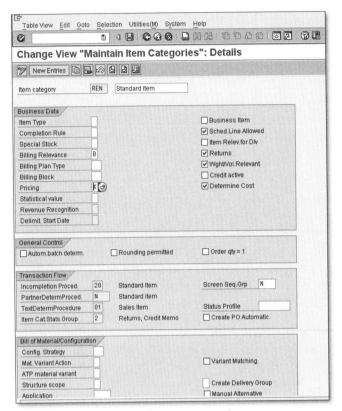

Figure 2.18 Configuration of a Returns Item Category

The field Sched.Line Allowed needs to be selected for delivery-relevant items such as materials in a sales order. Don't select this for returns that aren't relevant to delivery, such as a credit memo item or a text item.

Some data in the item category definition are provided as standard SAP ERP, such as the data under the Transaction Flow tab. The data in this tab acts as an input for many standard application programs in SAP ERP and provides information to the standard SAP ERP application programs to process the data in the item a specific way. When a new SAP item category is defined, this data gets copied over from the old item category into the new one.

SAP ERP also provides a standard Free Goods Item category called RENN. This is used when a free-of-charge item is returned. The pricing field shouldn't contain any data in the item category configuration for a free goods item, as shown in Figure 2.19.

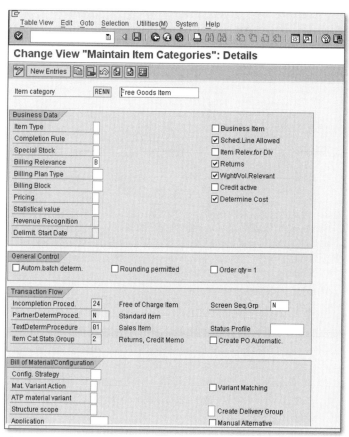

Figure 2.19 Configuration of a Free Goods Item Category

The next important configuration element is a schedule line category assigned to the schedule lines in the sales order that display the committed date of delivery of the product along with other important information. It's important to remember that the schedule line category determines the movement type that will be used to bring the part back into the company's network for returns. Let's look into the details of schedule lines and the schedule line category.

To display schedule lines in the sales order, you use Transaction VA03, select the line item to display, and then select the schedule lines for the item button as shown in Figure 2.20.

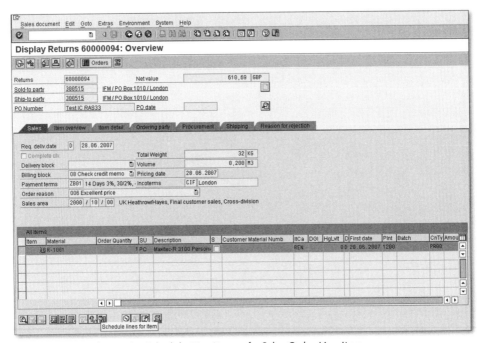

Figure 2.20 Displaying the Schedule Line Items of a Sales Order Line Item

In the detailed display of schedule lines, you'll find the Delivery Date, Order Quantity, Confirmed Qty, and Sched Line Cat., as shown in Figure 2.21. While the confirmed date is less meaningful in return orders than in forward orders, the schedule line category provides more data based on the configuration.

The schedule lines details also contain information about delivery block and movement type. As mentioned before, movement type determines which stock category the returns material will be posted into when brought into inventory and also the accounting entries that will be posted when the material is brought back into the inventory. Delivery block prevents further processing of the order until the delivery block is removed.

> **Example**
>
> If a copier component such as a drum is returned, the company can always block the delivery creation until the returns department approves the return. Blocking a delivery prevents logistics processes from starting until the approval is obtained. To prevent the delivery creation in SAP ERP, a delivery block can be defaulted in the order every time a return order is created.

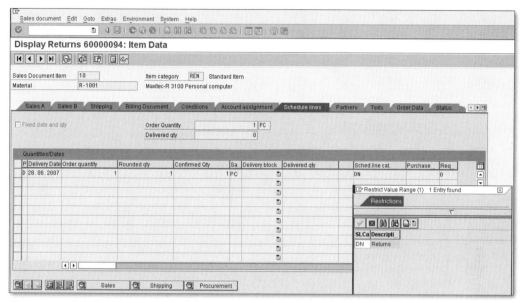

Figure 2.21 Detailed Display of Schedule Lines in a Returns Sales Order

To display the details of the delivery block, change the schedule line item to display, and select the Shipping tab in the schedule line display of a sales order as shown in Figure 2.22.

In the details of the Shipping data for schedule line data, SAP ERP displays the Delivery Block field. This field is relevant for reverse logistics because it enables users to block delivery creation if the order is incomplete or is pending further action. For example, if a customer ordered a part under warranty and wants to return the part for a replacement part, then a returns sales order is created to return the broken part under warranty and a forward order is created to replace the broken part free of charge. In certain scenarios, the customer might not want to send the returns part until the replacement part is sent and received at the customer end. In this case, the order entry representative might block the delivery creation until the customer has confirmed receipt of the replacement part. Delivery block is also important for reverse logistics when the return has to be approved by the reverse logistics, order management, planning, and other departments before the part is returned to the network.

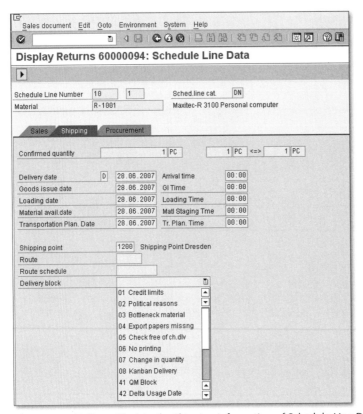

Figure 2.22 Delivery Block in the Shipping Information of Schedule Line Data

You can build the approval process using the SAP Business Workflow, where the data regarding the returns order is sent to the approvers. Once approved, the workflow triggers the removal of the delivery block to start the subsequent logistics subprocess. This process is followed in many companies where returns aren't automatically accepted from the customer. Some other requirements of delivery block at the order level for reverse logistics include ensuring the part returned is under customer warranty. Figure 2.22 shows the details of the Shipping tab for schedule line data that includes Delivery Block. To display the Shipping tab of the schedule line, you display the sales order details using Transaction VA03. You select the line item in the sales order and then choose the display schedule lines button at the bottom of the screen. In the next screen, you can select the schedule line that you want to review and select the shipping button at the bottom of the screen to display the Shipping tab details of the schedule line.

2.2.3 Movement Type

Movement type controls a lot of data and subsequent logistics processes in reverse logistics. In the sales order, the movement type is determined from the schedule line category. You can display the movement type selected in the sales order in the Schedule Line section. To display the movement type, select the schedule line, and then select the Procurement tab. The Movement Type field is displayed in the detailed procurement data as shown in Figure 2.23.

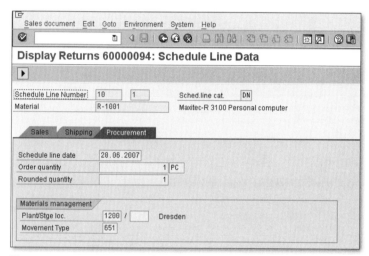

Figure 2.23 Movement Type Displayed in the Procurement Data in the Return Sales Order

The movement type determines the following for reverse logistics:

▶ Stock category of the returned stock. Movement type configuration determines whether the returned stock is returned to the returns stock category, blocked stock category, or unrestricted stock category.

▶ Which accounts will be affected by the goods movement transacted with that movement type.

As we mentioned previously, the movement type can't be changed at the sales order because it's defaulted into the order based on the schedule line category. Schedule line categories are defined in the configuration under SALES AND DIS-TRIBUTION • SALES • SALES DOCUMENTS • SCHEDULE LINES • DEFINE SCHEDULE LINE CATEGORIES.

In this screen, you can either display existing schedule line categories or create a new schedule line category by selecting the New Entries button. In the standard SAP-provided configuration, the schedule line category for returns is DN. To review the details, select and double-click the line item, as shown in Figure 2.24.

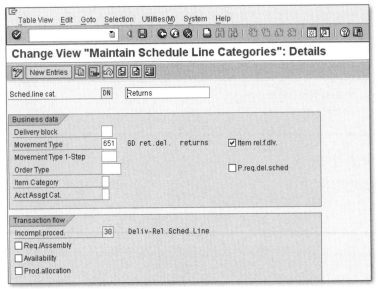

Figure 2.24 Detailed Display of the Schedule Line Category Configuration

As you notice in the configuration of the schedule line category, the movement type is assigned to the schedule line category. The standard movement type assigned to the returns schedule line category is 651. Using this movement type to process returns causes the received returns stock to be posted in the returns stock category. The receiving company doesn't own the returns stock until the inspection is completed. Then, the returns stock is converted to the company's own stock, and the ownership of the stock changes to the company.

In addition to containing the movement type, the schedule line category also allows you to default a delivery block that will be used in all sales order line items that use this schedule line category, as shown in Figure 2.25.

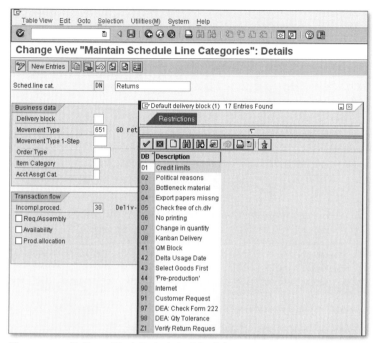

Figure 2.25 Delivery Block Default in Schedule Line Category Configuration

2.2.4 Incompletion Procedure

Incompletion procedures define the criteria that SAP ERP uses to determine if a sales order is considered incomplete for required data. For example, you can define Delivery Priority as one of the required fields for an order to be considered complete. You can choose any field that is available in the sales order tables in SAP ERP. You define incomplete procedures in the menu path SALES AND DISTRIBUTION • BASIC FUNCTIONS • LOG OF INCOMPLETE ITEMS • DEFINE INCOMPLETE PROCEDURES. Here, you can define a custom incomplete procedure based on the fields you choose in this configuration.

To define a custom incomplete procedure, you need to choose the incompletion group first. Incompletion groups are defined based on the document that the procedure will get assigned to and the level the procedure will be assigned to. For example, the sales order is the document, and the header level is where the procedure will be assigned.

To create a procedure, select the group from the Incompletion Groups section first, and then select the Procedure on the left-hand side, as shown in Figure 2.26.

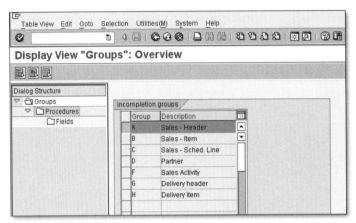

Figure 2.26 Definition of Incomplete Procedures at the Sales Order Header Level

After the incompletion group is chosen, you can define the fields for the procedure by choosing the procedure name and highlighting the Fields folder, as shown in Figure 2.27.

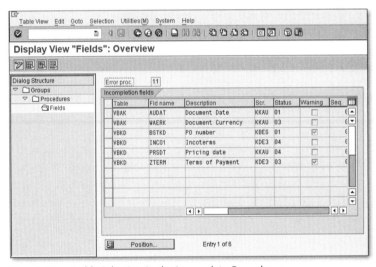

Figure 2.27 Fields Selection in the Incomplete Procedures

You can choose fields relevant for reverse logistics and assign them to the custom reverse logistics/returns incomplete procedure if your company requires that. For example, the reason for movement/return field can be made a part of the incompletion procedure to ensure that the reason for the return is captured before any subsequent processes can be started because the order would be considered incomplete without this field.

After the incompletion procedure is defined with the needed fields, the procedure is assigned to the schedule line category, as shown in Figure 2.28. To do this, you can use the following menu path in the configuration: SALES AND DISTRIBUTION • BASIC FUNCTIONS • LOG OF INCOMPLETE PROCEDURES • ASSIGN INCOMPLETE PRO-CEDURES. In this configuration, you can assign incompletion procedures for sales document types, item categories, schedule line categories, and partner functions.

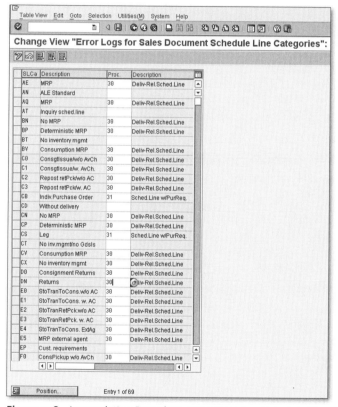

Figure 2.28 Incompletion Procedure Assignment to a Schedule Line Category

2.2.5 Movement Type Definition

As mentioned before, movement type is assigned in the schedule line category. Let's now consider how movement types are defined and what characteristics of movement types are relevant for reverse logistics.

Movement types are defined in the menu path MATERIALS MANAGEMENT • INVEN-
TORY MANAGEMENT AND PHYSICAL INVENTORY • MOVEMENT TYPES • COPY, CHANGE
MOVEMENT TYPES. SAP ERP provides predefined movement types that can be modified to meet specific requirements of some companies. In general, the accounting
links from the movement types are modified to meet the company's needs to post
the values to accounts different from the standard SAP ERP defined accounts.

In the detailed configuration screen of the movement type definition, you'll find
many subscreens where much more data can be defined for movement types. The
details of the movement type configuration are shown in Figure 2.29.

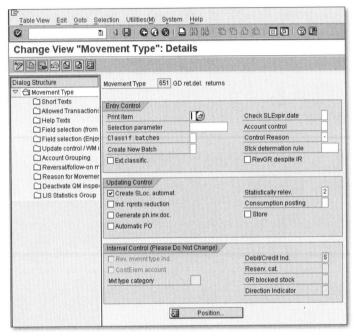

Figure 2.29 Detailed Configuration Screen for Movement Type 651

The Debit/Credit Ind. specifies which sides of the account transactions are updated.
For returns, the S debit indicator is chosen because the return is incoming. All
debit indicator movement types are incoming movements. The incoming product
can also be checked to ensure that it meets the shelf-life requirements by choosing
the required option in the Check SLExpir. Date field. The options in the standard
SAP ERP system are No Check, Enter and Check, Enter Only, and No Check at
Goods Issue.

Note

Shelf-life materials will be discussed in detail in Section 6.9, Batch Management, in Chapter 6, Serial Number Management in Reverse Logistics.

All delivery-based transactions should be maintained in the allowed transactions for the movement type to be able to execute a goods receipt against a delivery, as shown in Figure 2.30. To allow the transactions, you select the Allowed Transactions folder on the left side of the movement type definition shown earlier in Figure 2.29.

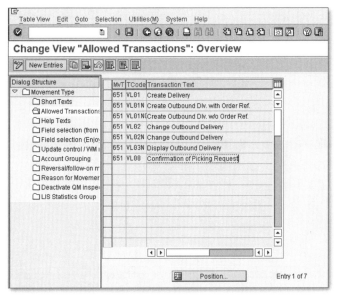

Figure 2.30 Allowed Transactions for Movement Type 651

You need to ensure the transaction code used for processing returns (e.g., PGI of a delivery using Transaction VL02N) is listed here to enable goods receipt of the returns stock.

The movement type determines the stock that the returns materials are going to be posted against. Following are the stock categories the returned material can be posted against:

▶ **Returns stock:** Returns stock are represented in SAP ERP as nonvaluated stock. Returns stock isn't owned by the company and is typically stored until it has been inspected and converted to the company's own stock. The stock category uses special stock indicator R for movements. Returns stock is displayed under the title Returns in the SAP ERP standard stock overview screen, as shown in Figure 2.31. This screen can be accessed in SAP using Transaction MMBE or by going to LOGISTICS • MATERIALS MANAGEMENT • INVENTORY MANAGEMENT • ENVIRONMENT • STOCK • STOCK OVERVIEW.

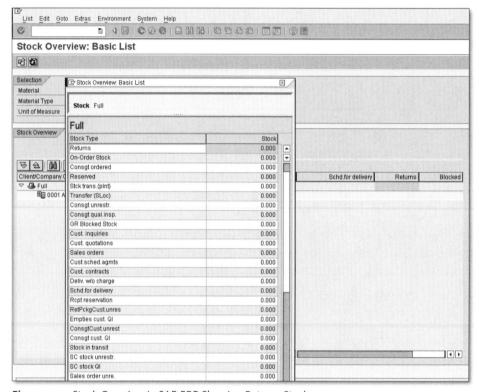

Figure 2.31 Stock Overview in SAP ERP Showing Returns Stock

▸ **Unrestricted stock:** This is the stock owned by the company. In general, you shouldn't receive stock being returned directly into the company's own stock before completing the inspection because if the inspection fails, you'll need to either return the part to the customer or try to get the credit back from the customer.

▸ **Blocked stock:** This stock is also owned by the company. Blocked stock refers to the category of stock that is in blocked status, which prevents the stock from being available for other processes and functions, such as planning or outbound delivery creation.

▶ **Quality stock:** This stock is also owned by the company and refers to the category of stock that is currently under stock review. Quality stock is also prevented from being available for other processes and functions.

When the returns stock is brought back from the customer, one of the key decisions that the company needs to make for reverse logistics is which stock category the returns material stock should be received into. Following are key characteristics for each stock category that can be used to make this decision:

▶ Returns stock category allows the stock to be received without any financial impact because the stock isn't valuated upon receipt. Although this gives you the flexibility of allowing the receiving location to hold the stock without financial impact, this stock needs to be processed quickly to determine the subsequent action that needs to be taken for the inspected stock.

▶ If the inspection fails, you can return the stock to the customer due to failed inspection and not pay the customer any credit for the material. For example, if a customer claims a returned product is in "New" condition but upon inspection you find the material was used, then the material can be returned from the returns stock back to the customer. The inventory value of the company isn't affected by this process because the material was never brought into company stock.

▶ If the returns stock processing stock isn't done on time, it impacts other processes such as planning. If the returned stock is considered in "New" condition, then planning can consider that stock as available and include that in materials requirement planning (MRP) to avoid ordering a new part from the vendor. So, it becomes critical to process stock in the returns stock category quickly.

▶ If the credit to the customer is pending inspection of the returns stock, then the inspection needs to be done in the time period specified in the sales agreement. If not, the customer has to be paid even if the inspection of the part fails.

▶ Although receiving the parts into the returns stock category has its benefits, it also adds additional transactions to process the returns stock to the company's own stock after the inspection. This is done using movement type 453 in the standard SAP ERP system. This movement type transfers the stock from returns to own and, in the process, triggers the accounting documents that post the cost of the material into the company's inventory.

▶ Receiving the stock as unrestricted is done typically when the company pays the customer for the part before the inspection is done. So whatever the condition of the part, the customer gets the credit. Obviously this creates a risk for the company because the part that is returned might not be good enough to be used by the company, but some companies prefer this approach based on the agreement with the customer or to maintain a good customer relationship. It's more important to perform quality inspection when you pay the customer ahead of time before the inspection to make sure only good parts are put back in the network and broken parts are scrapped or sent to repair.

▶ Receiving the stock in the blocked stock category is a better solution for most companies than receiving the stock into unrestricted. Blocked stock is also valuated, so receiving into blocked stock doesn't prevent the customer from being paid for the returned stock, but it provides a mechanism for a quick inspection by the company before the stock is considered available for other processes. Blocked stock is usually done for quick or visual inspections because if a thorough inspection is required, then the stock needs to be received into quality inspection stock to allow all quality checks to be performed on the part. In addition, receiving the stock into quality allows stock reporting to report the status of the stock accurately.

▶ Receiving into quality stock is done to provide the incoming inspection executed in detail as mentioned before. In addition to receiving the stock in the quality category, some material is received into quality stock automatically even though the configuration of the movement type assigned to the schedule line category indicates receipt into unrestricted stock. This is because the material has quality inspection defined as active in the material master.

▶ For materials that have inspection active, SAP ERP automatically receives the material into the quality stock category and creates an inspection lot automatically. Inspection lots provide an opportunity to do quality inspections based on predefined steps. The inspection checks whether the materials meet specific quality inspection criteria. Quality inspections, quality notifications, and inspections lots are described later in this chapter.

As we mentioned, which stock category material will be received into is a major decision that impacts reverse logistics. After you determine the stock category for the returns stock, then you change the movement type that receives the stock to post it into the desired stock category. You can then update the movement type information in the schedule line category configuration as discussed earlier in this chapter.

If you have multiple returns orders (i.e., return for credit, return for replacement, etc.), you can define multiple movement types to receive the materials being returned against these orders into different stock categories.

To accommodate the requirements of returning to multiple stock categories, you can create new schedule line categories, which you can in turn assign to new item categories that will be assigned to the relevant order types. The flow of returns stock category determination and movement type determination is described in Figure 2.32.

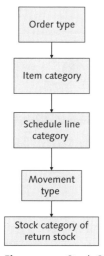

Figure 2.32 Stock Category Determination in Returns

Movement types in SAP ERP also determine the accounts that will be used for posting the costs and value of the material being returned. The accounting details for movement type are determined using account grouping definitions in the movement type configuration. To view the account grouping definitions in the movement type configuration, choose MATERIALS MANAGEMENT • INVENTORY MANAGEMENT AND PHYSICAL INVENTORY • MOVEMENT TYPES • COPY, CHANGE MOVEMENT TYPES. In this configuration, you select the movement type to be displayed or modified and then choose the Account Grouping definitions on the left side as shown in Figure 2.33.

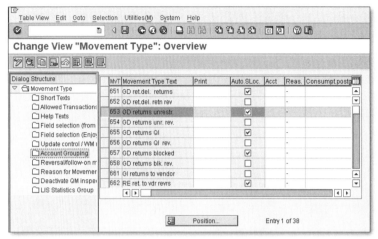

Figure 2.33 Display Details of Account Grouping for Movement Type

The Account Grouping details show the default setup for the movement type in standard SAP ERP. To modify the accounts being assigned, you can modify the account modifier (Acct. Modif column) in the movement type definition shown in Figure 2.34.

> **Note**
>
> We'll discuss the details of how an accounting document gets posted for returns by using the movement type definitions in Chapter 7, Finance in Reverse Logistics.

As you notice in Figure 2.34, you can select the movement type relevant for returns (653, in this example) and if needed modify the account modifiers (PRA, in this example).

The SAP system provides standard movement types that are configured to enable financial postings. In certain business scenarios, you may want to use a standard movement type, but you want to ensure using this movement does not create an accounting document or financial postings in SAP ERP.

> **Example**
>
> When copiers are returned to the company, the company decides to receive the copiers directly to the company's stock and not receive them into the returns stock category. So the SAP standard ERP configuration for the returns movement type should be changed to post the material to the company's stock and also perform accounting entries when receiving the stock because the stock received is going to be valuated as against a returns stock that isn't valuated.

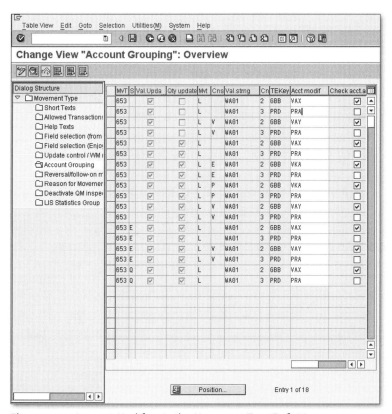

Figure 2.34 Account Modifiers in the Movement Type Definition

For example, if you want a movement type that enables a returns posting to set as blocked stock, but the stock remains nonvaluated until the inspection is done, then you can create a custom movement type that is a copy of the standard movement type and remove the entries in the Account Grouping folder. This ensures that there is no accounting document created, so the movement isn't valuated. For example, the movement type 651 posts the stock to the returns stock and that movement is nonvaluated and movement type 653 posts the stock to unrestricted stock and this movement type usage results in the goods movement being valuated and therefore the posting accounting entries. Figure 2.35 shows movement type 653 account grouping on the left side and movement type 651 account grouping information on the right side, and you can see the account grouping details are empty for movement type 651 because this movement type posting doesn't result in any accounting entries.

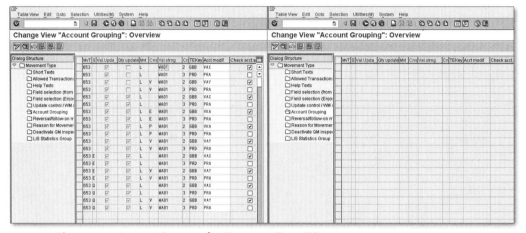

Figure 2.35 Account Grouping for Movement Type 653

Details of the actual accounts posting configuration can be displayed by going to MATERIALS MANAGEMENT • VALUATION AND ACCOUNT ASSIGNMENT • ACCOUNT DETERMINATION • ACCOUNT DETERMINATION WITHOUT WIZARD (OR) ACCOUNT DETERMINATION WITH WIZARD.

The account modifier defined in the movement type is one of the criteria used to determine the account that will be used in the accounting document. To validate the accounts that will be affected by a movement type, you can use the Simulation function in the account determination in the Automatic Postings configuration. To access this configuration, choose MATERIALS MANAGEMENT • VALUATION AND ACCOUNT ASSIGNMENT • ACCOUNT DETERMINATION • ACCOUNT DETERMINATION WIZARD. Then you select the Simulation function to show the account postings for a movement type as shown in Figure 2.36.

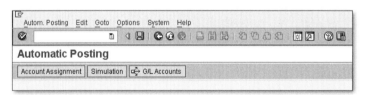

Figure 2.36 Simulation Function in Automatic Postings Configuration

To continue the simulation, enter the Plant, Material, and Movement Type for which you want to validate the accounts used, as shown in Figure 2.37.

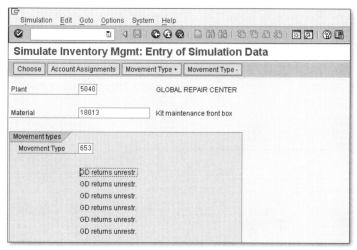

Figure 2.37 Simulation of Movement Type 653 in Automatic Postings

Choose the Account Assignments button to display which accounts are assigned to this transaction and movement type. Figure 2.38 shows the accounts assigned to this transaction in the simulation mode.

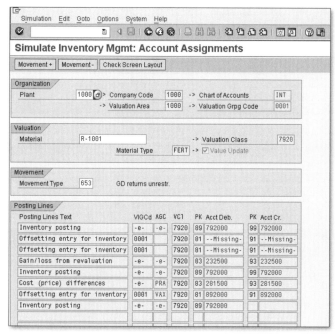

Figure 2.38 Details of Accounts Postings for Movement Type 653 for Returns to Unrestricted Use

The accounts determined and configured here are automatically used when a materials document posting is done using this movement type. The accounts details are displayed in the accounting document associated with the material document. To display a material document, use Transaction MIGO, choose Display Material Document in the selection screen, enter the Material document number, and execute the transaction. In the Doc Info tab, select the FI Documents button to show the details of the accounting document (see Figure 2.39).

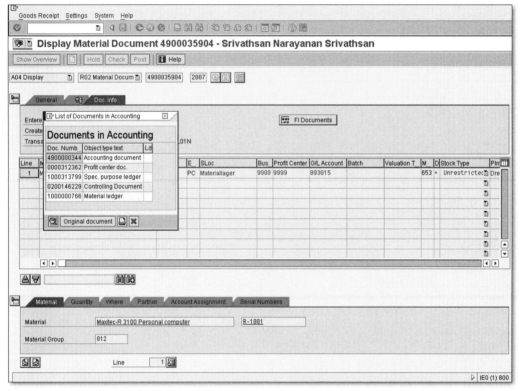

Figure 2.39 Display the Accounting Document from a Material Document

> **Note**
>
> To modify account assignments, work with an SAP Finance consultant to base the modifications on business requirements.

If you select the accounting document and display the details, you'll see that the accounts selected by the document are the same as the accounts from the automatic account posting displayed in Figure 2.38.

In the movement type configuration, you can select to deactivate quality inspection. This ensures that no quality inspection lots are created when material is received using this movement type, even if the material is activated for quality inspection in the material master. This is useful for reverse logistics and particularly for returns if you want to activate quality inspection with inspection lots for some materials only for inbound activities and not for returns. To deactivate quality inspection in the movement type configuration, choose the Deactivate QM Inspection/Delivery Category folder on the left side, and select the QM Not Active flag, as shown in Figure 2.40.

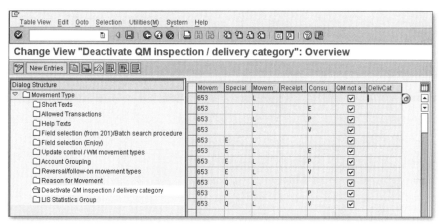

Figure 2.40 Deactivating Quality Inspection Lots for Movement Type 653 in the SAP ERP Configuration

You need to create a return order for both external and internal returns, with reference to a forward order to process returns. For internal returns, the return order can be made to reference a service order by enhancing the standard SAP system using ABAP development.

Once enhanced, the service order document flow will show the forward and the return orders, as illustrated in Figure 2.41.

Figure 2.41 Document Flow of Service Order with Both Forward and Return Orders

For external returns, the forward order document flow references the return order and vice versa, as shown in Figure 2.42.

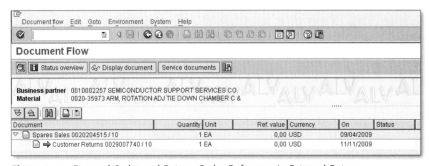

Figure 2.42 Forward Order and Return Order Reference in External Return

2.3   Returns Receipt and Processing

The warehousing team in all companies handles returns receipt and processing. The team receives the materials and if necessary passes them to the inspection team, and the process continues until a determination is made on the material condition. Let's now look at all of the functions within returns receipt and processing.

2.3.1   Receipt

Returns against a returns sales order are done by doing a goods receipt or by posting the goods issue of a return delivery. For items that aren't relevant for delivery, as indicated in the item category of that item in the sales order, the goods receipt is considered done at the time of the return order creation. Examples of items that don't need receipt using a delivery are text items and services. These items don't need a delivery-based receipt because no material was physically returned. For these items, a credit memo can be created immediately after the order creation to pay the customer back.

For items that need a receipt, you must create a delivery against the returns order. The delivery that gets created against a returns order is called a *returns delivery*. The returns delivery has a specific delivery type, which in standard SAP ERP is LR. The following are other delivery types that are relevant for reverse logistics and come preconfigured in the standard SAP system:

- **LO:** Delivery without reference
- **NCR:** Return stock transport order CC
- **RL:** Returns (per order)
- **RLL:** Return delivery to a vendor
- **SRNP:** New part returns
- **SRUP:** Used part returns

In addition to LR used for accepting returns from a customer, RLL is used for shipping parts back to a vendor for returns. Configuring the returns delivery type to meet your requirements is necessary to enable a smooth reverse logistics flow in the company.

Delivery Type

Configuring the delivery type is important because it contains a few relevant pieces of information for reverse logistics. To access the configuration for delivery type, go to Logistics Execution • Shipping • Deliveries • Define Delivery Types. The standard delivery type for returns is LR. The following fields are configured in the delivery type: Order Required and Storage Location Rule. Let's review these fields in detail.

Order Required

The Order Required field contains prerequisite information/order needed for all delivery types. For example, for external or internal returns from a customer against a return sales order, this field is defined with the sales order prerequisite information. This field contains several possible values for prerequisites:

▸ **B:** Purchase Order Required

▸ **R:** Return Delivery to Vendor

▸ **X:** Sales Order Required

▸ **[blank]:** No prerequisite documents required

Figure 2.43 shows the details behind the delivery type configuration for the LR Returns Delivery type.

For the example shown in Figure 2.43, you'll need to configure the returns sales order with the value –X to set the returns sales order as the reference document for a returns delivery.

Storage Location Rule

When returns deliveries are processed, the system proposes a storage location based on the storage location rule. The storage location rule can't be changed in the configuration of the delivery type, but you can change it by going to Logistics Execution • Shipping • Picking • Determine Picking Location • Define Rules for Picking Location Determination, in the configuration.

SAP ERP provides a standard location rule called MALA. This is by default assigned to most of the delivery types. For reverse logistics, the storage location rule can be used to meet complex requirements of the company. For example, if your company stores parts to be scrapped in a different location than parts that are still under inspection and parts that need to be returned to a vendor in a different location, then you can define a custom storage location rule to identify the storage location to be used in the delivery based on the delivery type.

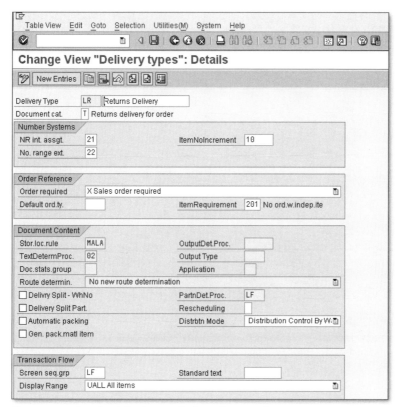

Figure 2.43 Details of the Returns Delivery Type Configuration

The custom storage location rule needs to be defined with the name, YY to ZZZZ, and the coding for the rule needs to be defined in the user exit in Program MV50AFZZ.

After the coding is done and the custom storage location rule is created, you can assign it to the delivery type in this table, as shown in the example for delivery type LR in Figure 2.44.

These are the important fields that need to be defined in the delivery type to make reverse logistics processes work correctly. All of the data configured in the delivery type impact the header details of the returns delivery. Let's now move on to the data that impact the item level details of the delivery.

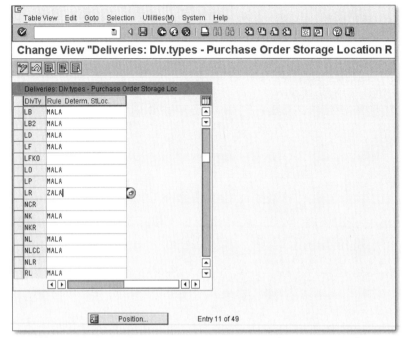

Figure 2.44 Custom Storage Location Determination Rule Being Assigned to Returns Delivery Type LR

Delivery Item Category

The standard delivery item category used for returns is REN. You can configure the delivery item category in the configuration by choosing Logistics Execution • Shipping • Deliveries • Devine Item Categories for Deliveries. Details of the item category REN configuration are shown in Figure 2.45.

Just two fields impact reverse logistics from a delivery item category definition:

▸ **StLocation required:** This field needs to be selected for a returns delivery if the material received needs to be stored or put away in a storage location.

▸ **Determine SLoc:** This field indicates if the system will do an automatic determination of the storage location. If the storage location determination rule is defined, then this field needs to be selected to ensure the location gets determined automatically in the returns delivery.

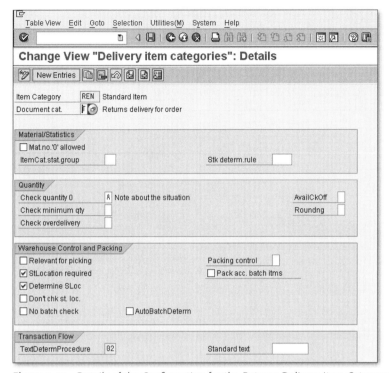

Figure 2.45 Details of the Configuration for the Returns Delivery Item Category

In addition to the delivery item category REN, SAP ERP also provides the RENN category used for free goods items, which is used when the goods are issued to the customer free of cost. The item category is determined based on the combination of delivery type, item category group, usage, and top-level item category. The item category determination can be configured by choosing LOGISTICS EXECUTION • SHIPPING • DELIVERIES • DEFINE ITEM CATEGORY DETERMINATION IN DELIVERIES.

The item category determination has little impact on the overall reverse logistics process because, in general, the returns delivery type LR is assigned to the returns item category REN. Based on this configuration, shown in Figure 2.46, the item category value gets defaulted in the returns delivery.

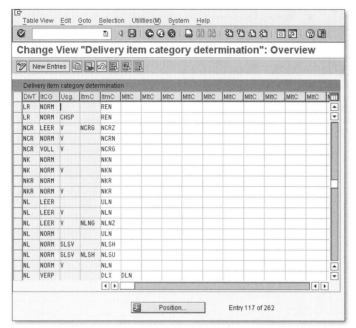

Figure 2.46 Delivery Item Category Determination Configuration

The next major piece of configuration in the shipping and delivery area that impacts reverse logistics is copying control.

Copying Control

Copying control is the SAP ERP mechanism to manage the data copy between two documents with one of them being the source (i.e., a sales order) and the other being the target (i.e., delivery).

The data that gets copied from the return order to the return delivery is defined within copying control. Copying control for deliveries is defined in the Implementation Guide (IMG) by going to LOGISTICS EXECUTION • SHIPPING • COPYING CONTROL • SPECIFY COPY CONTROL FOR DELIVERIES. Like copying control at the order level, data can be copied from orders to deliveries. In addition, custom checks can be done within the copy control.

For reverse logistics, this is an effective tool that will help you determine the basis of pricing and parts. For example, you can develop custom code in the copy routine if your company wants additional information that was coded in the order, such as instructions from the customer about contamination, to be copied over to the delivery so that the instruction can be printed in the delivery note that will be used as the shipping documentation.

To develop code, you'll need to select the combination of order type and delivery type that you want to modify from the copy control configuration table, as shown in Figure 2.47.

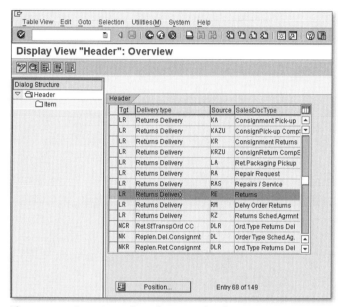

Figure 2.47 Copy Control Configuration for the Return Order to the Return Delivery

After you've selected the combination for which you want to change the copy control, you can assign the custom routine in the details screen of this selection.

Before you assign the new copy routine, the copy routine should have been created and built in a different location in the IMG. The menu path in the IMG to define copy routines is LOGISTICS EXECUTION • SHIPPING • COPYING CONTROL • DEFINE COPYING REQUIREMENTS.

You'll see a screen where you can define custom Copying Requirements, Data Transfer Routines, and Requirement Routines. In this screen, go to Copying Requirements, and select Deliveries to look up the existing routines or to define new routines for deliveries.

SAP ERP provides you with a few copy requirements such as 1, 2, 3, 51, 101, and so on. Each number represents a unique routine, and the detailed code for every routine describes the data that is being copied or any other checks that the company wants to have for copying data from an order to the delivery.

Custom routines are generally created with numbers starting from 900, as you see in Figure 2.48.

Figure 2.48 Copy Routines Available for Deliveries

After you decide to modify or create a new routine, for example, 902 for a header level, you can create the routine with the necessary description and build the source code to meet your requirements. For example, if you want to ensure that deliveries aren't created if there is a block on the sales order, you need to code the routine to meet that requirement and save the routine with the new routine number. Another copy routine that is useful for reverse logistics is used when the part is serialized, so that before the delivery is created, a custom check can be done to ensure that the serial number is provided by the customer and is captured at the order level. The delivery creation can be stopped or blocked if the serial number isn't provided at the header level for returns orders. The details of the location to code the copy routine are shown in Figure 2.49.

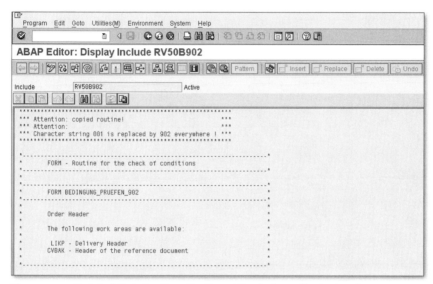

Figure 2.49 Detailed Code for Copy Routine at the Delivery Header Level

After the code is developed and the routine is ready to be assigned, the assignment should be done in the configuration by going to LOGISTICS EXECUTION • SHIPPING • COPYING CONTROL • SPECIFY COPY CONTROL FOR DELIVERIES.

After selecting the combination of the return order type RE and the return delivery type LR, the detailed screen shows the routines assigned to this combination. This is where you can change or add the new routine that you've created. In the example shown in Figure 2.50, header routine 001 provided by SAP is being replaced by a custom routine 901, where there is an additional code to prevent delivery creation if there is a block in the sales order. To replace the routine, use the pull-down menu on the field you want to change, and choose the new entry that you want to use.

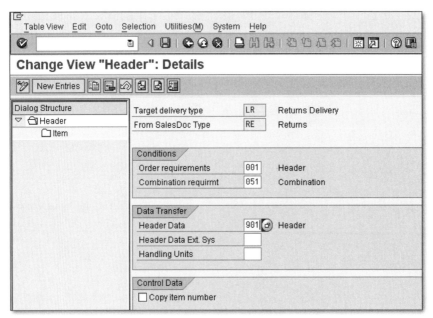

Figure 2.50 Copy Routine Being Changed at the Delivery Header Level

Now that we've discussed the configuration of order types, item categories for orders, delivery types, item categories for delivery, schedule line categories, and movement types, let's proceed to the complete returns business process.

Both the internal and external returns process start with the creation of a returns sales order. After the return sales order is created, a returns delivery is created. A returns delivery can be created from the order change screen itself, using Transaction VA02 if you're using order change or Transaction VL01N if you're trying to create the delivery as a standalone object. To create a delivery from order change, you'll need to select SALES DOCUMENT • DELIVER from the sales order change menu as shown in Figure 2.51.

To create a delivery from a standalone transaction, you can use Transaction VL01N. Enter the return sales Order number and the Shipping Point, as shown in Figure 2.52.

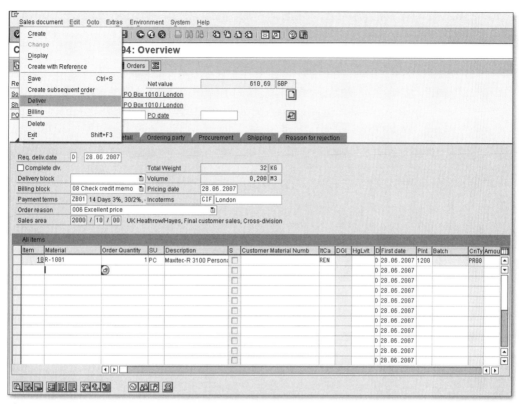

Figure 2.51   Creating a Return Delivery from Returns Sales Order

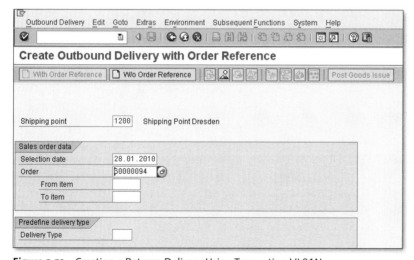

Figure 2.52   Creating a Returns Delivery Using Transaction VL01N

The delivery configuration contains a key piece of information that will be used for reverse logistics. The delivery contains data regarding the returns plant, returns storage location, and route.

▶ **Returns plant:** The returns plant in the delivery is determined from the sales order. Typically this plant is entered during the sales order creation process, and can be defaulted using custom development or by the SAP Supply Chain Management (SAP SCM) component, Global Available to Promise (GATP).

▶ **Returns storage location:** The returns storage location is also determined from the sales order or by SAP ERP automatically using a storage location determination rule, which we discussed earlier.

▶ **Route:** Route is an important piece of information for reverse logistics if your company is paying the shipping cost from the customer back to your company. In this case, the route contains information regarding the carrier that should be used to deliver the product. The carrier is assigned to the route in the configuration of the routes, which can be access by going to LOGISTICS EXECUTION • SHIPPING • BASIC SHIPPING FUNCTIONS • ROUTES • DEFINE ROUTES. Here you define the route and also assign the service agent to the route, as shown in Figure 2.53.

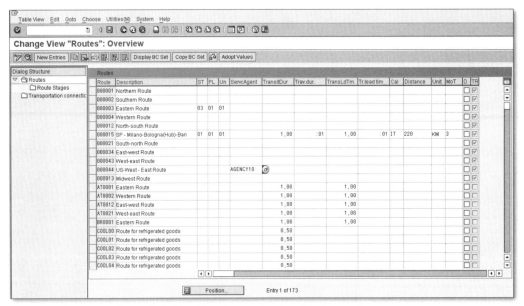

Figure 2.53 Route Definition Showing Service Agent Assignment

2.3.2   Returns Receiving

Returns receipts are created by processing the returns delivery. When you post the goods issue to a returns delivery, it results in a goods receipt of the returned product. The stock category of the returns stock is determined based on the movement typed used in the delivery. If the returning plant and storage location are associated with a warehouse, then a warehouse transfer requirement or a transfer order is created depending on the configuration of the warehouse in SAP ERP.

In the warehouse, you use the delivery note output or a sales order output that accompanies the shipment to process the returns receipt.

Because the product is being returned in a returns delivery, you don't need to use picking. Instead, putaway of the product needs to be done in the warehouse.

To process the returns delivery, the warehouse employees need to verify the product to ensure the correct product is being received and then select the Post Good Issue button in the delivery, as shown in Figure 2.54.

Figure 2.54   Post Goods Issue of a Returns Delivery

If a post goods issue is successful, a goods receipt document is created in the background.

The goods receipt document gets updated in the delivery document flow. The document flow shows the history of actions in the SAP system for the delivery. You can access the delivery document flow by going to ENVIRONMENT • DOCUMENT FLOW, as shown in Figure 2.55.

Figure 2.55 Accessing the Document Flow in a Returns Delivery

In the document flow display, you'll see all of the documents associated with the order, including delivery and goods receipt document, as shown in Figure 2.56.

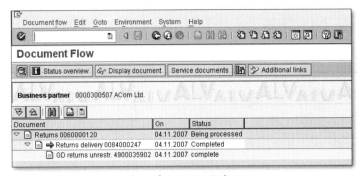

Figure 2.56 Document Flow of a Returns Delivery

As you notice in Figure 2.56, the return order is 0060000120, the associated return delivery is 008400027, and the goods receipt document into the unrestricted stock is 4900035902. The material document displays the details of the movement, including the movement type, material, plant, and storage location.

2.3.3 Warehouse Processing

Warehouse processing for returns starts with creating a transfer order with reference to the transfer requirement that was created when the delivery was post goods issued. To look up all open transfer requirements in a transfer order, you can use Transaction LB10, as shown in Figure 2.57. This transaction lists all of the open transfer requirements for which transfer orders haven't been created.

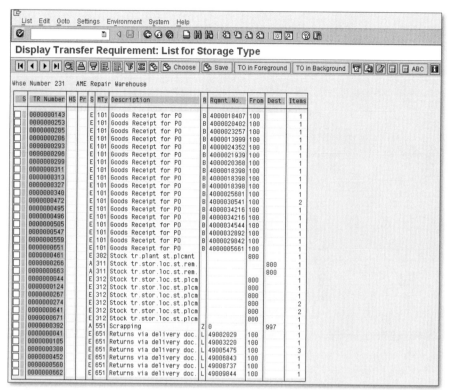

Figure 2.57 List of Open Transfer Requirements for the Warehouse Using Transaction LB10

To start the put away or placement process, you need to select the transfer requirement that you want to process and select either the TO in Foreground button or the TO in Background button to create the transfer order.

The transfer order is a document that proposes a bin to complete the placement process. As a part of the transfer order process, a transfer order printout can be enabled that identifies the destination bin where the material needs to be placed.

Based on the recommendations of the transfer order, you'll need to complete the putaway into the destination bin. The SAP system can also be set up to confirm the transfer order that will complete the putaway process. Depending on the requirements of the confirmation, you can either enable Confirmation Required or Confirmation Not Required in the warehouse management configuration.

Figure 2.58 shows the details of a transfer order with the source storage type, source bin, destination storage type, and destination storage bin.

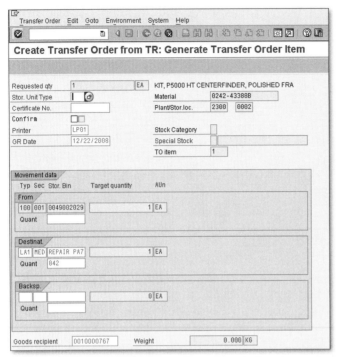

Figure 2.58 Transfer Order Creation from a Transfer Requirement

The transfer order also shows the stock category and the printer details where the transfer order is going to be printed out.

For materials that are being returned to the returns stock and that need to be converted into own stock after the inspection process, the quality inspection can be done in a quality staging area in the warehouse. After the inspection is complete, then another transfer order can be created to move the material from the quality staging area to the regular putaway storage bin.

2.3.4 Parts Segregation and Identification

Returns parts need to be clearly identified to keep track of the inspection process and also not to mix the parts that haven't cleared inspection with good parts stock.

To identify the parts, you can create a label that identifies the material, which is typically called the material identifier tag. This tag can be custom coded to include any specific requirement of your company such as the goods receipt date, material, quantity, batch, and serial number if the part is serialized.

The description of the part is also printed as part of the material identifier tag. Depending on how your company identifies the broken or defective part — by part number or any other material master attribute — it should be clearly printed on the material identifier tag.

The material identifier tag can be set up to print when the goods issue is posted against the return delivery. This enables the receiver to attach the material identifier tag when the part is received in the warehouse.

We'll now review the quality inspection processes that are usually performed for returns parts.

2.3.5 Quality Management

The quality management process in the warehouse can be visual or very detailed, based on how you check certain characteristics of the material.

To perform just a visual inspection, the materials need to be received into quality stock and not quality inspection stock. Quality inspection stock involves creating inspection lots that involve multiple steps of performing tests and recording them in the results of the inspection lot. Then a usage decision is made based on the test results. The subsequent movements for the materials are determined based on these test results.

> **Example**
>
> When a part is received into inspection stock, an inspection lot is created. After inspection processing, if the part is found to meet the inspection results, a usage decision to accept the inspection lot can be made, and the goods movement for this usage decision can be configured to move the stock from the returns stock to the company's own stock.

Inspection lots are created for specific inspection types. Inspection types define the type of inspection that needs to be done. Inspection types are defined in the IMG as a part of the quality inspection configuration. You can access the inspection types by going to QUALITY MANAGEMENT • QUALITY INSPECTION • INSPECTION LOT CREATION • MAINTAIN INSPECTION TYPES.

SAP ERP provides a specific inspection type for inspecting customer returns, which is inspection type 06. Figure 2.59 provides the detailed configuration of Inspection Type 06.

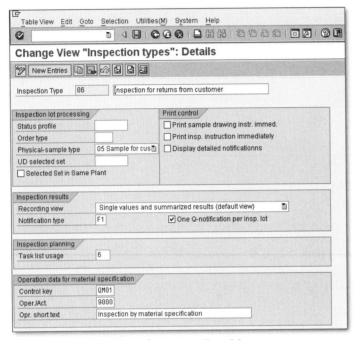

Figure 2.59 Configuration of Inspection Type 06

When you set the inspection lot of Inspection Type 06, it allows for the material to be returned and an inspection lot to be created for that material. To do so, the material master needs to be modified to add and activate Inspection Type 06 in the quality view of the material master. Figure 2.60 shows the Quality Management tab of the material master. To access this view, use Transaction MM03, and enter the material number information. To post the received stock into a quality stock category, select the Post to Insp. Stock field in the material master.

In the Quality Management tab, you'll need to select the Insp. Setup button to add and activate inspection types and maintain data specific to the inspection type and the material. To activate the inspection type, click on the Active flag in the inspection type subscreen, as shown in Figure 2.61.

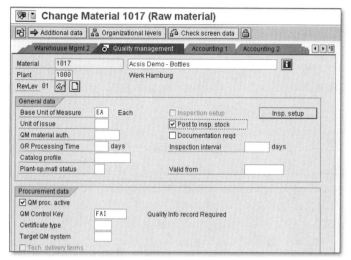

Figure 2.60 Quality View of the Material Master

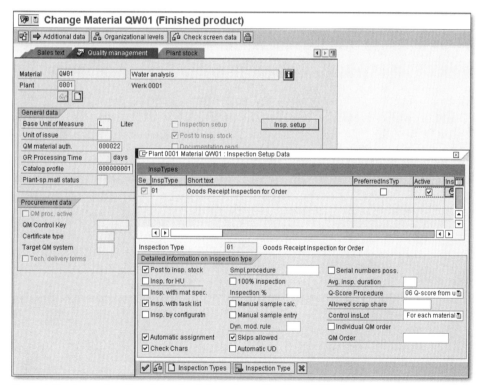

Figure 2.61 Inspection Type Setup for Returns Inspection Type 06 in the Material Master Quality View

In the material master, you can also set up the inspection procedures and how sampling needs to be done for inspecting this material. All of these data are used to create an inspection lot for inspecting returned parts from customers. After the inspection is completed, the parts are released to be stored in the warehouse for subsequent processing.

2.4 Summary

In this chapter, we covered how returns are processed in SAP ERP and the configuration options to allow returns to be processed differently based on your company's requirements. Using the information provided in this chapter, you should be able to do the following:

▶ Configure return order types

▶ Configure return delivery types

▶ Configure return order item category

▶ Configure return order schedule line category

▶ Configure movement types

▶ Configure accounting information for returns

Based on the configuration options and a clear understanding of the business process of returns order processing, returns processing in the warehouse, and also quality inspection, you should be able to configure the requirements for these processes in your company effectively in SAP ERP.

The next chapter discusses how you can enable and process refurbishment in SAP ERP.

Refurbishment is the process of receiving a failed or broken part returned by the customer, repairing it, and selling it back at full or discounted price. In this chapter, we'll discuss the different possibilities that enable rework or refurbishment, along with the SAP ERP functions and options to enable refurbishment.

3 Refurbishment

Refurbishment is the process where returned products are repaired and sold to customers. Typically, if the part is under warranty, the parts are returned by the customer, and the company accepts the failed part back into the network to either scrap or repair. The repaired part is generally sold at a less expensive price or the original price with additional warranty. There are a variety of types of refurbishment, including internal repair for refurbishment and external repair for refurbishment.

3.1 Internal Repair

For internal repair, the customer returns a part to the company, and the company repairs the product internally. The company procures the necessary components and supplies for the repair, performs the repair, and returns the product to the inventory as a refurbished product. The refurbished product is identified as such so that it can be sold at a different price or with an extended warranty. Figure 3.1 shows the simplified business process of receiving a failed part from the customer or engineer, repairing it, and adding it into the inventory. In some cases, the customer pays for the repair process if the product is owned by the customer, which is referred to as a paid repair or customer paid repair. We'll discuss this process further in Chapter 4, Customer Paid Repair Process in SAP ERP.

As you can see in Figure 3.1, different organizations in the company are involved in getting the returned product repaired and sold back to customers. Let's take a look at each of the roles played by these organizations in more detail.

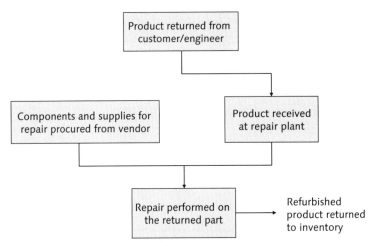

Figure 3.1 Internal Repair for Refurbishment Business Process

Example of Internal Repair

A toy manufacturing company makes toy wagons for sale in retail stores. On certain occasions due to bad handling of the product during transportation from the warehouse to the retail stores, the wheels of the wagon are broken and customers return the wagon to the store, which in turn returns it to the central returns processing center of the company. The company then inspects the wagon and determines that the wheels need to be replaced. Because the wheels for the wagon are produced in house, the repair center obtains a replacement wheel from the manufacturing warehouse of the company and packs the new wheels in the toy box with the wagon and sells the product as a refurbished toy wagon. The wagon is sold as refurbished because the product was already sold to the customer and was returned. So the company sells the product as a refurbished product at 50% of the original price but with the same warranty terms used at the sale of the original product.

The internal repair for refurbishment is accomplished in SAP ERP using various system processes and tools. The warranty check is done using a warranty claim document in SAP ERP. When checking for a warranty claim, the system uses the functions available in the warranty claim process in combination with the validation/substitution rules (VSR) checks to ensure that the product is under warranty and is acceptable for return based on the material condition. You can build custom requirements for checking the return in the VSR action checks, so that the product is allowed to be returned to the network for internal repair. After the warranty claim has been created and the product is accepted for return, a return order is created in SAP ERP using Transaction VA01 with reference to the forward order. The details of the return order are discussed in detail in Chapter 2, Returns. After the creation of the return order, the return is processed into the network by creating a return delivery and receiving the product into the warehouse against the return delivery. The returns delivery processing contains a step to post the goods receipt in SAP ERP against a return delivery using Transaction VL02N (LOGISTICS • LOGISTICS EXECUTION • OUTBOUND PROCESS • GOODS ISSUE FOR OUTBOUND DELIVERY • OUTBOUND DELIVERY • CHANGE • SINGLE DOCUMENT).

After the product is received, quality inspection on the product is completed using a combination of quality notifications and inspection lots in SAP ERP. The result of the inspection determines the product to be repairable. Sometimes, at this point, if the product is deemed nonrepairable, the product is scrapped locally in the repair plant or sent to the scrap plant. The receiving warehouse isn't always the repair facility, so if the product is repairable, it's sent to the repair facility by using a stock transport order (STO) if the repair plant is in the same company code as the receiving warehouse. If the repairing plant is in a different company code, then the product is transferred using an intercompany transport order (ICTO). Figure 3.2 shows the process of accepting a return and returning the product into the network and into the repair facility in SAP ERP.

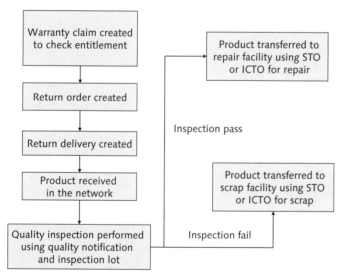

Figure 3.2 SAP ERP Process to Receive the Returned Product and Transfer It to the Repair Location

After the product is received in the repair location, the repair location uses a SAP ERP production order to repair the product by disassembling it to remove the broken component and replacing the product with new components. When the repair is just cleaning the product, a production order can be used to capture the materials and labor used to clean the product.

The repair process can be broken down into subprocesses, such as cleaning, disassembly, and repair as shown in Figure 3.3.

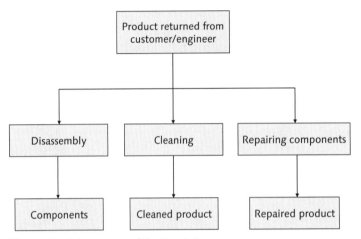

Figure 3.3 Subprocesses of the Repair Process

3.1.1   Cleaning a Product

Certain repairs actually involve cleaning the product. For example, a customer returns the dirty product that has been used and can't be used further without cleaning. The company provides a replacement product that is already cleaned, and the customer pays for the service and not for the product itself. This process is handled in SAP ERP by creating contracts for providing clean products in exchange for dirty products for a fixed price to the customer.

> **Example of Cleaning**
>
> In the semiconductor industry, kits are cleaned after continuous use to remove residues and chemical deposits before they can be reused again. The cleaning consists of sandblasting or some other form of cleaning to remove the residue and deposits. This cleaning is considered a form of repair and can be performed in SAP ERP using a production order to indicate consumption of consumables, labor, and machine time if the company completes the cleaning process in house.

In SAP ERP, you can create a production order using Transaction CO01 (LOGISTICS • PRODUCTION • SHOP FLOOR CONTROL • ORDER • CREATE • WITH MATERIAL). Figure 3.4 shows a production order created for cleaning a wafer in the semiconductor industry. This production order is displayed using SAP ERP Transaction CO03 (LOGISTICS • PRODUCTION • SHOP FLOOR CONTROL • ORDER • DISPLAY). The figure displays the different repair operations, such as Film Stripping, Visual Inspection, Polishing, Pre-Cleaning, and Final Clean.

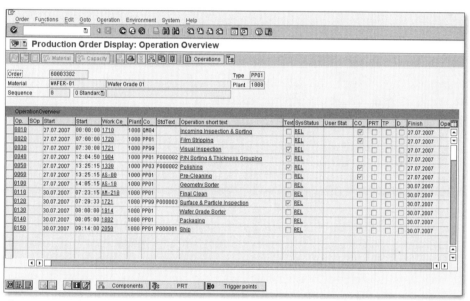

Figure 3.4 Production Order Operations in SAP ERP Used for Cleaning a Wafer

The types of operations performed are defined in the control key displayed in the operations of the production order. For example, in the production order displayed in Figure 3.4, the first operation is Incoming Inspection & Sorting. To display the details of this operation, you can use the pull-down menu of the control key, and select the control key QM04 as shown in Figure 3.5.

The control key also indicates if the operation is costing relevant, if inspection characteristics are to be maintained for the operation, and if the operation is a rework. The control keys are configured in the IMG in SAP ERP that is accessed using Transaction SPRO. In the IMG, you can go to PRODUCTION • SHOP FLOOR CONTROL • MASTER DATA • ROUTING DATA • DEFINE CONTROL KEY to configure control keys.

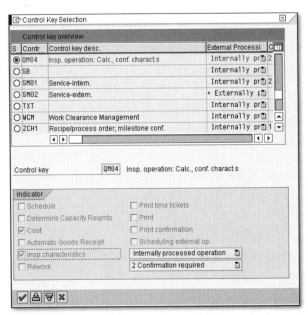

Figure 3.5 Details of the Control Key of the Incoming Inspection Operation of a Production Order

Here you can define the characteristics of the control key shown in Figure 3.5. In addition to the control key, the work center where the operation is performed is also specified in the operations of a production order. The work center is the organization unit where the operations are performed. Work centers also have a limited capacity that is defined during their creation. A work center can refer to machines or people. In Figure 3.4, shown earlier, the work center for operation 0010 is 1710, which is defined for goods receipt inspection for plant 1000 where the operation 0010 will be performed.

To perform every operation, some components or materials are used. The components used for the production order displayed in Figure 3.4 can be displayed by choosing the GOTO • OVERVIEWS • COMPONENTS option in the menu of the production order.

Figure 3.6 shows the components of the production order used in the example shown earlier in Figure 3.4. Component 0010-RW0014 is used in operation 0010 to perform an incoming inspection.

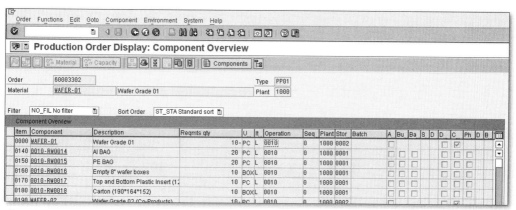

Figure 3.6 Components of a Production Order

The production order captures the cost of cleaning based on the costing information provided in the control data of the production order. The control data can be accessed from the production order display by choosing the Control Data tab in the production order header. The control data of the production order displayed in Figure 3.4 is shown in Figure 3.7.

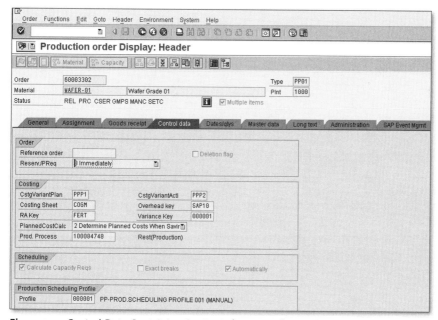

Figure 3.7 Control Data Containing Costing Information for Production Orders

Costing information includes the costing variant for planned costs and the costing variant for actual costs as shown in Figure 3.7. To display the costs itemized for the production order, you can choose GOTO • COSTS • ITEMIZATION from the production order display menu. The itemized costs of the production order displayed in Figure 3.4 are shown in Figure 3.8.

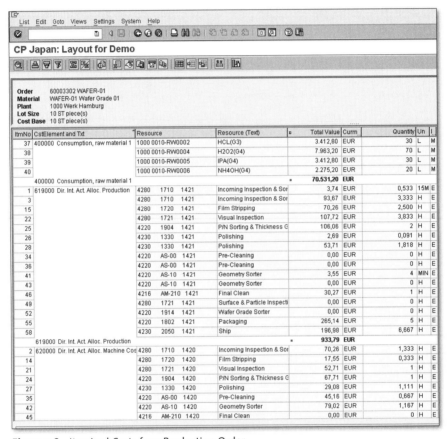

Figure 3.8 Itemized Costs for a Production Order

The costs for different cost elements are allocated based on the consumption of materials and use of the resources in the production order as displayed in Figure 3.8.

3.1.2   Disassembly

Disassembly is another process where a component in a kit can be removed and sold again even though the kit itself has to be scrapped. The disassembly process can be done in SAP ERP using a production order. In the production order, the kit is entered as a component, and the kit's components that can be removed and sold are classified as by-products or co-products. When the production order is confirmed, the components that were classified as co-products and by-products are received into inventory against the production order.

If you don't want to use a production order, you can create a custom movement type to consume the kit against a general ledger account or a cost center and a reversal custom movement type that references the same general ledger account or costs center that you can to receive the components. This will ensure that the kit value is consumed, and the component value is deducted from the same general ledger account or cost center, resulting in the difference of the kit value and the component value being left out in the general ledger account or the cost center.

The advantage of using a production order for disassembly is that the production order can automatically determine components that can be disassembled based on a BOM (bill of material), whereas the custom movement type solution requires the user to enter the component manually in the SAP ERP system.

Co-products and by-products can be specified in the BOM of the kit. For co-products, the material master needs to be set up to indicate that the material can be produced as a co-product. Co-products provide additional flexibility because the actual costs of the co-products can be displayed at the co-product level, which isn't possible with by-products. In SAP ERP, co-products are indicated by the co-product indicator in the production order line item. By-products are indicated by the negative quantity of the component in the production order without the co-product indicator. Figure 3.9 shows a list of by-products in a production order.

As described earlier, by-products are items that are present in the components of the production order with negative quantity without the co-product indicator. Figure 3.10 shows a production order with components that include co-products.

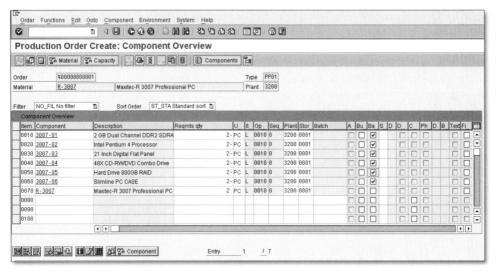

Figure 3.9 By-Products Listed in a Production Order

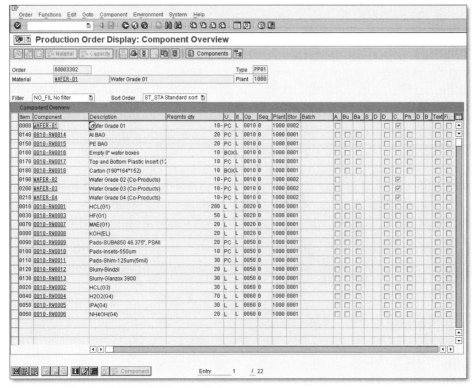

Figure 3.10 Co-Products in a Production Order

To consume the kit against the custom movement type, you use the SAP ERP Transaction MIGO, choose the Goods Issue – Other option, enter the custom movement type (XXX in Figure 3.11) in the GI for Cost Center field, and enter either the G/L Account or Cost Center information in the Account Assignment tab of the line item as shown in Figure 3.11. Transaction MIGO can be accessed by going to LOGISTICS • MATERIALS MANAGEMENT • INVENTORY MANAGEMENT • GOODS MOVEMENT • GOODS MOVEMENT (MIGO).

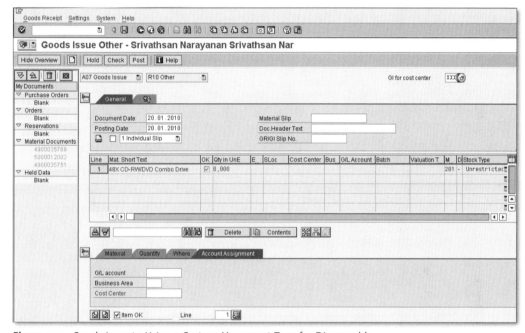

Figure 3.11 Goods Issue to Using a Custom Movement Type for Disassembly

After the kit or the parent material is consumed then using the reversal movement type or another custom movement type, the components can be received back into inventory. To create the receipt, you can use the same Transaction MIGO, choose the Goods Receipt – Other option, and then use the custom movement type and the general ledger account to complete the transaction.

3.1.3   Repair

In certain assemblies that are returned, only one component of the assembly is defective, and the rest of the assembly is good. In this case, the assembly is disassembled, and the defective component is removed and replaced. This whole process is done in SAP ERP using a production order to disassemble and then another production order to assemble the product with good components. The defective component is then scrapped using Transaction MIGO with the Goods Issue – Other option and movement type 551. The scrap movement can also be allocated to a general ledger account or a cost center using the Account Assignment tab in Transaction MIGO.

Now that you have a solid understanding of internal repair, let's move on to discuss external repair.

3.2   External Repair

For external repair, the returned product is received into the network, an external vendor is contacted, and a quote is obtained for performing the repair. If the quote is accepted, then the product is sent to the vendor who performs the repair and returns the product to the company. The company then sells the product as a refurbished product.

> **Example of External Repair**
>
> A computer manufacturing company receives a laptop that has failed from a customer. Upon return and inspection, the problem is identified to be the motherboard. The manufacturer then contacts a vendor who is qualified to repair motherboards to obtain a quote. Upon approval, the product is sent for repair, and afterwards, the product is returned to the company. The company then advertises the product as a refurbished laptop with a selling price that is 50% off the original price with the original manufacturer's warranty of 1 year from the sale.

The difference between internal and external repair is that for internal repair, the activities for repairing the product happen within the company, so the financial impact is within the company. For external repairs, where a vendor invoices for the service, the cost needs to be considered for external repair reporting. Sometimes, there are opportunities to repair products inside the company, and the product is still repaired by the vendor because of the lower cost of repairing externally. In addition, for OEM products, the vendor has equipment qualified to do certain kinds of repair that the company can't perform in house. Also, most companies today prefer to have a contract with a third-party logistics (3PL) provider that handles the repairs for the company. The 3PL in turn either repairs the product or subcontracts the repair to another vendor. The 3PL bills the company on a periodic basis for the repairs instead of billing for every repair activity. Figure 3.12 provides the overview of the external repair business process.

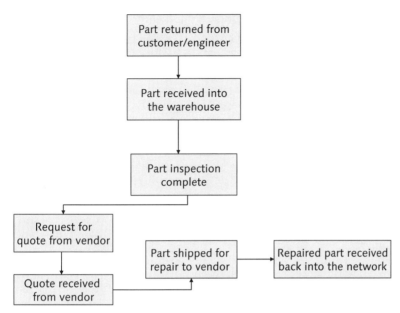

Figure 3.12 External Repair Business Process Overview

In SAP ERP, the external repair process is accomplished using the following tools and process flows. The starting point for both external and internal repairs is the same. The order entry team obtains the information from the customer or the engineer and creates a return sales order. But after the product has been returned to the warehouse and the inspection is complete, if the product is deemed repairable, the procurement team identifies a vendor that can repair the material and contacts the vendor to get a quote. The request is done in the SAP system by using the request for quote (RFQ) transaction. An RFQ can be created in SAP ERP using Transaction ME41. This transaction can also be accessed by going to LOGISTICS • MATERIALS MANAGEMENT • PURCHASING • RFQ/QUOTATION • REQUEST FOR QUOTATION • CREATE.

After the quote is obtained and accepted by the company, then a subcontracting purchase order or an expense purchase order is created to send the part for service. The difference between a subcontracting purchase order and an expense purchase order lies in the tracking and the cost. For a subcontracting purchase order, the material movement to and from the vendor is tracked in SAP ERP; for the expense purchase order, the material movement isn't tracked, and only the cost associated with the service provided by the vendor is captured in SAP ERP. Because the subcontracting purchase order provides the option to track both the materials and the cost of service from the vendor, it's the preferred solution to handle external repairs. In the subcontracting purchase order, if the company is providing any components for the service, the components are listed in the purchase order. If the part alone is shipped to the vendor and received back, then the part is listed both as the received part or the main part as well as the component. SAP ERP standard serialization doesn't allow for the same material number/serial number to be both sent as a component and received as a repaired part. To overcome this issue, serialization can be turned off for certain movement types, as discussed in Chapter 6, Serial Number Management in Reverse Logistics.

After the purchase order has been approved based on the release strategy, the part is then shipped from the warehouse by using a delivery against the subcontracting purchase order. After this delivery is processed and the post goods issued, the stock shows up in a stock category called stock with vendor. The stock stays in this category until the repair is complete and the repaired part is returned to the company. Upon receipt of the repaired part, the component stock is consumed from the stock with vendor category, and the repaired material is stored in the warehouse. If additional material was used by the vendor, then another transaction for subsequent adjustment can be created to provide the additional material to the vendor. To do subsequent adjustments, you use Transaction MIGO, and choose the Subsequent Adjustment option. Figure 3.13 shows the process of external repair in SAP ERP.

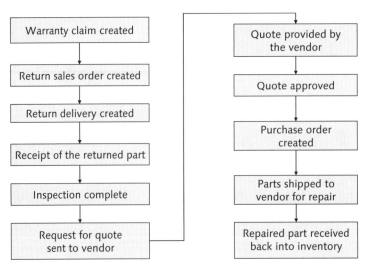

Figure 3.13 External Repair Process in SAP ERP

3.2.1 Products Returned from Service Engineers

In many industries, products are stored on the customer's premises to provide support to the service engineers who provide support and are responsible for maintaining equipment. These products are used by the service engineers to fix issues in the machines and return the broken machine parts back to the network if they are repairable. If they are repairable, then the product follows the same process of the internal and external repair described previously. The service engineer returns the product to the closest repair location that is capable of performing quality inspection.

The service engineer return process starts with the product being removed from the machine that has stopped due to a defective part. The removal of the product from the machine is shown in SAP ERP by performing Transaction MIGO, using movement type 262 in the transaction to reverse the goods issue, or performing a goods receipt against a service order. In some companies, because the stock was consumed against a forward sales order against a service order, the removal of the product from the machine is done in SAP ERP by creating a returns sales order and performing the goods receipt against the returns delivery. For contracts provided to the customers where the company is responsible for maintaining the machine and ensuring problems are fixed in the machine ASAP, the company owns and is responsible for all of the components in the machine. The inventory of all spare parts that are owned by the company and are stored in the customer's location shows in the stock report of the company in the maintenance plant. The maintenance plant is the location where the machine and the parts used for services are stored in SAP ERP. This is the plant against which service order operations are created and performed against.

For returns from the service engineer, the parts are returned to the maintenance plant first by performing a goods movement transaction with movement type 262 with reference to a service order or by using the return sales order process. After this return, the part is either returned to the local warehouse or a repair facility using a STO or an ICTO. From that point on, the process is the same as internal or external repair. Figure 3.14 shows service order header details in SAP ERP. The service order can be displayed using Transaction IW33 or by going to LOGISTICS • CUSTOMER SERVICE • SERVICE PROCESSING • ORDER • SERVICE ORDER • DISPLAY.

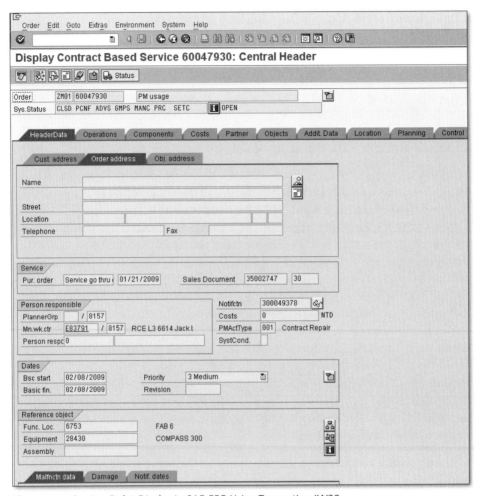

Figure 3.14 Service Order Display in SAP ERP Using Transaction IW33

The service order has components that are entered by the service engineer that will be used to perform the maintenance on the machine. Every material in the line item that is used for maintenance may have a corresponding material that can be returned because the material being installed on a machine means the failed or defective material with the same material number is removed from the machine. Figure 3.15 shows the service order header displaying the maintenance plant.

The maintenance plant stores the spare parts that will be used for servicing the machines in that location.

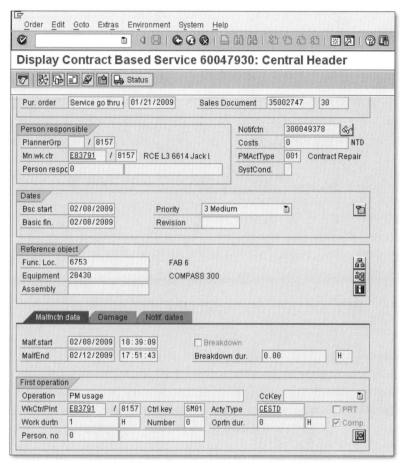

Figure 3.15 Service Order Display Showing the Maintenance Plant

All of the parts ordered in the service order are displayed in the components screen of the service order. These are the parts ordered by the service engineer to perform maintenance. Figure 3.16 shows the component screen with a list of all of the materials ordered against a service order. The plant and storage location listed in the component screen typically refer to the maintenance plant where the material is stored until the service engineer uses it to perform the service.

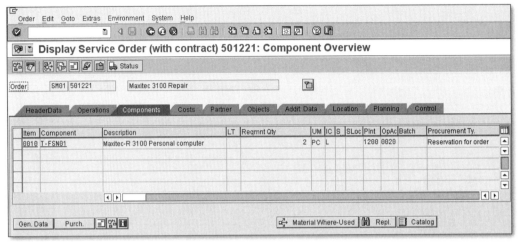

Figure 3.16 Component Listed in the Service Order

The costs associated with the service order are listed in the Costs tab and the costs subscreen that shows costs associated with labor, material, and services. Figure 3.17 shows the Costs tab and costs subscreen with the costs breakdown of External Services, Internal Labor, Overhead, and Spares (Own Production).

Figure 3.18 shows Transaction MIGO used with movement type 262 to receive the returned part. You can see the material document that was posted for the 262 movement type.

As you can see, the service order is referenced in the material document under the Account Assignment tab. The Profit Center and Functional Area are also specified to ensure proper valuation and accounting. Figure 3.19 shows the material document display with the Plant, Storage Location, and the Movement Type in the Where tab at the item level.

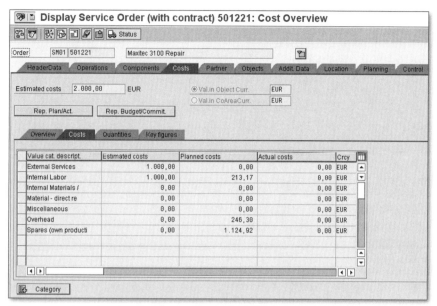

Figure 3.17 Costs Displayed in the Service Order

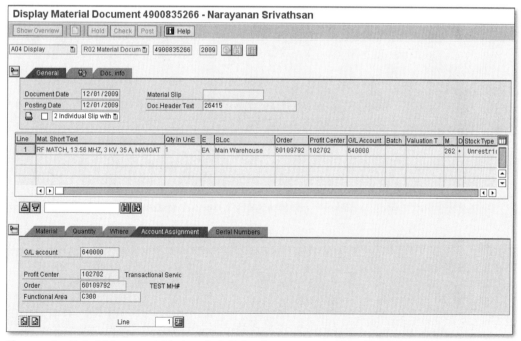

Figure 3.18 Material Document Display of a 262 Goods Movement with Reference to a Service Order

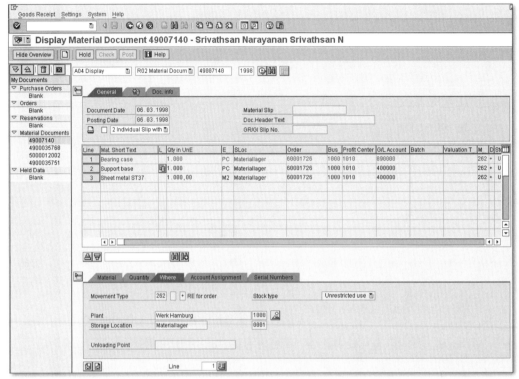

Figure 3.19 Material Document Display with Plant, Storage Location, and Movement Type Displayed

In certain situations, the stock for the service order is received using a sales order. This process is based on stock being issued for a sales order that has a reference to the service order and ensures the value of the material is accounted against a service order and isn't billed directly to the customer. In this scenario, the return from a service engineer is done using a return sales order, and the receipt of the return sales order is done by goods receipt against a returns delivery. After the receipt is completed, a quality inspection follows, which is then followed by contacting the vendor for a quote, and so on.

3.3 Organization Impact on Refurbishment Processes

Different organizations are involved in enabling the refurbishment process to perform smoothly. In this section, we'll discuss the impact of these organizations.

3.3.1 Order Administration

Order administration involves collecting data from the customer and creating the warranty claim document to validate the customer entitlement. After the customer warranty is confirmed, the customer service representative (or the order administrator) creates a return sales order. Figure 3.20 shows the warranty claim creation process with the display of actions to check for customer entitlement and to create a return sales order.

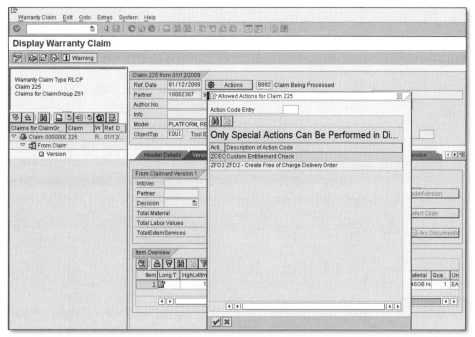

Figure 3.20 Warranty Claim Checking for Customer Entitlement and Creating a Returns Sales Order Using Action Codes

Order administrators also check the return acceptance of the part by the planning department by using the warranty check against data in the material master. The planning group updates this data to ensure only products that can be reworked or repaired are allowed to be returned into the network.

After the return order is created, it's sent for approval using the workflow process to ensure the order is approved before the return is received from the customer.

3.3.2   Planning

The planning team provides the necessary decisions regarding accepting returns of materials based on the condition, version, and use of the part in the network. Current inventory levels are checked against the incoming inventory of the part to determine whether to accept the part. In addition, the planning group is responsible for enabling the STOs and ICTOs that allow materials to be moved between two plants. To allow materials to ship using STOs, the destination plant is defined as a customer in the configuration. Along with defining the plant as the customer, the customer is also attached to a default sales organization, distribution channel, and division.

For STOs, you also create the checking rules in the configuration. Checking rules are defined for the availability check for STOs. The checking rule defines what parameters are considered for moving materials using STOs. Checking rules are combined with availability checks to determine the criteria used for checking parameters for availability. Figure 3.21 shows the details of the configuration linking the availability check to the checking rule.

In the checking rule and availability check configuration, you can define which in/out movements and which stock category should be considered when calculating availability of a material for committing to STOs shipments.

The other important configuration for STOs is the assignment of the delivery type and checking rule to the purchase order type and supplying plant. This configuration controls which delivery type is used for the supplying plant by the purchase order type. This is a very important configuration from a reverse logistics perspective because you can define different checking rules for reverse logistics than you can for forward logistics. This allows the availability check to work differently for the movement of defective material as compared to new or good material.

> **Example of the Checking Rule and the Availability Check for Reverse Logistics**
>
> The return stock received from a customer in a computer manufacturing company is stored in a local warehouse where inspections are done. After the inspection is complete, the stock needs to be transferred to a repair warehouse. The return stock is stored in the blocked stock category because this stock shouldn't be considered for shipping as regular stock. But this stock should be available for shipments to the repair warehouse. To accomplish this, you can define a custom rule for STOs/ICTOs for reverse logistics and assign a checking rule that considers blocked stock when considering available stock, thus allowing the creation of a delivery for the STO.

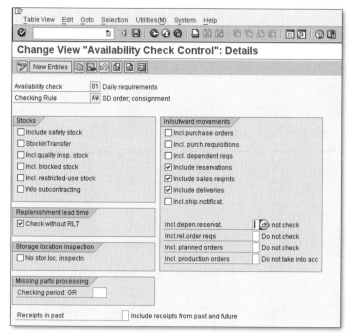

Figure 3.21 Configuring the Link Between the Availability Check and the Checking Rule in SAP ERP for STOs

The preceding example requires the checking rule for the STO/ICTO for reverse logistics to consider blocked stock. Figure 3.22 shows the checking rule configuration. On the left side, you can see the allowed stock category to be considered for stock, and you can select the Incl. Blocked Stock flag to indicate that blocked stock needs to be considered.

After the checking rule is defined, it can be assigned to a custom or standard delivery type for reverse logistics. You might define a custom delivery type for reverse logistics if the delivery type needs to be assigned to a custom movement type that in turn is assigned to the company's required account assignments.

Another configuration that is commonly used in reverse logistics is the single-step procedure for moving stock between plants. Most often when transferring stock between regular plants to repair plants that are close by or transferring stock from one side of the building to the other where the cleaning machines are located, you'll need to perform a lot of transactions during shipping, such as post goods issue and receiving the material on the receiving plant. The one-step configuration allows the goods receipt to be done automatically in the receiving plant as soon as the post goods issue is done on the supplying plant. This ensures that there is no goods receipt transaction needed at the receiving plant and no stock in transit. To set up this configuration, use MATERIALS MANAGEMENT • PURCHASING • PURCHASE ORDER • SETUP STOCK TRANSPORT ORDER • ASSIGN DOCUMENT TYPE, ONE STEP PROCEDURE, UNDERDELIVERY TOLERANCE, as shown in Figure 3.23.

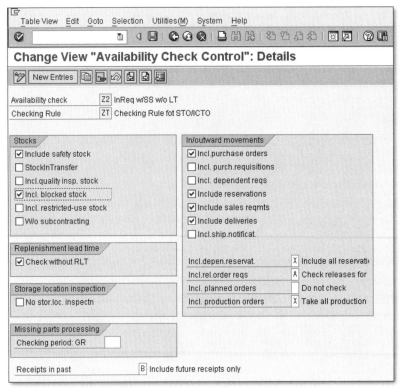

Figure 3.22 Selecting Blocked Stock for the Availability Check and Checking Rule for the STO/ICTO

In addition to allowing the one-step procedure, the document types for STOs are also specified in this configuration. The document type is specified for the combination of supplying plant and receiving plant in this configuration. In the standard SAP ERP system, the document type used for STOs between two plants in the same company is UB; if the plants are in different company codes, then it's NB. You can specify a custom document type if you've created one for any combination of plants here.

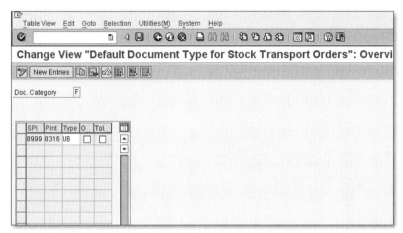

Figure 3.23 One-Step Procedure Configuration for STOs

The purchase order document types are defined in the configuration using MATE-
RIALS MANAGEMENT • PURCHASING • PURCHASE ORDER • DEFINE DOCUMENT TYPES,
as shown in Figure 3.24.

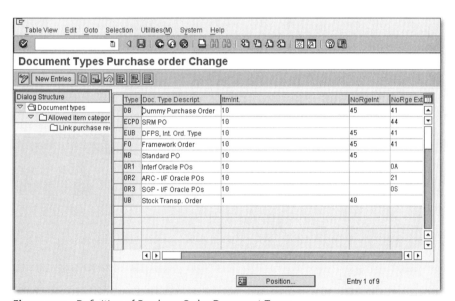

Figure 3.24 Definition of Purchase Order Document Types

Along with the definition of the purchase order document type, this configuration contains information about the allowed item categories for the purchase order document type. To view the allowed item categories, select the purchase order document type (Standard PO) and the Allowed Item Categories folder on the left side of the screen, as shown in Figure 3.25.

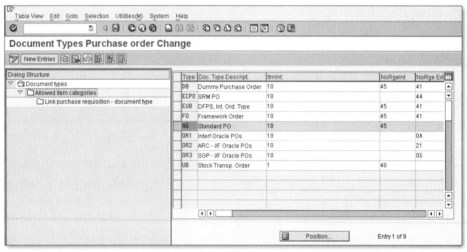

Figure 3.25 Allowed Item Categories for the Purchase Order Document Type

Figure 3.26 shows the allowed item categories for the standard NB purchase order document type in SAP ERP.

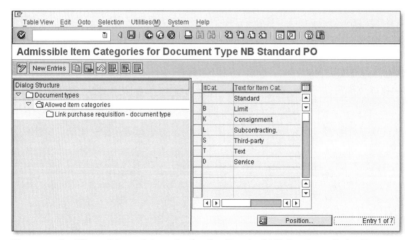

Figure 3.26 Allowed Item Categories for the Standard NB Purchase Order Document Type

The subcontracting item category L is specified here as an allowed item category. The subcontracting purchase order process will be discussed in detail later in this chapter.

3.3.3 Procurement in Internal and External Repair

The procurement team is involved in both internal and external repair. For internal repair, they are responsible for procuring the necessary components or materials needed for repairing or cleaning the product. The process for internal repair involves creating a production order for the repair, disassembly, and cleaning. Based on the production order requirements, if the components need to be bought from a vendor, then purchase requisitions are created automatically. Figure 3.27 shows the display of a production order with multiple components.

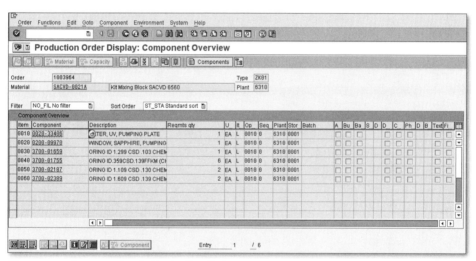

Figure 3.27 Components of a Production Order

The production order material and the components are displayed in the MRP stock requirements list in SAP ERP using Transaction MD04. For example, the final material in the production order shows the incoming quantity of the material with respect to the production order in the stock requirements list, as shown in Figure 3.28.

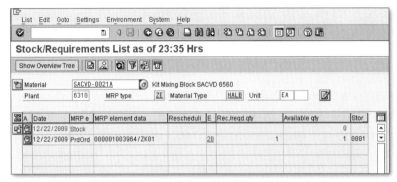

Figure 3.28 Stock Requirements List for a Material in a Production Order

The components of the production order also appear in the stock requirements list as reservations for the production order. These reservations can be converted to purchase requisitions, which in turn can be converted to purchase orders.

Figure 3.29 shows the stock requirements list for a component in a production order.

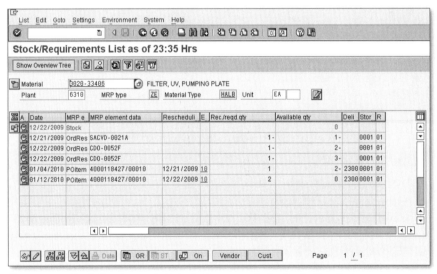

Figure 3.29 Stock Requirements List of a Component of a Production Order

A purchase requisition is created to indicate the need to procure a product. The procurement department needs to convert the purchase requisition to a purchase order to procure the product. When converting the purchase requisition, the procurement team also identifies the procurement vendor. When configuring, you can define the defaults for the conversion of the purchase requisition to purchase orders by going to MATERIALS MANAGEMENT • CONSUMPTION-BASED PLANNING • PROCUREMENT PROPOSALS • DEFINE CONVERSION OF PURCHASE REQUISITION INTO PURCHASE ORDER, as shown in Figure 3.30.

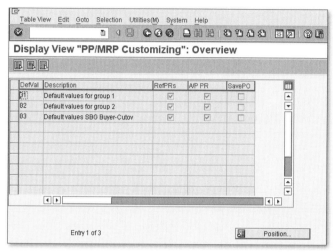

Figure 3.30 Default Settings for Converting Purchase Requisitions to Purchase Orders

For external repairs, the procurement team is responsible for the following:

▶ Creating the ICTO to obtain a quote for subcontracting services from a vendor.

▶ Creating a purchase order with reference to the quote.

▶ Notifying the warehouse about the purchase order so that they can ship the product.

▶ Ensuring the purchase order gets approved by all necessary managers, which is done in SAP ERP by using SAP Business Workflow.

Request for Quote (RFQ)

A request for quote (RFQ) is a document created to request a quote from a vendor for a product or service. Figure 3.31 shows the header for an RFQ created in SAP ERP.

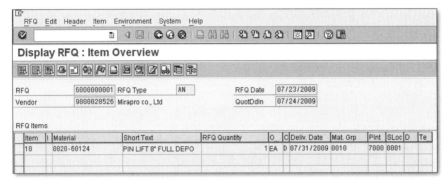

Figure 3.31 Request for Quotation in SAP ERP

The item category describes the type of item being requested for a quote from the vendor. Figure 3.32 shows the different item categories in SAP ERP in an RFQ, which includes Standard, Third-Party, and Service.

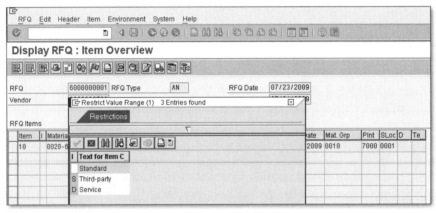

Figure 3.32 Display of Item Category in Request for Quote

For subcontracting purposes, the standard item category is used in the RFQ to obtain a quote for repair. In addition to entering data, the procurement team can also enter text describing the kind of service expected to be performed on the part, as shown in Figure 3.33.

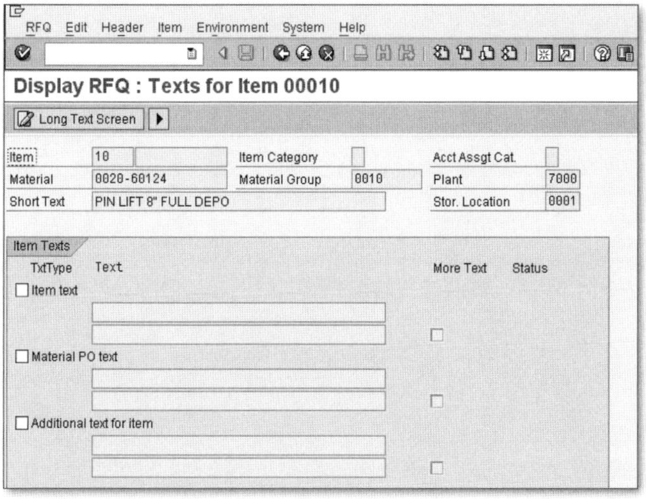

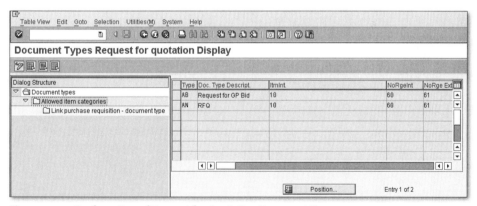

Figure 3.33 Text Entry in a Request for Quote

The document types for RFQs are configured in customizing, along with the allowed item categories and linking the purchase requisition type with the RFQ document type. This configuration is done by going to MATERIALS MANAGEMENT • PURCHASING • RFQ/QUOTATION • DEFINE DOCUMENT TYPES, as shown in Figure 3.34.

Figure 3.34 Configuration of Request for Quotation Document Type

To configure the purchase requisition type to the RFQ document type, select the request for quotation document type, and select the Link Purchase Requisition folder on the left side of the screen, as shown in Figure 3.35.

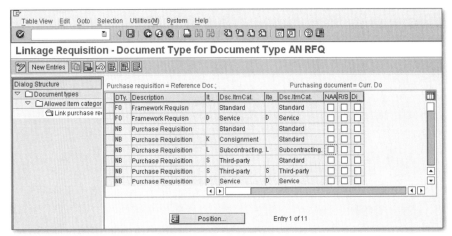

Figure 3.35 Linking the Purchase Requisition Document Type to the Request for Quotation Document Type

The item category for the RFQ is linked to the purchase requisition document's item category. The RFQ also has a release procedure and release strategy that can be assigned to it. The release procedure for the RQF is configured in the Purchasing area, by going to MATERIALS MANAGEMENT • PURCHASING • RFQ/QUOTATION • RELEASE PROCEDURE FOR RFQS • DEFINE RELEASE PROCEDURE FOR RFQS, as shown in Figure 3.36.

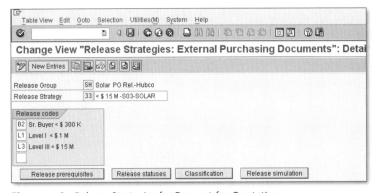

Figure 3.36 Release Strategies for Request for Quotation

Subcontracting Order

A subcontracting purchase order is identified by the item category of the purchase order. The item category is L, which indicates the line item in the purchase order is created for subcontracting. The subcontracting purchase orders always have components where the list of materials that are used for servicing or subcontracting are listed. Figure 3.37 shows the subcontracting purchase order with the subcontracting line item.

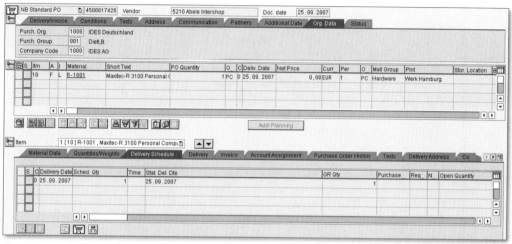

Figure 3.37   Create a Subcontracting Purchase Order

The components sent to the vendors are entered in the components screen of the subcontracting purchase order. Figure 3.38 shows the components of a subcontract purchase order.

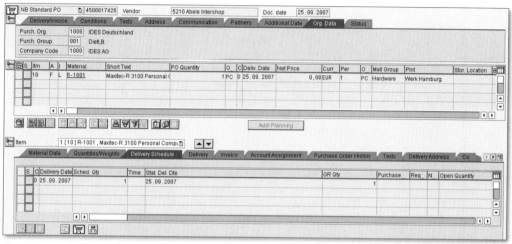

Figure 3.38   Components in a Subcontracting Purchase Order

The configuration for the subcontracting purchase order is accessed by going to MATERIALS MANAGEMENT • PURCHASING • PURCHASE ORDER • SET UP SUBCONTRACT ORDER.

In this configuration, the delivery type for shipping products on a subcontracting delivery is assigned by the supplying plant. The delivery type to the purchase order type is important if you want to use the standard process that uses deliveries and shipments to send components to your vendors just like you ship products to your customer. You can also ship products to the vendor without deliveries just by doing a material movement in SAP ERP, but following a standard shipping process that uses the delivery document and shipment document is the preferred method. Figure 3.39 shows the configuration for the subcontract purchase order to the delivery type. As you'll notice in the figure, you can assign different delivery types based on the supplying plant. This will help you handle complex requirements such as using a different movement type to the supplying plant if needed.

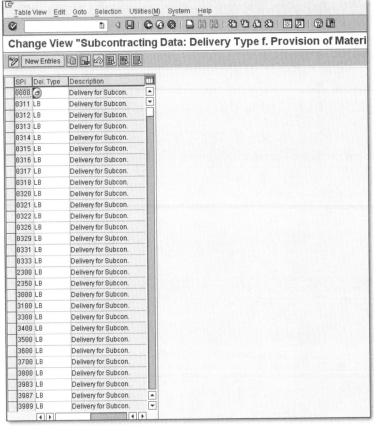

Figure 3.39 Assignment of Delivery Type to Supplying Plant for Subcontracting

3.4 Summary

Refurbishment is a very common process performed in many companies. The SAP system, if configured properly, can enable you to maximize the returns from the refurbishment process. Both internal and external repair can be configured in SAP ERP using standard tools. The subprocesses for refurbishment such as cleaning, repair, and disassembly can also be handled by configuring production orders and material movements against service orders. Production orders are important for internal repair and need to be configured to meet the requirements of the company's planning and finance teams.

Both materials returned from the customer and materials returned from the service engineers can be refurbished. With the help of the SAP system, you can perform both types of repair to meet your refurbishment needs.

In the next chapter, we'll move on to discuss the customer paid repair process with SAP ERP.

Customer paid repair is a subprocess in reverse logistics that provides an additional revenue stream by enabling a company to repair the customer's products and get paid for the service provided. In this chapter, we'll review the repair process in detail and learn about the various objects involved in repair.

4   Customer Paid Repair

The customer paid repair process refers to a company repairing and returning a customer-owned material and then billing the customer for the repair. Understanding how the repairs process works in SAP ERP and also gaining the SAP configuration knowledge on the repair processes and objects will help you configure SAP to meet all your company's repair needs.

4.1   Customer Paid Repair

Customer paid repair involves obtaining a defective product or material from a customer, repairing it internally or externally, returning the repaired product to the customer, and billing the customer for the repair service. Let's now proceed to see the business process and the system processes for customer paid repair in detail.

4.1.1   Business Process of Customer Paid Repair

In the customer repair process, the customer contacts the company and provides information to request a repair of one or many of the products owned by the company to the customer. Typically, this is done only for products that aren't covered by any warranty because the product has been used past its warranty expiry date. The company then receives the material from the customer, and the material is inspected or analyzed to determine if the repair is possible. If repair is possible, then the company provides an estimate to the customer, who determines whether to go ahead with the repair. If so, then the company starts the repair process. To repair the product, the company can perform the repair within the company, subcontract the product to a vendor and get the product repaired, or use a combination of both. If the product isn't repairable, then it can either be returned to the customer or scrapped at the company. Figure 4.1 shows the overview of the customer paid repair business process.

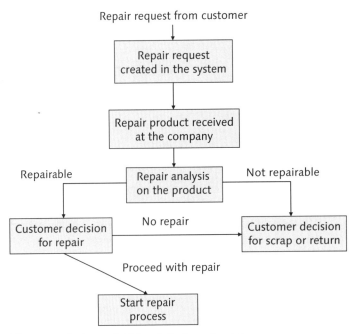

Figure 4.1 Customer Paid Repair Business Process

In Figure 4.1, a repair request is created when the customer contacts the company for the repair process. Let's now look at an example of a customer paid repair in a computer manufacturer.

Example of Customer Paid Repair

A customer buys a desktop computer directly from a computer manufacturing company. The company provides a warranty on the desktop and the components of the desktop for a year. After a year, the customer runs into the problem that the desktop shuts off automatically several times during the day. He calls the manufacturer to get the desktop fixed, and the manufacturer provides a shipping box with shipping information and also informs the customer of a flat charge of $100 to analyze the issue and provide an estimate to fix the desktop. So, the customer ships the desktop to the manufacturer, and the company determines that the motherboard has a defect and notifies the customer with the additional estimate of $200 to fix the desktop. The customer agrees to pay the amount, so the manufacturer fixes the desktop and returns it back to the customer. In the meantime, the customer is billed for the total amount of $300.

The important difference between the external and internal repair processes is that for external repair or customer paid repair, the product is owned by the customer. For internal repairs, the company owns the product being repaired.

Because the customer owns the product in customer paid repair, this product needs to be clearly identified throughout the repair process. This can be done by using serialization to use serial numbers to identify the material that belongs to the customer. If the product isn't serialized, then the identification can be done by using a different material number to identify the customer-owned product or by using a different material characteristic in the system that differentiates the material returned from the customer to the product owned by the company. Serialization is discussed in detail in Chapter 6, Serial Number Management in Reverse Logistics. Each approach has both pros and cons that need to be considered, but one approach has to be taken to avoid confusion between the defective customer-owned product and the good (new condition) product stored in the company's inventory.

Table 4.1 lists the pros and cons of using the three different approaches mentioned in this section.

Approach	Pro	Con
Serialization to identify customer-owned repair material.	Standard option available in the SAP ERP system. Easily tracked in the system through the standard end-to-end repair process in SAP ERP.	Serialization isn't linked to the inventory at the Warehouse Management (WM) level in SAP so picking isn't possible by serial number. Serialization increases transaction costs due to the additional information that needs to be entered and maintained in all transactions. Valuation of the inventory is an issue because the product should not be valuated, since it's owned by the customer. So valuation by using the material number is difficult because only the serial number is different; the material number is the same for both the customer-owned material and the company-owned material.

Table 4.1 Pros and Cons of Different Material Identification Options in the Customer Paid Repair Options

Approach	Pro	Con
Different material number to identify customer-owned material sent to the company for repair.	Clear identification physically using the material number in the material identifier tag, and also the material number is available in SAP ERP at all levels of inventory reporting including Warehouse Management (WM). Picking and storage can be easily done and identified. This is the logistics preferred solution and also the finance preferred solution due to the valuation impact. When storing the returned products, the materials can be directed to a different location in the warehouse based on the material master settings in the WM view in SAP ERP. Pricing and valuation can be easily maintained because the cost is maintained at the material level, and typically the cost of a customer-owned product in the system will be zero.	System performance could be affected due to the volume of data that needs to be maintained across all processes for the new material numbers. Because material numbers identify the ownership of the product, the SAP ERP system reports need to be run based on material numbers to report data.
Using a material master attribute in the SAP ERP system such as material status or material group to identify customer-owned material returned for repair.	The data maintenance effort will be far less compared to maintaining new materials.	Standard system processes aren't built to identify materials by attributes, so a lot of enhancements are needed to identify the customer-owned materials. Outputs have to be customized to include this attribute so that the physical warehouse processes can use this to identify and segregate these parts and not mix with the regular inventory that the company owns.

Table 4.1 Pros and Cons of Different Material Identification Options in the Customer Paid Repair Options (Cont.)

4.2　SAP Processes for Customer Paid Repair

In SAP ERP, the customer paid repair process uses the repair order to register the repair and, in the case of customer paid repair, this is the first step where the repair request is captured. In some instances, the repair process is also started with a service estimate or a service quotation, such as when the company decides to start the repair process and sends the estimate to the customer first for approval before starting the actual repair. Figures 4.2 and 4.3 show the SAP process for customer paid repair in a typical case.

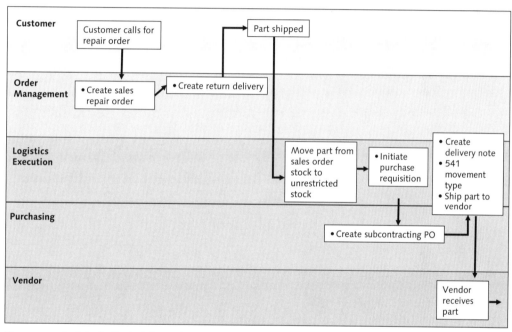

Figure 4.2　Part 1 of a Typical Case of Customer Paid Repair Processing in SAP ERP

In Figures 4.2 and 4.3, the repair order is the starting point of the customer paid repair process in most companies. After the repair order is created with all of the relevant data, including the product to be repaired and the type of repair that needs to be performed, then a return delivery is created to obtain the product from the customer back to the company. After the product reaches the company, the goods receipt is posted, and the product is received into inventory. The goods are received into a special stock category called the sales order stock as shown earlier in Figure 4.2. Because the product is owned by the customer, the goods receipt is generally nonvaluated, resulting in a material document and no corresponding accounting document with reference to the material document. The stock category of the returned material is determined by the configuration of the receipt movement type. It's best to receive the returned or defective product into a sales order stock category to indicate that the defective items are customer owned to prevent other processes, such as the materials requirement planning (MRP) process, from using this product.

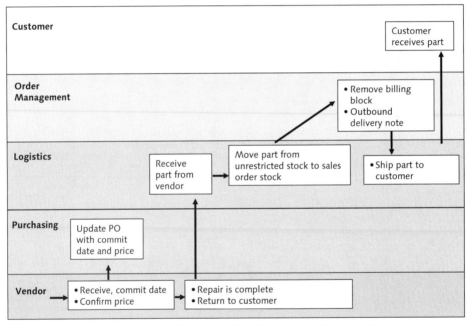

Figure 4.3 Part 2 of a Typical Case of Customer Paid Repair Processing in SAP ERP

After the product is received, a technical check is performed against the material to determine what actions need to be performed, such as perform repair, scrap the material, and/or send a replacement material to the customer if needed.

If the repair process is continued, then a service order is created with reference to the repair order to capture costs, materials consumed, and labor time used. From the service order, an external purchase order can be generated to obtain subcontracting services. After the repair process is complete, the service order is completed, and the product is moved from the current stock category to the sales order stock category. From here, the product is shipped back to the customer against the repair order. The costs collected in the service order for both external and internal activities are settled to a repair order item.

The repair order, as shown in Figure 4.4, provides a robust mechanism that allows users to capture the end-to-end repair process using the repair order as the main document and all of the additional documents as a part of the document flow of the repair order. The repair order also provides ways to capture costs from both external and internal sources and to calculate the overall cost of the repair. This enables the company to do profitability analysis on the repair business and adjust prices accordingly.

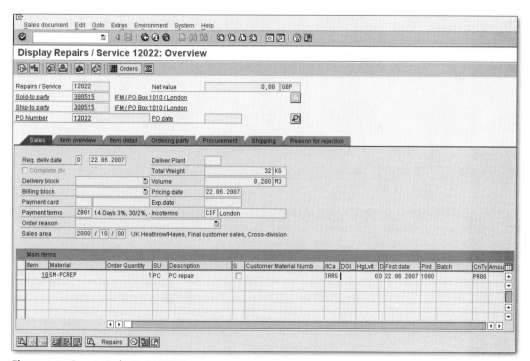

Figure 4.4 Repair Order in SAP ERP

The repair order contains information about the customer (Ship-to Party and Sold-to Party), material being repaired, quantity, plant where the repair part is received, and item category information as shown in Figure 4.4. In some instances, the external repair process can be started or generated using a service notification. Figure 4.5 shows a service notification.

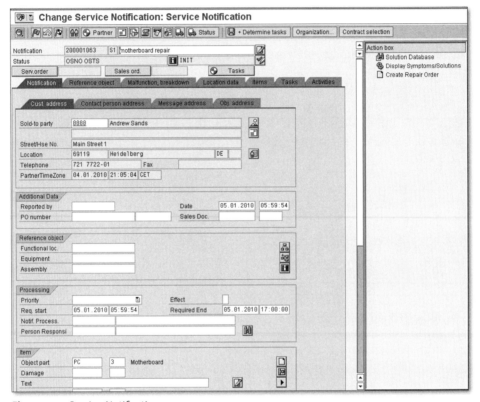

Figure 4.5 Service Notification

A service order or a repair order can be generated from a service notification in SAP ERP. The Action Box column on the right side is important because it has an action to create a repair order from the service notification. This example shown in Figure 4.5 is for repairing a motherboard in a desktop computer for Sold-to Party 8888. Figure 4.6 shows the items listed for service with the code group PC and the object set as the motherboard.

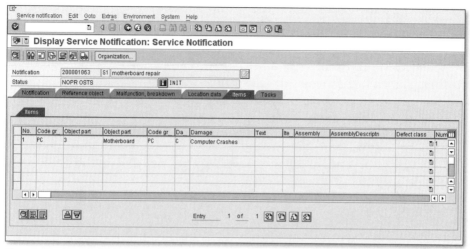

Figure 4.6 The Code Group and the Object in the Items of a Service Notification

Based on the code group and the object being repaired, the SAP ERP system can be configured to automatically determine the list of tasks that needs to be performed for fixing the motherboard on the PC, as you can see in Figure 4.7.

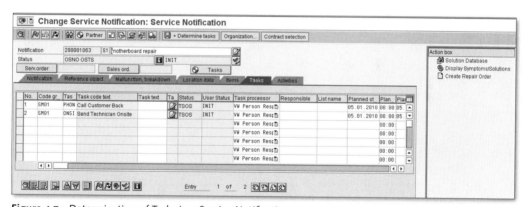

Figure 4.7 Determination of Tasks in a Service Notification

In the example in Figure 4.7, the tasks determined are the following:

▶ **PHON:** To call customer back.

▶ **ONSI:** To send a technician onsite.

Now, let's move on to view the configuration that enabled the list of tasks that are automatically determined for a service notification based on the line item in the service notification.

The code group PC is defined for a catalog "9" that belongs to object types. Catalogs are main categories under which code groups and codes are classified according to their content. In SAP ERP, there are standard catalogs for Tasks, Usage Decisions, Defect Types, Events, and other objects. The catalog types are defined in the configuration in the following menu path: PLANT MAINTENANCE AND CUSTOMER SERVICE • MAINTENANCE AND SERVICE PROCESSING • MAINTENANCE AND SERVICE NOTIFICATIONS • NOTIFICATION CREATION • NOTIFICATION CONTENT • MAINTAIN CATALOGS. Figure 4.8 shows the list of standard catalog types available in SAP ERP.

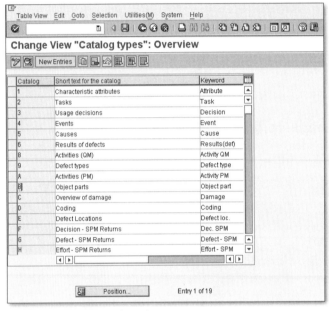

Figure 4.8 Definition of Catalog Types

In Figure 4.9, there is a catalog defined for object parts B, which is where you'll define the code group PC that was used in the service notification in Figure 4.6.

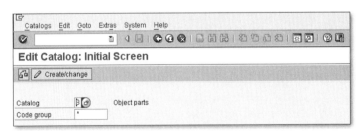

Figure 4.9 Editing the Catalog and the Code Group

In the next screen, you can either create or change code groups for the chosen catalog profile, as shown in Figure 4.9. In this example, we've chosen Catalog B – Object parts.

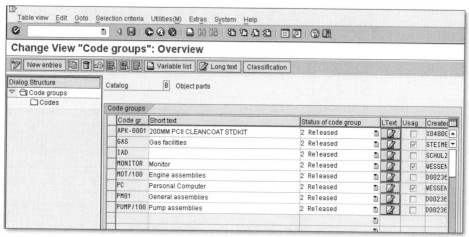

Figure 4.10 Create/Change Catalog 8 Used for Object Parts and Contains Code Group PC

From here, you can define and edit the code groups. The code group PC used in this example is shown with the description in Figure 4.10.

Along with defining the code group, the code group is also described here. In addition, a long text of the code group can also be added by selecting the Long Text button. The text entered here gets copied over automatically to the service notification and to subsequent documents that use this object. After defining the code group, the codes under the code groups can also be created at the same configuration point. To do this, you can select the code group and highlight the Codes folder on the left side. From here, you'll see the list of codes or services that can be provided under the code group selected. In Figure 4.11, you'll see that the Code Group PC and the code 3 – Motherboard that was used in the earlier example are defined.

After the service notification is created, you can create a repair order by selecting Create Repair Order in the Action Box, as shown in Figure 4.12.

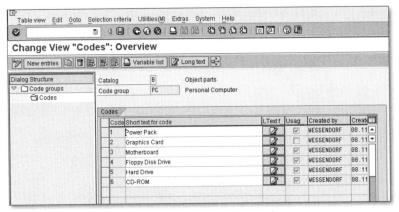

Figure 4.11 Codes Defined Under Code Groups for Catalog 8

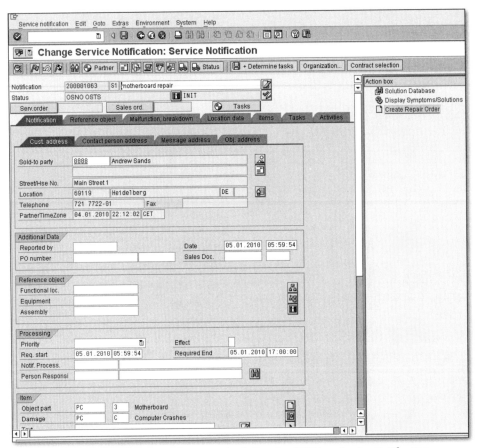

Figure 4.12 Creating the Repair Order Using the Action Box Within a Service Notification

After selecting the action for creating the repair order, a pop-up screen appears with the relevant data entry for creating the repair order, as shown in Figure 4.13.

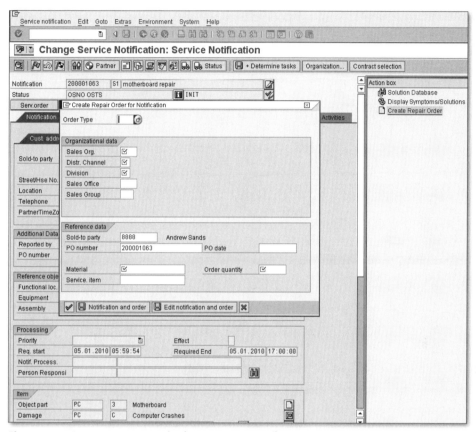

Figure 4.13 Creating a Repair Order from a Service Notification

You need to enter the repair order type in the Order Type field at the top of the dialog box. In the standard SAP ERP system, the repair order type for repair request is RA. After entering the order type and the information in the Organizational Data tab, you can enter the material that is going to be serviced. After you've entered all of the data, a task is created in the service notification with the action to create a follow-on repair order, as show in Figure 4.14.

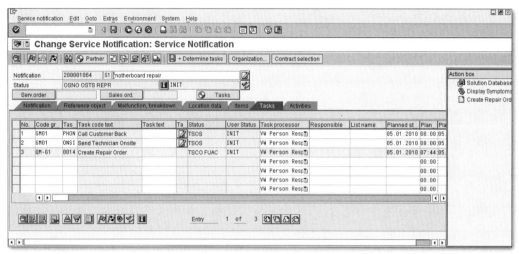

Figure 4.14 Task Created in a Service Notification to Create a Follow-on Repair Order

In Figure 4.14, the task 0014 has been created with the intent of creating a repair order. The follow-on repair order gets created as soon as the service notification is saved. After the repair order is created, the order is shown in the document flow of the service notification, as you can see in Figure 4.15.

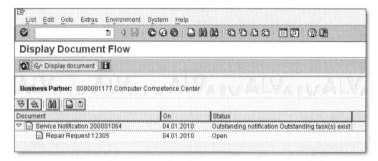

Figure 4.15 Repair Request Displayed in the Document Flow of the Service Notification

The Action Box and the actions allowed are also defined in the configuration of the service notification by choosing PLANT MAINTENANCE AND CUSTOMER SERVICE • MAINTENANCE AND SERVICE PROCESSING • MAINTENANCE AND SERVICE NOTIFICATIONS • NOTIFICATION PROCESSING • ADDITIONAL FUNCTIONS • DEFINE ACTION BOX.

In this configuration, you can define the follow-up functions (generated tasks and activities) for the service notification type as shown in Figure 4.16. In the example described previously, the service notification type S1 was used.

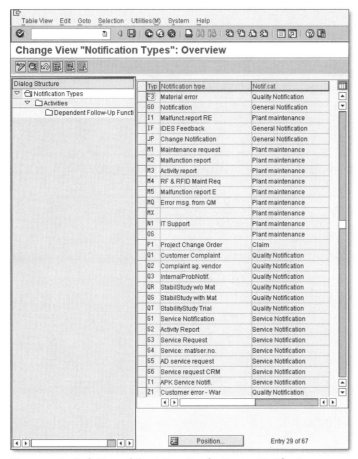

	Typ	Notification type	Notif.cat
	F3	Material error	Quality Notification
	60	Notification	General Notification
	I1	Malfunct.report RE	Plant maintenance
	IF	IDES Feedback	General Notification
	JP	Change Notification	General Notification
	M1	Maintenance request	Plant maintenance
	M2	Malfunction report	Plant maintenance
	M3	Activity report	Plant maintenance
	M4	RF & RFID Maint Req	Plant maintenance
	M5	Malfunction report E	Plant maintenance
	MQ	Error msg. from QM	Plant maintenance
	MX		Plant maintenance
	N1	IT Support	Plant maintenance
	OS		Plant maintenance
	P1	Project Change Order	Claim
	Q1	Customer Complaint	Quality Notification
	Q2	Complaint ag. vendor	Quality Notification
	Q3	InternalProbNotif.	Quality Notification
	QR	StabilStudy w/o Mat	Quality Notification
	QS	StabilStudy with Mat	Quality Notification
	QT	StabilityStudy Trial	Quality Notification
	S1	Service Notification	Service Notification
	S2	Activity Report	Service Notification
	S3	Service Request	Service Notification
	S4	Service: mat/ser.no.	Service Notification
	S5	AD service request	Service Notification
	S6	Service request CRM	Service Notification
	T1	APK Service Notifi.	Service Notification
	Z1	Customer error - War	Quality Notification

Figure 4.16 Definition of the Action Box for Service Notifications

To define the possible actions or activities for a particular service notification, select the activities on the left side of the service notification type. In the example, we used the notification type S1, which is shown in Figure 4.17.

For every activity, the technical definition is also included in this configuration. You can view the technical task for every activity by double-clicking on the activity. In this example, we've used the Create Repair Order activity, as shown in Figure 4.18.

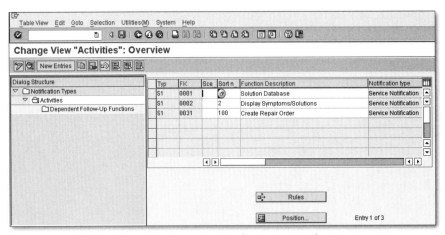

Figure 4.17 Activities Allowed in the Action Box for Service Notification Type S1

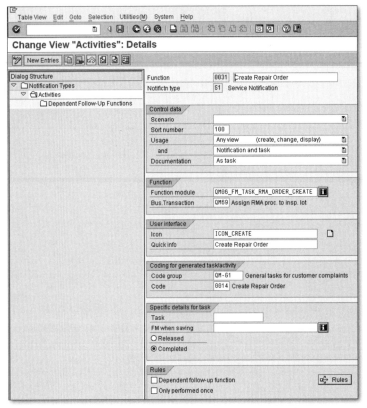

Figure 4.18 Technical Details Definition for the Activities in the Service Notification Action box.

This example uses the function module QM06_FM_TASK_RMA_ORDER_CREATE and Transaction QM69. You can either use a standard function module or custom function module to perform the task that needs to be executed when this action is selected in the Action Box of the service notification.

Before we move on to the details of the repair order and further repair processing, let's review the customer paid repair process flow in SAP ERP.

As you can see in Figure 4.19, the repair order plays an important part in an end-to-end customer paid repair scenario.

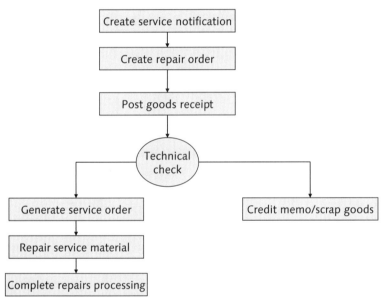

Figure 4.19 Customer Paid Repairs Processing in SAP ERP

The repair order is another sales order in SAP ERP, but the configuration indicates that the sales order is used for repairs instead of a sale. In the definition of the order type in the standard SAP ERP system, two order types are provided for repairs: RA for repair requests and RAS for repairs/service orders. The details of the configuration of these order type don't differ much from the other types. To view the order type definition of these order types, choose SALES AND DISTRIBUTION • SALES • SALES DOCUMENTS • SALES DOCUMENT HEADER • DEFINE SALES DOCUMENT TYPE.

You can define the details of the order type in this configuration. Figure 4.20 shows the configuration of the standard repairs order type RAS in SAP ERP.

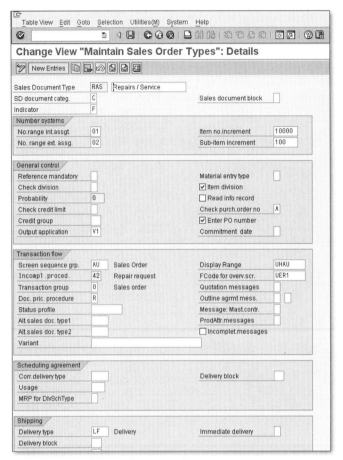

Figure 4.20 Definition of Repair Order Type RAS

In addition to creating the repair order type from the service notification, the repair order can also be created as a standalone order by using Transaction VA01. The repair order contains more than one line item for one complete repair. The different line items in a repair order are created for different purposes. The main level line item is usually of item category IRRA in the standard SAP EPR system, and it's used to collect repair costs. The other line item is IRRE, which indicates the item used to create a return delivery to bring the item back from the customer. Similarly, the line item used to indicate repair uses the item category IRRP, and so on. The item category definition determines if the item category is a return or not. In the case of IRRE, it's defined as a return item category to indicate a return movement of the part from the customer back into the company. Item category definition was discussed in detail in Chapter 2, Returns, but as a reminder, you can reach the item category definition in the configuration by going to SALES AND DISTRIBUTION • SALES • SALES DOCUMENTS • SALES DOCUMENT ITEM • DEFINE ITEM CATEGORIES.

Figure 4.21 shows the definition of the item category IRRA used for repair costs in a repair order. One important field that is relevant for repair processing is the repair procedure assignment (Repair Proced.) in the item category. The other field that plays an important role in the item category definition is the DIP profile (DIP Prof.). In the example in Figure 4.21, the DIP profile is 00000003. DIP (dynamic item processor) profile will be discussed a little later in Section 4.3, Repair Costs. Also in Figure 4.21, you can see the Repair Proc. 0001 assigned to the item category IRRA.

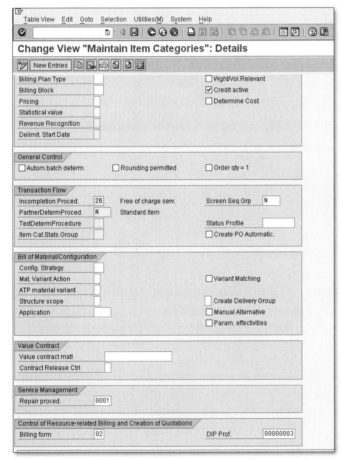

Figure 4.21 Assignment of the Repair Procedure and DIP in the Item Category Definition of IRRA to Capture Repair Costs

Now let's discuss the purpose of the repair procedure in the customer paid repair process.

4.2.1 Repair Procedure and Repair Actions

The repair procedure defines the list of actions that can be defaulted, be performed manually, or be generated by the system. All of these actions are determined in the repair procedures, which are assigned to the sales order item category as defined in the previous section. The repair procedures are defined in the configuration by using SALES AND DISTRIBUTION • SALES • SALES DOCUMENTS • CUSTOMER SERVICE • RETURNS AND REPAIRS PROCESSING • DEFINE REPAIRS PROCEDURE.

In this screen, you can define a repair procedure, as shown in Figure 4.22.

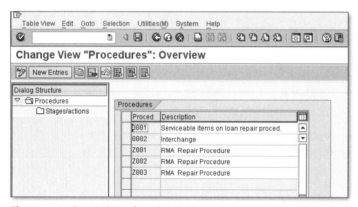

Figure 4.22 Repair Procedure Creation

Along with the definition of the repair procedure, you can also define the stages/actions in the same configuration point. To do this, you select the procedure you want to edit and click on the Stages/Actions folder on the left side. Figure 4.23 shows the stages and actions for Repair Procedure 0001 used in this example.

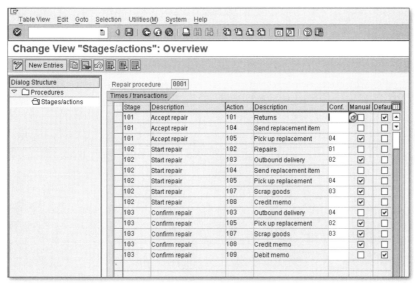

Figure 4.23 Stages/Actions for a Repair Procedure

Figure 4.23 shows the actions for Repair Procedure 0001, which is a procedure for serviceable items on loan repair. Because it involves providing replacement parts to the customer, there are actions that allow sending and picking up replacements as shown in Stage 101 and Action 105 in Figure 4.23. You can also define your own custom procedure, like the one shown in Figure 4.24, which is a simple repair that contains only three actions.

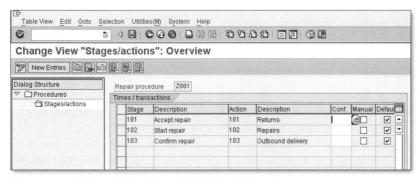

Figure 4.24 Actions Defined for a Simple Repair Procedure

All of the defined actions are displayed in the actual repair order per the configuration shown in Figure 4.24. Figure 4.25 shows a repair order of type RAS, which is displayed via Transaction VA03. There are two lines in this order. The main Item 10, with item category IRRS, is used to capture repair costs. The material listed here isn't a repairable item but a material that is used to capture repair costs and is a main line item in the repair order. The actual material that can be repaired is called *serviceable material in SAP*. In the example, material R-1001 in line Item 110 has an item category IRRE, which is the material that is picked up from the customer to be returned. The item category of this material is IRRE, which is used for return for repairs.

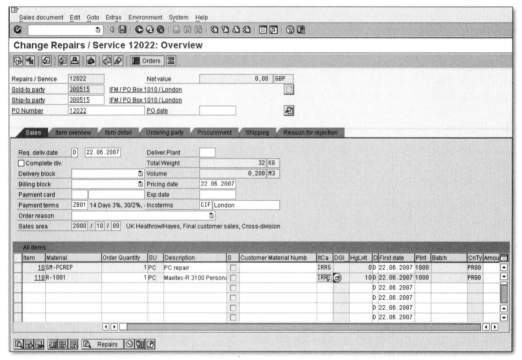

Figure 4.25 Repair Order Showing the Main Line Item and the Returns Line Item

The actions in the repair procedure are displayed according to the stage of the repair order. To display the actions, select the Repairs button in the bottom of the repair order screen. The next screen shows the actions (see Figure 4.26).

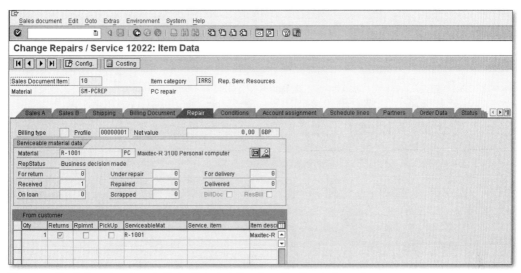

Figure 4.26 Actions in a Repair Order Selected Based on the Repair Procedure

Because the returns line item has already been processed, and the returns are completed, the actions displayed in the order indicate that the returns step has been completed. In addition to the selected Returns checkbox, you can see the returns were received with the quantity 1, indicated in the Received field above the actions listed in Figure 4.26.

To process the repair order further, a service order can be generated from the repair order, which can be used to create a service purchase order or a subcontract purchase order as required to complete the repair of the product.

To view the service order created for repair from a repair order display, use Transaction VA03. In the repair order, select the Repairs button at the bottom of the screen. The next screen shows all actions associated with the repair order. Here you need to choose the SM Order button. If the repairs stage in the repair order is processed, then a service order should be displayed. In the service order operations screen, you can define whether the component required for the operation in the service order needs to be procured externally or internally by selecting the operation and choosing either the External or Internal button in Figure 4.27.

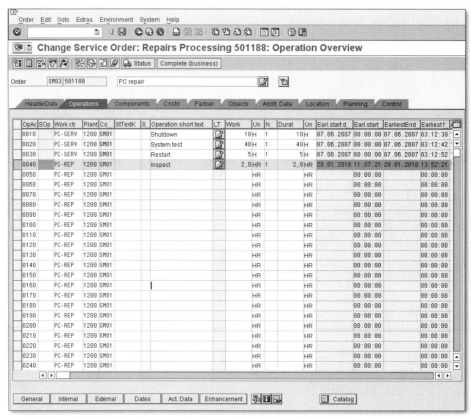

Figure 4.27 Operations in a Service Order Related to Customer Paid Repair

One of the important uses or advantages of the repair order in SAP ERP is the capability to capture repair costs and the integration to the billing process that allows the customer to be billed for the repair costs. The repair order can be configured to capture the service order costs that contain both internal and external operations. Let's now discuss how repair costs are calculated in a repair order.

4.3   Repair Cost

The repair order contains pricing information that is stored in the Conditions tab of the order. This can be displayed by accessing the repair order using Transaction VA03 in SAP ERP. Here you enter the repair order number and then select the Item Conditions button to display the pricing conditions relevant for the item. The repair order may contain the following items:

- Item with item category IRRS, which is used for repair service resources
- Item with item category IRRE, which is used for receiving the repair product from the customer
- Item with item category IRRP, which is the repair service
- Item with item category IRAL, which denotes the delivery of the repaired goods to the customer

The repair order may also contain other items with item categories IRRA (repair costs), IRLA (pickup replacement), and so on.

Some of these items are relevant for pricing, and you can access the pricing information by selecting the item and then choosing the Item Conditions button. Figure 4.28 shows the pricing information for the item with item category IRRS in a repair order.

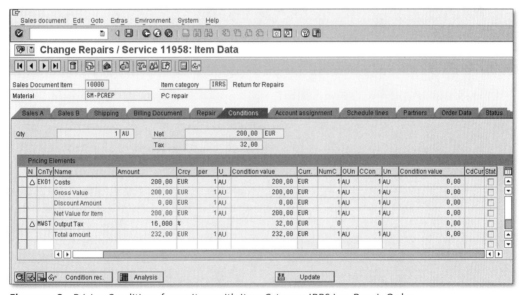

Figure 4.28 Pricing Conditions for an Item with Item Category IRRS in a Repair Order

The pricing condition EK01 in the example displayed in Figure 4.28 indicates the condition for costs. This condition is defined at the sales document type level. In this example, the sales document type is the repair order type RAS. The condition for costs is defined in the configuration by choosing SALES AND DISTRIBUTION • SALES • SALES DOCUMENTS • CUSTOMER SERVICE • SERVICE QUOTATION/RESOURCE RELATED BILLING • ASSIGN CONDITIONS TO SALES DOCUMENT TYPES.

In this configuration, you can assign the condition type used in all sales document for the costs. Figure 4.29 shows this configuration in SAP ERP.

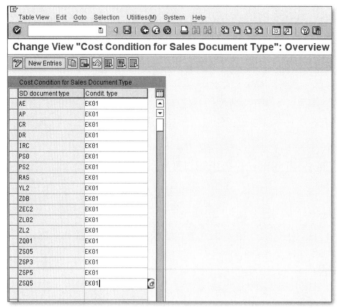

Figure 4.29 Assignment of the Condition Type for Costs to the Sales Document Type

The condition type for costs for the repair order type RAS is EK01 as shown in Figure 4.29.

The material number displayed in the item with item category IRRP isn't the material that can be repaired; this is a material number that represents the activity type used in the service order within the repair order. To display the configuration of this material's link to the costing elements, choose SALES AND DISTRIBUTION • SALES • SALES DOCUMENTS • CUSTOMER SERVICE • SERVICE QUOTATION/ RESOURCE RELATED BILLING • PROFILES FOR RESOURCE RELATED BILLING/QUOTATION CREATION.

The pricing in a repair order is calculated for items based on the item category. The item category contains the DIP that was discussed earlier in this section. The DIP is used in the configuration to allow billing against a repair order. The document used to bill a repair order and the credit memo type used are also defined for the DIP in the configuration specified in the preceding menu path. Here you can define for every DIP the sales document type for either billing or quotation.

Figure 4.30 shows the usage of DIP 00000002 for billing purposes assigned to the billing document type IRC, which is a standard debit memo request.

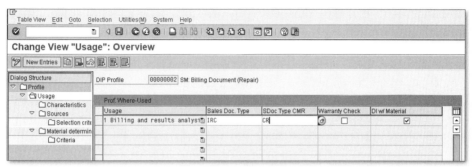

Figure 4.30   Assignment of Billing Document Type to the DIP

In the same configuration, the DIP usage is also assigned to material determination that in turn determines the cost element that will be used for service materials costing. Choose the usage, and select the Material Determination folder on the left side to see the service materials list. Select the service material you want to view in detail, and then choose the Criteria folder on the left side to view the cost element details of the service material. Figure 4.31 shows the cost element assignment for service material SM-PCREP.

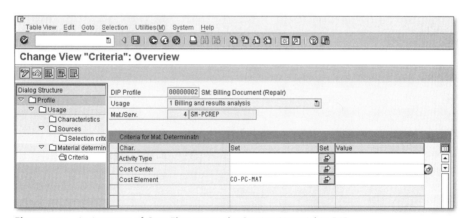

Figure 4.31   Assignment of Cost Element to the Service Material in DIP

We'll discuss more about pricing procedures and conditions in Chapter 7, Finance in Reverse Logistics. Let's now proceed to look at enhancement options in the customer paid repair process.

4.4   Enhancements in the Customer Paid Repair Process

While the repairs functionality in SAP ERP is robust, it can be enhanced by some modifications. One of the enhancements is used to allow the service order created against a repair order to generate a subcontract purchase order. While the service order allows external purchase, you'll usually need a subcontract purchase order so the repair can be performed externally using a vendor. To enable this, SAP ERP requires an additional code from the aerospace module that provides a MRO (maintenance, repair, and overhaul) solution containing a repair workbench. To avoid the additional implementation of this functionality, companies can build the capability to create a subcontract purchase order and then link the data to the service order via the account assignment capability of the service order. This ensures the cost of the purchase order is allocated back to the service order, and the company can use the standard SAP subcontract purchase order that provides the capability to ship the repair product to the vendor and track the process in the system. Once repaired, the product can again be received back into the inventory, be converted back into the sales order stock category, and then be shipped back to the customer.

4.5   Summary

The customer paid repair process is very important for the company providing this service to a customer. SAP ERP standard repair order functionality is integrated with service orders and purchase orders to allow both internal and external operations to be performed on the customer-owned product. SAP ERP also allows you to capture costs for all operations and report those costs in the repair order. In this chapter we discussed the following:

- ▶ The customer paid repair business process
- ▶ The customer paid repair process in SAP ERP
- ▶ Configuration of the repair order
- ▶ Configuration of the catalogs and codes
- ▶ Repair procedure and actions
- ▶ Repair costs
- ▶ Enhancements in the repair process

You should now be able to configure the customer paid repair process for your company to meet the necessary repair requirements. The next chapter reviews another important subprocess in reverse logistics: warranty processing.

Warranty claim is one of the most underused tools in SAP ERP. If used properly, it can ensure that your company offers excellent customer service by providing warranty recovery for your customers. The warranty claim enables you to recover a warranty from vendors, which ensures reduced inventory and procurement costs.

5   Warranty Claim Processing

The warranty claim is a process that customers use to recover warranties from their suppliers. It's a common practice across all industries since companies provide warranties on their products as a way to guarantee product quality. Customers typically are provided either a replacement part or credit for the purchase amount if a product is returned to the supplier within the specified warranty period. In this chapter, we'll discuss how a warranty is provided to a customer, how customers can reclaim the warranty, how a company can also reclaim a warranty from their vendors, and how these processes are executed in SAP ERP.

5.1   What A Warranty Claim Is

The warranty claim tool validates the warranty provided to the customer and also tracks the warranty provided by the vendor. The warranty claim process works differently depending on the type of industry, which is illustrated in the following examples.

Examples

Example 1: A foundry that manufactures castings buys raw materials such as iron from a supplier, produces castings, and offers a warranty on the castings to the customer. In turn, the customer can use the castings as is or as one of the components in an assembly that is sold to another customer. For the foundry, the vendor who supplied the iron provides a warranty on the quality of the iron and guarantees that the iron meets the specifications required by the foundry. The vendor also guarantees no failure of the product due to the iron used for a set time period (i.e., two years). The foundry then provides that set warranty period of two years to the customer. If the customer returns a product due to a failure or bad quality, the foundry provides a replacement or credit and checks the product to find the reason for the failure. If the foundry finds that the failure is due to the iron quality, it requests replacement or credit from the iron supplier. In this example, the foundry needs to do the analysis and prove that bad quality iron was the reason for failure before it can claim warranty from the vendor.

Example 2: A car manufacturing company obtains several components or subassemblies from its subcontractors. For example, the company gets brake assemblies from a subcontractor, and if the car brake fails for any reason, the customer gets a replacement brake, and the company passes this information or the assembly to the vendor to get a replacement or credit. As you notice in this case, there was no analysis needed by the car manufacturer to start the warranty claim process with the vendor because the vendor supplied the brake assembly as a whole. This may not be the case if the warranty is provided based on certain conditions, such as if the failure happened due to impact or if the brake failed due to the incorrect installation in the car.

Example 3: A semiconductor manufacturing customer buys a service from a subcontractor for fixing an air chamber in a machine. If the machine fails again during the warranty period provided for the service, the customer is entitled to a reimbursement of the service costs, or the machine is fixed again at no cost by the vendor.

In short, the warranty claim concept is the same across all industries, and it involves a supplier providing a warranty and a guarantee of the product quality for a set period of time. The customer can request a replacement or credit if the product fails during the warranty period.

Figure 5.1 illustrates the concept of a warranty claim between a vendor and a customer at a high level.

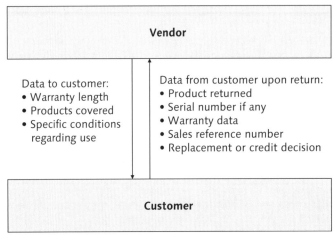

Figure 5.1 Warranty Claim Process Data Interaction Between a Vendor and Customer in SAP ERP

As you can see in Figure 5.1, the vendor provides the data regarding the length of the warranty for the product and the conditions for the use of the product for the warranty provided. The customer needs to provide the data regarding the serial number and the forward order reference to the vendor for warranty recovery from the vendor.

5.2 Warranty Claim Document in SAP

The definition of a warranty claim, according to SAP, is as follows:

> A warranty claim is a claim for reimbursement of material, labor, and external service costs that are incurred for the purpose of rectifying faults in an object with a valid warranty.

A warranty claim in SAP ERP is a cross-application component that is completely integrated with different areas in SAP, including Materials Management, Sales and Distribution, Customer Service, Plant Maintenance, Pricing, and Finance.

Warranty claim processing in SAP ERP can be done easily for a large number of items because you can automate the needed checks for warranty processing. Manual processing can also be done for items that fail the checks and need manual authorization to proceed.

Let's move on to look at the integration of warranty processing in SAP ERP.

5.2.1 Integration for Master Data

There are three types of master data that should be integrated with warranty claim processing:

▶ Material master
▶ Customer master
▶ Vendor master

Material Master

For materials to be returned or processed through a warranty claim, the material master records need to be created. A material master can be created using Transaction MM01. In the material master, there are different views that affect warranty processing. For an external service return, a service material record needs to be created. For returned parts in the material master, the fields Product Attribute 9 and Product Attribute 10 in the Product Attributes tab of the Sales Organization Data view of the material master needs to be used. Product Attribute 9 indicates the duty of the claimant to return the parts to the claim processor. Product Attribute 10 indicates the duty of the processor to the reimburser. Figure 5.2 shows the material master Sales Organization Data view displaying the product attribute fields.

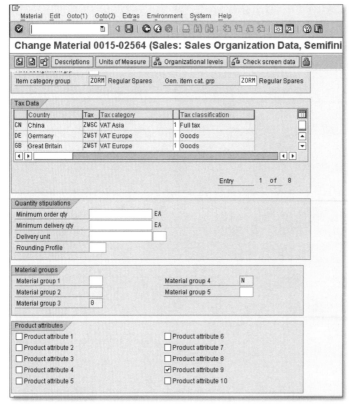

Figure 5.2 Sales Organization View Showing Product Attributes Value in the Material Master

Vendor Master

The vendor master is maintained with the details of the supplier, including address, payment information, and purchasing data.

Vendors are considered *reimbursers* in the warranty process. So, all vendors that provide a replacement or credit need to be created in SAP ERP as a vendor with a vendor master and a vendor account number. In a warranty claim document in SAP ERP, vendors are included as partners so that when warranty claims are posted, credit and debit memos can be created. The credit and debit are posted to the appropriate accounts based on the information maintained in the vendor master.

Note

Each vendor/creditor also has to be assigned to itself as a partner, or debtor, in the vendor master record. If this doesn't happen, problems occur in pricing and during finance postings. The debtor must be created in the appropriate sales organization.

You can use Transaction XK01 to create a vendor master in SAP ERP, use Transaction XK02 to change it, and use Transaction XK03 to display a vendor master. Figure 5.3 shows the display of control data of a vendor master record in SAP ERP.

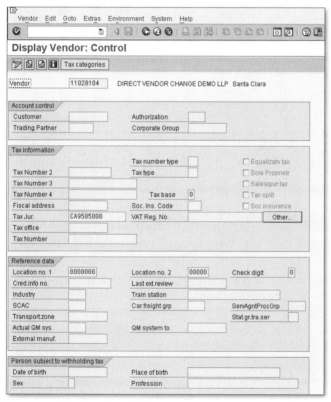

Figure 5.3 Vendor Control Parameters

Customer Master

Customer masters are master records for customers that contain the customer's address, control data, payment transactions, and company code data. The vendor can also be linked to the customer in the customer master. Figure 5.4 shows the customer master data in SAP ERP and the field where the vendor is linked to the customer.

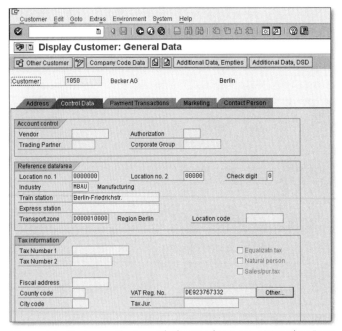

Figure 5.4 Customer Master with the Vendor Account Number Entry

As you can see in Figure 5.4, the vendor account number in the vendor master can be entered in the customer master so that the vendor master and the customer master are linked. This is an important requirement in subcontracting processes because when a delivery is created for a vendor, the customer master information is used for identifying the shipping parameters.

5.2.2 Warranty Objects

Warranty objects are all objects for which warranties can be maintained. Depending on the length of the warranty, these objects may be in under warranty at any point of time. In SAP ERP, several technical objects can be maintained as warranty objects, including equipment, functional locations, installed bases, and material numbers with active serialization. Let's review the SAP definitions of these objects and their relevance to warranties:

▶ **Equipment:** An equipment object is an individual object maintained as an autonomous unit, for example, a production resource, personal computer, testing machine, building, or tool. Equipment can be built into or out of functional locations. Each equipment item is maintained in the system with individual data. This means that the equipment items have data unique to them, such as the warranty period exclusive to the warranty.

Example of Equipment

A cleaning machine that cleans dirty wafers in a semiconductor manufacturing company can be created as an equipment item. This equipment will have its own characteristics, such as the warranty length for the machine and the individual components that make up the machine.

▶ **Functional location:** A functional location is an organization unit in Logistics and represents the place where a maintenance task is performed. For example, the location where the cleaning machines are installed to perform cleaning on a wafer of a semiconductor company is set up as a functional location in SAP ERP.

▶ **Installed base:** The installed base is an object for which a service can be provided. It's a multilevel structure of components for managing both products at the customer site and products that are used internally. The installed base describes the structure of these products and their components. The following master records can be part of a component: material, equipment, functional location, installed base, and document. An equipment item that can have servicing done on it is a good example of an installed base. The same example used for equipment — a cleaning machine — is also a good example of an installed base in SAP ERP.

▶ **Material number with serial number:** The material master record contains all of the data for describing and managing a material but doesn't offer any options for differentiating between individual items. The combination of material number and serial number defines individual material items and renders them distinguishable. Serialization is discussed in detail in Chapter 6, Serial Number Management in Reverse Logistics.

If you want to work with material numbers/serial numbers in a warranty claim, you have to link the screen groups S6100 (serial number/material number) and

S6101 (main object plus serial number/material number) to the screen layout of your warranty claim type by using LAYOUT • DEFINE SCREEN LAYOUTS in the warranty claim configuration. Warranty claim configuration can be accessed using Transaction OWTY.

Warranty claim types are defined using Transaction OWTY, as you can see in Figure 5.5.

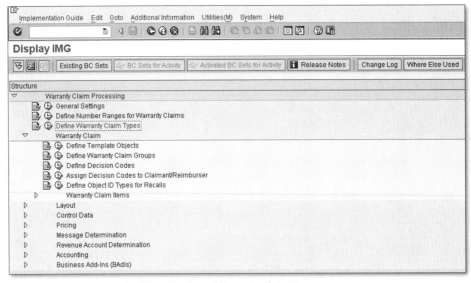

Figure 5.5 Transaction OWTY to Configure Warranty Claim Types

Transaction OWTY controls all of the configurations related to the warranty claim and has nodes and subnodes where all individual configuration items are present, as shown in Figure 5.5.

In the definition of the warranty claim type, you can specify both layouts without the navigation tree and the layouts with the navigation tree. The details of the warranty claim definition are shown in Figure 5.6. The warranty claim type determines the processing procedure that a warranty claim goes through (i.e., precrediting, postcrediting, authorization, recall). It contains default values for the organizational data and control parameters.

The screen groups provided in the standard SAP ERP system can be defined in the layout for the warranty claim types using Transaction OWTY, or by going to WARRANTY CLAIM PROCESSING • LAYOUT • DEFINE SCREEN LAYOUTS.

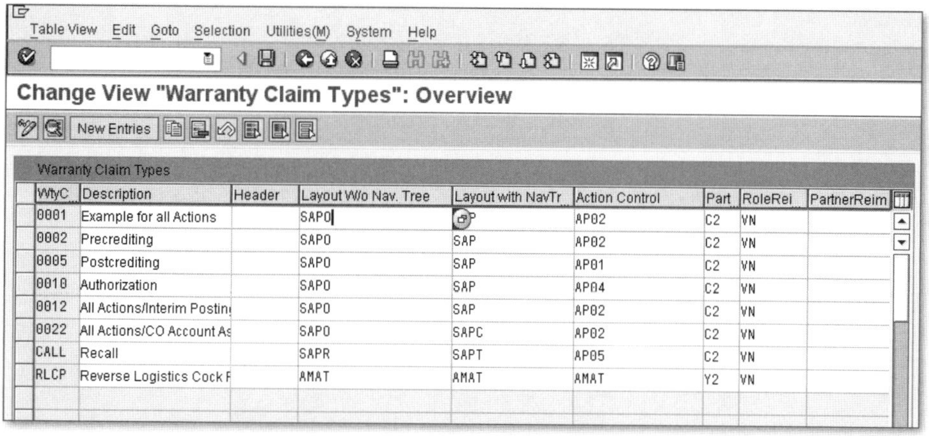

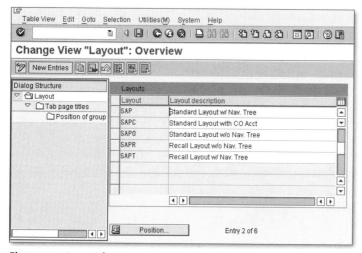

Figure 5.6   Definition of Warranty Claim Type with the Layouts Specified

Figure 5.7 shows the configuration of the layouts for warranty claim processing.

Figure 5.7   Layout for Warranty Claim Type Definition

In the configuration, you can choose the layout that you want to change or create a new one. After you choose the layout, select the Tab Page Titles folder on the left. In the Tab Page Titles folder, there are different tab details displayed, including Header Details, Version Detail, Prices – Version, Item Details, and so on, as shown in Figure 5.8.

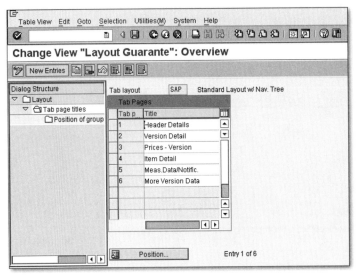

Figure 5.8 Tab Page Titles for the Screen Group

Here you select the tab where the screen groups need to be modified and high-light the line item. After the item is highlighted, select the Position of Groups on the Tab Pages folder on the left. Figure 5.9 shows the configuration for the screen groups.

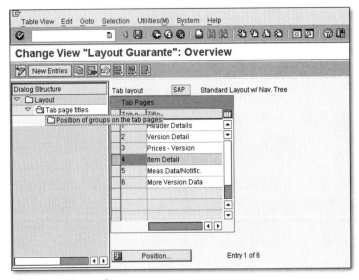

Figure 5.9 Screen Groups

In this screen, you can define or add the screen group that you want to include for the tab selected. Figure 5.10 shows the addition of screen groups S6100 and S6101 to the Item Detail screen.

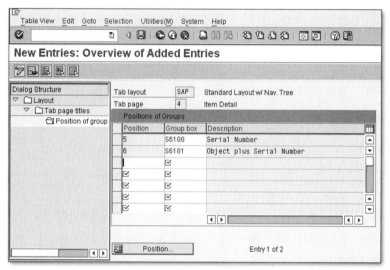

Figure 5.10 Screen Groups S6100 and S6101 in the Item Detail Screen for Layout

There are a variety of transactions in SAP ERP that are useful at this point. The following list provides the transaction code and the corresponding action:

- ▶ **IE01:** Creating equipment
- ▶ **IL01:** Functional location
- ▶ **IB51:** Installed base
- ▶ **MM01:** Material number
- ▶ **IQ01:** Serial number

You assign these objects using the object type in the warranty claim creation process. The warranty claim document is created using Transaction WTY as shown in Figure 5.11.

In the initial screen, you enter the warranty claim type (WtyClmType). Figure 5.12 shows the different warranty claim types (including Example for all Actions, Precrediting, Postcrediting, etc.).

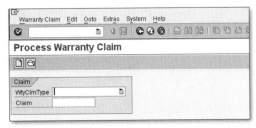

Figure 5.11 Creating a Warranty Claim Document

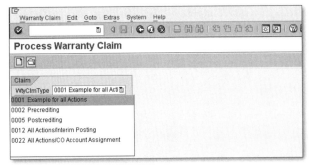

Figure 5.12 Warranty Claim Types

The warranty claim types are defined in the same transaction (OWTY) where the screen groups and layouts are defined. In that transaction, you use the menu WAR-RANTY CLAIM PROCESSING • DEFINE WARRANTY CLAIM TYPES.

SAP ERP provides some warranty claim types in the standard system, but you can define your own warranty claim types as well. Figure 5.13 shows standard as well as custom warranty types.

WtyC	Description	Header	Layout W/o Nav	Layout with NavTr	Action Control	Part	RoleRei	PartnerReim	RoleClmnt	PrSchem
0001	Example for all Actions		SAP0	SAP	002		VN		AS	WT0001
0002	Precrediting		SAP0	SAP	AP02		VN		AS	WT0002
0005	Postcrediting		SAP0	SAP	AP01		VN		AS	WT0001
0010	Authorization		SAP0	SAP	AP04		VN		AS	WT0002
0012	All Actions/Interim Postin		SAP0	SAP	AP02		VN		AS	WT0012
0022	All Actions/CO Account As		SAP0	SAPC	AP02		VN		AS	WT0022
CALL	Recall		SAPR	SAPT	AP05		VN		AS	WT0002
CUST	custom warranty type		SAPR	SAPT	AP05		VN		AS	WT0002

Figure 5.13 Standard and Custom Warranty Claim Types in SAP ERP

As you can see in Figure 5.13, SAP ERP provides warranty claim types for postcrediting and precrediting. These are two different processes that provide the option for the company to either credit the customer before obtaining the credit from the vendor or after. This will be discussed in detail a little later in this section.

Example
A tire company requires warranty checks on the returns. This check is performed against a material and source sales document because the materials aren't serialized. The company provides an exception to some customers, where they provide materials for the customer to use, and the customer provides the data after use. The customer doesn't provide serial numbers even though the material being returned is serialized. In addition to this, the company also has serialized materials that need to go through the standard warranty process for checking the warranty length (based on the end warranty date for other customers). The customers returning the product without providing serial numbers provide the return details via a file with the material and sales document reference. To differentiate the warranty claim from the exception customers versus the other customers, the company can create a custom warranty type, as displayed in Figure 5.13. In this figure, you can choose the Custom Warranty Type (CUST) and use the regular warranty claim type 0002 and 0005 (Precrediting and Postcrediting).

Let's move on to the business process of warranty recovery.

5.2.3   Warranty Recovery

There are two types of warranties for a company: a customer warranty and a vendor warranty. Regarding the customer warranty, in general the company uses a serial number or a sales document reference to provide a warranty. Figure 5.14 provides a process flow of how a customer warranty process works.

In the customer warranty process shown in Figure 5.14, the claimant (which would typically be the customer who is claiming the warranty) contacts the company with the information needed to reclaim the warranty (a material number, quantity, serial number, sales document reference) and condition of the part. Based on the information provided, the data is checked against the warranty check requirements, and the company decides to accept or reject the claim for warranty.

For a vendor warranty process, the company becomes the claimant, and the vendor becomes the party responsible for either crediting the money back or sending the replacement (reimburser). Figure 5.15 shows a standard vendor warranty process.

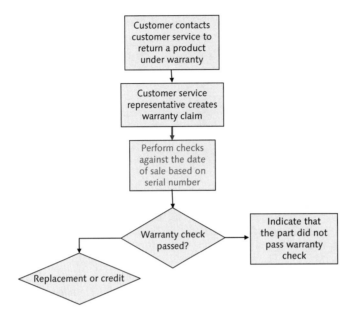

Figure 5.14 Customer Warranty Process

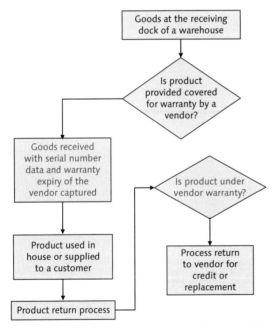

Figure 5.15 Vendor Warranty Process to Recover a Warranty

As you can see in Figure 5.15, the new product is received in the warehouse and then either used in house or shipped to the customer for a sale. If a defective product is returned from the customer or from an internal source, the product is checked for vendor warranty information. If the defective or returned product is still under vendor warranty, then a vendor is contacted, a return material authorization (RMA) is obtained from a vendor, and the product is shipped to the vendor for either a replacement or credit.

In SAP ERP, both the customer and vendor warranty process can be accomplished by using a combination of warranty claim document and the validation/substitution rule (VSR), which we'll discuss further in Section 5.3, Control Data Definition in Customizing. With the combination of the two objects, SAP ERP can handle complex requirements in the warranty area and provide you with a powerful tool.

Figure 5.16 shows the SAP ERP process to handle a customer warranty scenario.

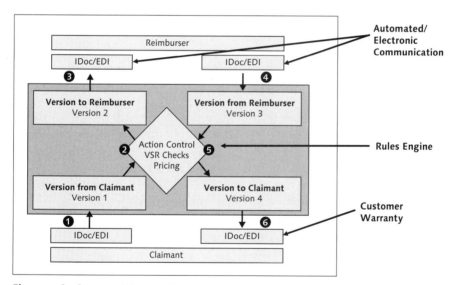

Figure 5.16 Customer Warranty Process Using a Warranty Claim in SAP ERP

In Figure 5.16, the process starts out with communication from the customer (claimant) to the company, captured in the form of a warranty claim (Version 1). After communications and discussions with the vendor, the final decision for replacement or credit is sent to the customer (claimant) again, using a different version of the warranty claim (Version 4).

SAP ERP also provides a similar process for vendor warranty processing, as displayed in Figure 5.17.

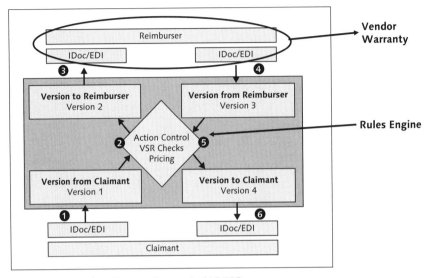

Figure 5.17 Vendor Warranty Process in SAP ERP

The processes for both customer and vendor warranty are well integrated using the action control VSR checks. The vendor warranty check can be performed as a standalone operation, in which the company acts as a claimant and sends data to a vendor manually or through EDI to obtain either a replacement or credit.

When processing warranty claims, you can process with postcredting/precrediting or process with recalls or technical campaigns, depending on the relationship that you have with your customer or vendor.

Processing with Postcredting/Precrediting

Processing with postcrediting/precrediting is also referred to as standard processing:

► Postcrediting happens when a customer isn't credited until the part is sent to the vendor and a decision has been obtained from the vendor or reimburser.

► Precrediting is the process when the customer is credited before the reimburser or the vendor provides a decision regarding the recovery of warranty.

Example of Postcrediting

A tool manufacturing company buys OEM (original equipment manufacturer) parts from vendors and supplies them as spare parts to its customers. The company offers the same warranty on the parts as the vendor does to its customers. In addition to offering a warranty on parts, the company also offers a maintenance service. The company has different types of contracts with its customers, depending on the type of product or service the customer has purchased. If the company is selling only a product, then the warranty provides conditions that have to be met before the customer can get either a credit or a replacement. These conditions include the proper use and maintenance of the part. Failure to meet these conditions means that the customer won't get credit or replacement. Because the company gets the part from the vendor and sells it to the customer, the company is covered for the warranty with similar terms by the vendor, so when a customer sends the part back to the company, the company sends the data to the vendor and waits for the vendor's approval of warranty before giving credit to the customer. This process in warranty claim is called postcrediting.

Example of Precrediting

A semiconductor tool maintenance company provides services through contracts to maintain customer tools. The contract covers both parts and service, and the company is responsible for recovering the warranty of the parts that fail or break before their warranty expires from the vendors. Customers that buy these contract services don't want to perform warranty recovery and instead want this to be included in the service provided by the company. So, in this case, if a part fails during the warranty period, the customer is immediately credited when the warranty claim is processed from the claimant (in this case, a customer). The company then creates another version to obtain the credit from the reimburser. Precrediting might cause issues to some companies because, in some cases, the vendor might not provide the credit to the company for various reasons. The company provides the reimbursement to the customer, but if this credit isn't provided back from the vendor due to the contract terms, then the company bears the cost of the product.

The process flow in a warranty claim is to create different versions of the claim depending on whom the communication is between. For precrediting, the following sequence of versions is created and processed in the warranty claim:

- **Version 1:** Version from claimant (customer)
- **Version 2:** Version to claimant (customer)
- **Version 3:** Version to reimburser (vendor)
- **Version 4:** Version from reimburser (vendor)

For postcrediting, the versions are as follows:

- **Version 1:** Version from claimant
- **Version 2:** Version to reimburser
- **Version 3:** Version from reimburser
- **Version 4:** Version to claimant

A version is a part of the warranty claim that contains specific information about the partner and has details about the entitlement of warranty from the partner.

In general, when a warranty claim gets created, the first version is the version from the claimant. The version contains one or more items for which the partner is requesting reimbursement. More versions are created during the processing of the warranty claim, as described previously, depending on the postcreding or precrediting process used. The versions are either created manually or electronically using EDI and IDOCs. In most cases, only the current version is active, but sometimes there can be more than one version that is active. This happens when you're using warranty claim with split processing. You split the process in a warranty claim when the customer requests reimbursement for more than one item, and the items were purchased from different vendors.

> **Example of Warranty Claim with Split Processing**
>
> A car manufacturer sells cars to customers and provides the warranty on the brake assembly for two years. The end customer who buys the car returns the brake assembly because both the brake pad and the brake disc failed to meet the standards. The car manufacturer had assembled the brake assembly by buying the disc and the pad from two different suppliers. So, when the warranty claim is created with version 1 (the version from the claimant), there are two items: the disc and the pad. Now the next versions created are for two different suppliers, so there will be two current versions active, and both of them will be versions to the reimburser.

Figure 5.18 shows a warranty claim being created with version 1, which is the version from the claimant.

A category is a subdivision within a warranty claim that defines a specific part process. Examples of categories include versions from the claimant, versions to the reimburser, and so on.

You define the starting category for every warranty type in the customization of the warranty claim type. The warranty claim types are defined by Transaction OWTY, or by going to WARRANTY CLAIM PROCESSING • WARRANTY CLAIM TYPES.

Figure 5.19 shows the warranty claim type definition where the starting category (StartCateg.) is specified.

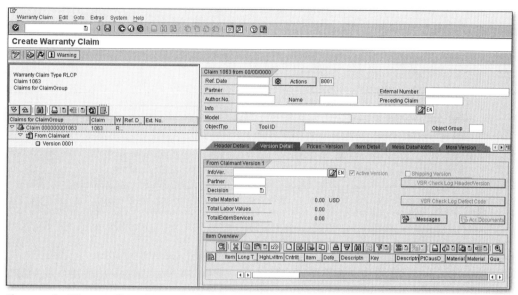

Figure 5.18 Warranty Claim Creation with Version 1 from Claimant

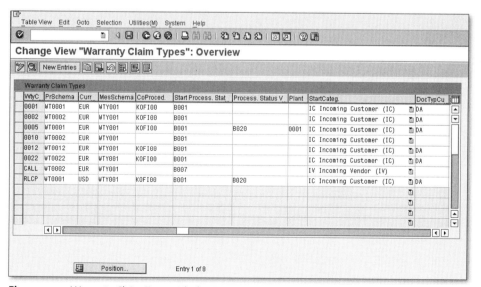

Figure 5.19 Warranty Claim Type with the Starting Category Specified

As you can see in Figure 5.19, the starting category defined for warranty claim (WtyC) 0001 is Incoming Customer (IC), which is the claim from the claimant or the customer. The warranty claim type controls many of the processing actions for the warranty claim created with that claim type. In addition to postcrediting and precrediting, other processes also use warranty claims, including processing with authorized goodwill and processing with recalls or technical campaigns. When processing with authorized goodwill, the claimant or the customer initiates the warranty claim, and the warranty check fails but you still provide the warranty. In other words, you want to make use of goodwill. You'll have to define a specific warranty claim type for this process. To process this type of warranty claim, you need to create an authorization in the system using Transaction WTYAUT. In this transaction, you'll need to enter the authorization type that is in turn created for the warranty claim type. After the authorization is created, then this authorization data can be provided to the claimant. The claimant then initiates the warranty claim by providing the authorization number, and the warranty check is done using VSR. Action controls use this authorization to process the warranty claim even though the warranty checks fail. The VSR check ensures that the objects in the authorization are the same as the objects in the warranty claim; if they are, the claim process continues.

Figure 5.20 shows the creation of an authorization for warranty claim type 0010.

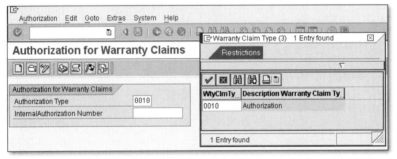

Figure 5.20 Creation of an Authorization for Warranty Claim Type 0010 Using Transaction WTYAUT

In the next screen, additional data such as the object type, partner number, and so on are entered. The partner data for the version from claimant is also specified in the authorization. Figure 5.21 shows the additional data entered for the creation of an authorization of warranty claim.

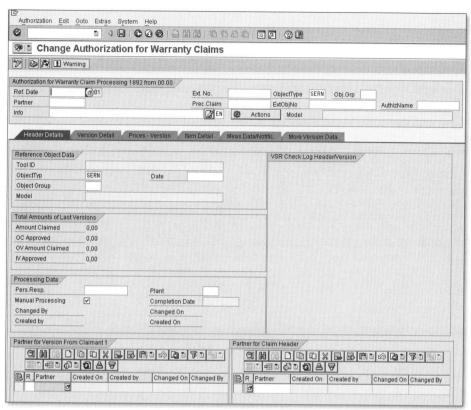

Figure 5.21 Additional Data Entered During the Authorization Creation for a Warranty Claim

Processing with Recalls or Technical Campaigns

The other process possibility for warranty claims is called processing with recalls or technical campaigns:

▶ **Processing with a recall:** This process is used for products that are subject to a recall. To handle this, a new warranty claim type has to be created. This process is special because the claim is created so the reimburser or the vendor can fix defects in the products sold. The warranty claim is processed even if the warranty check fails. You process warranty claims of this type using Transaction WTYRCL.

▶ **Processing with claim split:** We touched on this earlier in this chapter, but this occurs when there is more than one reimburser, and multiple versions need to be created to handle the claim. In the warranty claim type definition in Customizing, you can define the criteria used to split a claim. For example, you can use either a vendor or a defect to split the claim. Figure 5.22 shows the customization of a warranty claim type and where the split criteria are defined. You can choose from several fields to split the warranty claim for split processing.

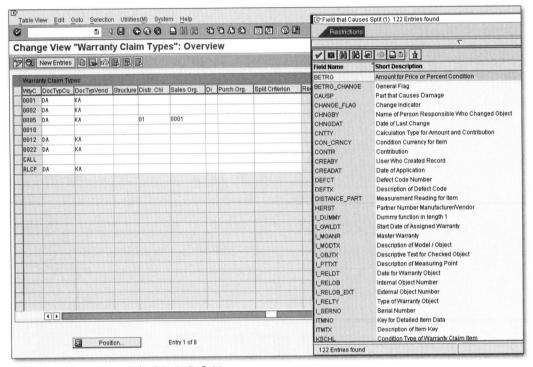

Figure 5.22 Split Criteria Definition

- ► **Processing with parts to be returned:** In this process, the claimant returns the product along with the warranty claim for the claim processor and the reimburser to inspect the product before a credit or replacement is provided. For this process, the parts are returned, and the possible status of the returned parts is defined in the customization of warranty claim processing. This is defined using Transaction OWTY or by going to WARRANTY CLAIM PROCESSING • WARRANTY CLAIM • WARRANTY CLAIM ITEMS • DEFINE STATUS FOR PARTS TO BE RETURNS. Figure 5.23 shows the configuration for the status of the parts.

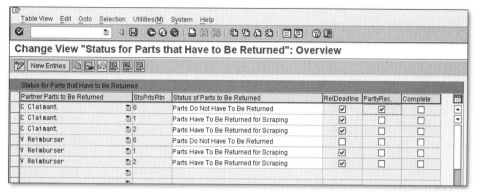

Figure 5.23 Configuration of the Status of the Parts

Other Warranty Checks

In addition to defining the status of the materials in the configuration, there are also checks that you can perform, including relevant for deadline, parts to be returned (partially received), and parts to be returned (delivered completely). If relevant for deadline is selected, then the parts are subject to a deadline for return. The actual number of days for the deadline is defined in the general settings in customization. The field status of the parts return is available in the warranty claim document in the Version Details tab at the item level.

There are a few fields that can be specified in the General Settings for Warranty Processing tab by using Transaction OWTY or by going to WARRANTY CLAIM PRO-CESSING • GENERAL SETTINGS.

The following fields are important for calculating deadlines for both the claimant and reimburser. For the claimant or customer, the Deadline Parts to Be Returned field is the length of the period by which the parts need to be returned. For the reimburser or vendor, the Answer Period Reimb. Version field is the length of the period by which the vendor or the reimburser needs to provide a credit or replacement decision.

The General Settings also define the pricing condition types, such as the Condition Type Amount Part IC and Condition Type Amount Part OV, which refers to the pricing condition type for inbound from the claimant and the pricing condition type for outbound to the reimburser, respectively.

Figure 5.24 shows the general configuration settings in SAP ERP.

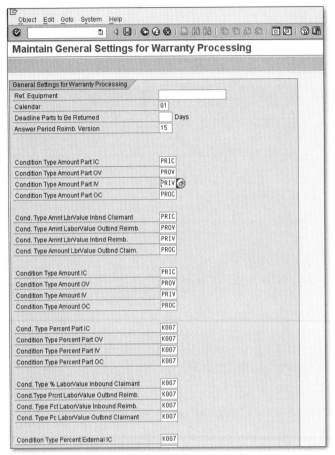

Figure 5.24 General Configuration Settings

The warranty process checks whether the object is still under warranty or not. To check for warranty, a master warranty should exist with warranty counters. The measurement positions with characteristics in the object and measuring points for these positions should have also been created. Master warranties are created using the Transaction BGM1. Master warranty creation is discussed in detail in Chapter 6, Serial Number Management in Reverse Logistics. When a warranty check is performed, the system compares the measurement readings in the measurement documents with the warranty counter limit values in the master warranties.

Now let's proceed to look at the control data that is used in the warranty claim document.

5.3   Control Data Definition in Customizing

The four sections in the control data definition for warranty claim processing configuration are as follows:

- ▶ Process control that contains actions and action controls
- ▶ Copying control that defines copy procedures
- ▶ VSR checks that define validations and substitutions
- ▶ Warranty checks

Let's take a closer look at a couple of these:

- ▶ **Process control:** This section contains the important actions and action controls that work along with VSR to provide a comprehensive mechanism for warranty claim processing.
- ▶ **Actions:** An action is a business part process in warranty claim processing. You define actions and processing statuses in the control data portion of the customization.

5.3.1   Actions

Actions can be elementary actions or interlinking actions, which consist of two or more actions that are linked to one another, the latter can be either elementary actions or interlinking actions themselves.

Actions can be differentiated according to whether or not they should be displayed in the action box in the warranty claim. The actions that are processed only automatically and not manually shouldn't be displayed in the actions box. Figure 5.25 displays the warranty claim document with the actions box where actions can be selected to be executed.

As you can see, the actions are displayed in the action box for you to select and execute during warranty claim processing. Figure 5.26 shows the definition of actions in Customization. You can define actions using Transaction OWTY under the menu path WARRANTY CLAIM PROCESSING • CONTROL DATA • PROCESS CONTROL • DEFINE ACTIONS.

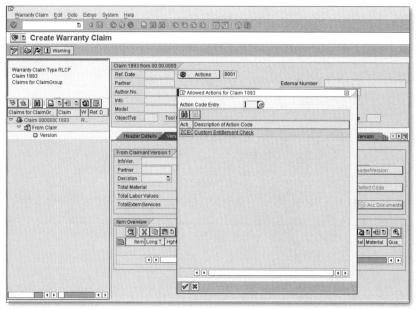

Figure 5.25 Action Box with Actions

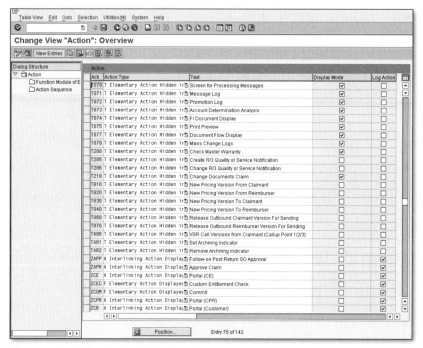

Figure 5.26 Actions in the Customization

In addition to defining the Actions, you can link the actions to a function module that performs the check defined in the actions. For example, to define an action to create a quality notification, you create the action ZE01 and link the action to a custom function module called ZQUALNOTIF_CREATE. Figure 5.27 shows the function module assigned to a custom action ZHUP and the action linked to a function module that packs materials into a handling unit in SAP ERP. To link the function module, select the action and function module of the elementary action on the left side tab. In the next screen, enter the function module name.

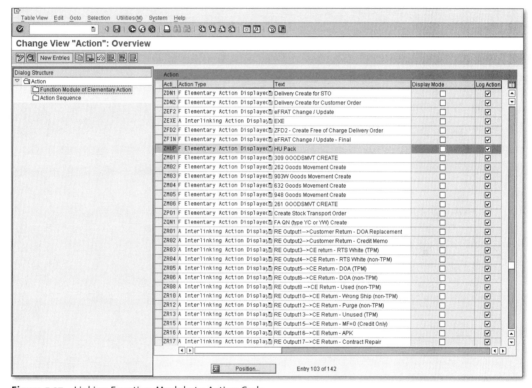

Figure 5.27 Linking Function Module to Action Code

To define whether the action is displayed in the action box, you need to choose the action type. There are four action types available:

- ▶ **A:** Interlinking Action Displayed in Action Box
- ▶ **F:** Elementary Action Displayed in Action Box

- **T:** Elementary Action Hidden in Action Box
- **V:** Interlinking Action Hidden in Action Box

Figure 5.28 shows the action type options in the configuration.

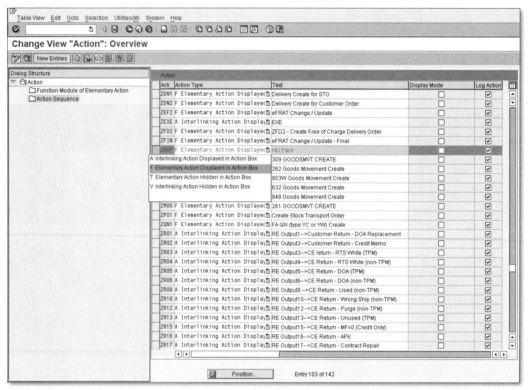

Figure 5.28 Action Types

Action controls are processes defined for automatic and manual processing that are assigned to a warranty claim type. An action matrix contains a series of actions defined for every action control, and it also defines the start and end processing statuses that should be reached before an action is started or ended, respectively.

Figure 5.29 shows the definition of the action control in customization, which you can get to using Transaction OWTY or by going to WARRANTY CLAIM PROCESSING • CONTROL DATA • DEFINE ACTION CONTROLS. In short, the action control defines how the system behaves when executing different action codes and the statuses when executing different actions.

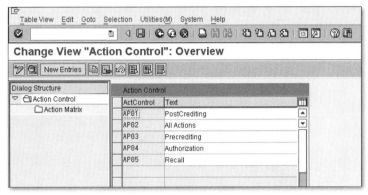

Figure 5.29 Action Controls

To review the action matrix assigned to the action control, you need to select the action control and choose the Action Matrix folder at. In the details of the action matrix, you'll notice the start processing and end processing status along with the action code. You can also define action codes that need to be called up automatically by selecting the Automatically (Autom.) checkbox in the action matrix configuration, as shown in Figure 5.30.

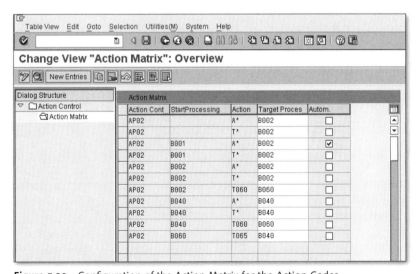

Figure 5.30 Configuration of the Action Matrix for the Action Codes

In this configuration, you can choose to specify all actions that start with T by selecting T* instead of entering all of the action codes. The processing statuses and their meanings are defined in the previous configuration, under WARRANTY CLAIM PROCESSING • CONTROL DATA • PROCESS CONTROL • DEFINE PROCESSING STATUSES.

Here you'll define the processing status codes and their meanings. Figure 5.31 shows the configuration in detail.

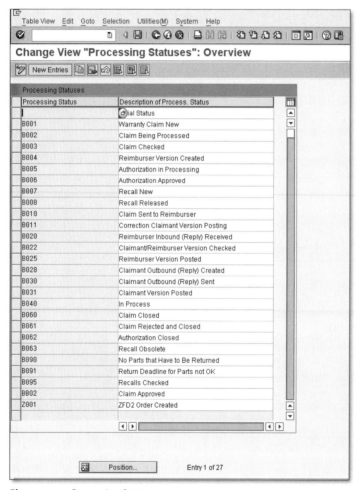

Figure 5.31 Processing Statuses

Finally, you need to assign the action controls to the warranty claim type definition discussed earlier in the configuration. Figure 5.32 shows the definition of the warranty claim type and the assignment of the action control to the warranty claim type.

```
┌─────────────────────────────────────────────────────────────────────────┐
│ Table View  Edit  Goto  Selection  Utilities(M)  System  Help             │
│ ⊘ _____ ▣ ◁ 🖫 ❘ ❂ ❷ ❸ ❘ 🖴 🖬 🖩 ❘ ❀ ❀ ❀ ❀ ❘ 🗷 🗷 ❘ ⑦ 🖫   │
│ Change View "Warranty Claim Types": Overview                              │
│ 📝 🔍  New Entries  🗍 🖫 ✑ 🖫 🖫 🖫                                       │
└─────────────────────────────────────────────────────────────────────────┘
```

WtyC	Description	Header	Layout W/o Nav	Layout with NavTr	Action Control	Part	RoleRei	PartnerReim	RoleClmnt	PrSchem
0001	Example for all Actions		SAP0	SAP	AP02	C2	VN		AS	WT0001
0002	Precrediting		SAP0	SAP	AP02	C2	VN		AS	WT0002
0005	Postcrediting		SAP0	SAP	AP01	C2	VN		AS	WT0001
0010	Authorization		SAP0	SAP	AP04	📷	VN		AS	WT0002
0012	All Actions/Interim Postin		SAP0	SAP	AP02	C2	VN		AS	WT0012
0022	All Actions/CO Account As		SAP0	SAPC	AP02	C2	VN		AS	WT0022
CALL	Recall		SAPR	SAPT	AP05	C2	VN		AS	WT0002
RLCP	Reverse Logistics Cock F		AMAT	AMAT	AMAT	Y2	VN		SP	WT0001

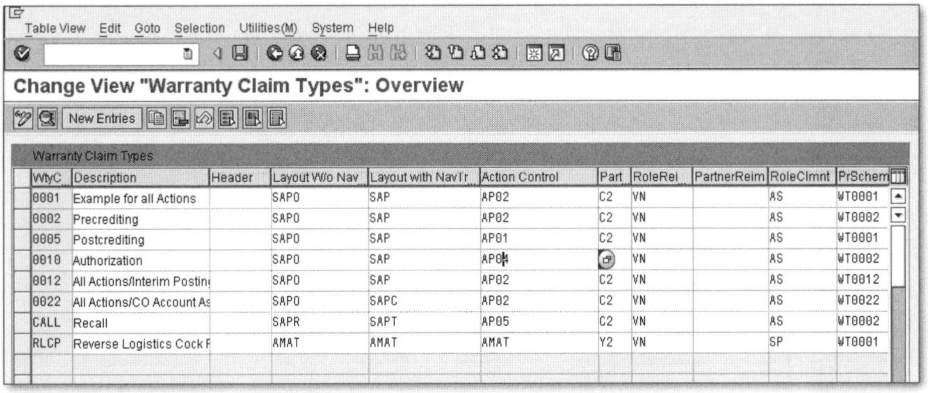

Figure 5.32 Assignment of Action Control in the Warranty Claim Type

5.4   Validation/Substitution Rules (VSRs)

Validation/substitution rules (VSRs) serve to check the validity of the data entered. They are critical to ensuring the automatic processing of warranty claims. Validation includes at least one step, and substitution also includes at least one more step. Each validation step has three components: prerequisite, check, and message. A check is carried out only if the prerequisites are fulfilled; if the check fails, then a message is displayed. A substitution has two components: prerequisite and substitution. The substitution is only carried out if the prerequisite is met.

The VSR checks used in the warranty claim processing are the same as those used in the finance special ledger processing. With the capability of doing VSR, the SAP ERP system offers a platform that the customer can use to add custom checks, referred to as a rules engine.

VSR checks are built and included in the function modules, which are assigned to action codes. To build VSR checks, you can define them in Customizing in the warranty claim processing by going to WARRANTY CLAIM PROCESSING • CONTROL DATA • VSR CHECKS or by using Transaction OWTY.

In this configuration, you can specify validations by selecting the area as warranty on the left side tab. From there, you can choose the Validation button on the top menu to see the screen to enter the validation name and description. In addition, you can also enter an authorization for the validation. Figure 5.33 shows the initial screen for creating the validation.

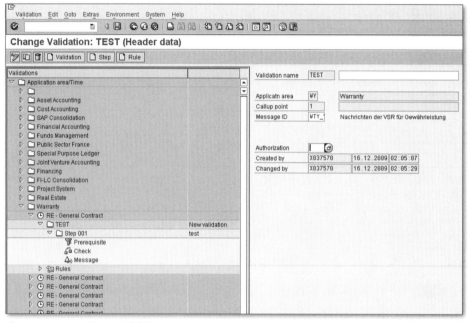

Figure 5.33 Creating a Validation

After you've entered the basic data for the validation, you can then enter the details of the prerequisite, check, and message by choosing them from the left side tab under the validation you just created. You can create multiple steps for the validation, or you can choose to have only one. For each step, you need to enter data for the three components, prerequisite, check, and message. When defining the prerequisite data, you can have table fields, rules, and exits, as shown in Figure 5.34. You can include the operators available, such as AND and OR, to build the custom checks needed.

After you've finished entering the data for validation, you can proceed to the check component. Next, you can define the data for the messages component, including the message number and message variables. You can use any of the fields available, as shown in Figure 5.35, to build message variables.

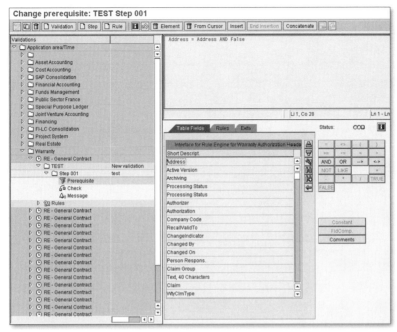

Figure 5.34 Building the Prerequisite for Validations

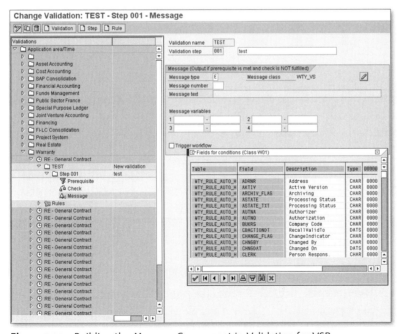

Figure 5.35 Building the Message Component in Validation for VSR

After you've completed the validation step, you need to build a substitution step similar to the validation step. Figure 5.36 shows the definition of a substitution component in the VSR.

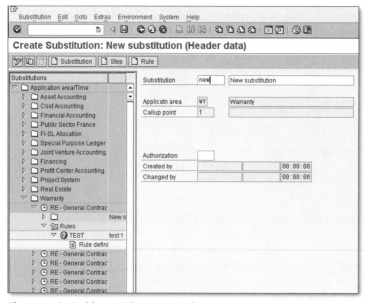

Figure 5.36 Building a Substitution Rule

Using the VSR (or rules engine) allows your company to improve reverse logistics dramatically.

> **Example**
>
> In a semiconductor company, returned products could be contaminated, and this information needs to be understood clearly to make decisions on where the returned products should be sent. By building the validation rule to make decisions based on the contamination data and by mapping customer information to the closest processing center that can handle contamination data, the rules engine can process the return and identify the return to location with all of the necessary documents for transport.

5.5 Summary

In this chapter, we've discussed the different components of warranty claim processing and how they relate to each other. As a review, the following is a reminder of the elements and components associated with warranty claim processing:

▸ **Warranty claim:** This is the document created to process warranty claims.

▸ **Warranty claim type:** This is the configuration that defines the type of warranty claim, such as postcrediting or precrediting. This claim type also contains the action control definition that defines the actions performed for this claim type.

▸ **Action control:** This contains the action matrix that includes the action codes.

▸ **Action codes:** These contain the function modules that define the actions in detail. The customer can code customer requirements in the function modules.

▸ **VSR:** This allows validations and substitutions that can be included in the function modules, which in turn are assigned to the action codes.

By using all of these mechanisms, you can build a completely automatic warranty claim and reverse logistics mechanism that can request information from a customer during a return to perform the necessary checks, issue the messages, and ultimately complete the entire warranty claim processing automatically.

In the next chapter, we'll discuss serial number management and batch management. You'll learn how to configure serial number management and batch management to improve reverse logistics.

The decision to serialize or not to serialize materials determines how companies handle warranty control, quality control, and several business processes. In this chapter, we'll review serialization requirements, configuration, and tips on making serialization work for specific business processes.

6 Serial Number Management in Reverse Logistics

Serialization is the process of enabling serial number tracking for materials. With serial numbers, materials can be tracked across all business processes, capturing and recording important information regarding quality, warranty, and other information in the system. In SAP ERP, serial number management is enabled in the configuration, where you can define the serial number management processes and how the serial numbers will be used across the network.

> **Example**
>
> In a computer manufacturing company, the end product sold to the customer is a computer. The company monitors all customer sales. Using serial numbers to identify the individual computers sold to the customers is very important to ensure that a computer returned by the customer was sold recently and that the product is still under warranty. In addition to this, the customer could have bought an extended warranty, which is also stored in the company's SAP ERP system with reference to the serial number. Some of the components within the computer are also serialized, for example, the hard drive and the memory. The serialization information of the components is very useful for many applications. For example, if there is a product recall of all of the hard drives bought from a vendor on a particular date, the hard drive serial numbers can be used to locate the computers where they were used and help the company send the recall information to the customers to request returns.

Companies consider several requirements before making a decision to serialize materials in the network. Serialization of the material creates additional steps in the business process that then adds to the overall product cost. Following are some of the reasons that a company chooses to serialize a material:

▶ The company wants to monitor the high cost of product returns to ensure that the quality of the product can be improved to reduce returns.

▶ The vendor provides serial numbers for materials and requires that serial numbers are provided during the returns process to the vendor.

▶ The vendor provides the warranty for its products, and this warranty data needs to be stored in the system so that when the product is returned, a replacement or credit is obtained from the vendor.

▶ New products need to be tracked through the complete cycle from procurement to sale to return. This helps the company improve product design or quality.

▶ The product performance needs to be analyzed so that it can be continuously improved.

▶ If products are to be recalled, the serial number information can be used to identify the current location information of the product.

When selecting parts for serialization, the following characteristics of the product are considered:

▶ Cost of the product
▶ Usage of the product
▶ Warranty provided by the vendor
▶ Warranty provided to the customer
▶ Repair/refurbish options for the product

Now that you understand serialization and when it's advantageous for your company to use and configure, let's take a deeper look, starting with serial number records in SAP ERP.

6.1   Serial Numbers

A serial number is a unique number that provides details about a material at different points in the supply chain. In SAP ERP, the serial number details are stored in the serial number master record.

A serial number record contains key details such as the material number, serial number, stock type, plant, storage location, vendor warranty, and customer warranty information, as show in Figure 6.1. The serial number record can be displayed in SAP ERP by using Transaction IQ03. You can also display the serial number record by choosing LOGISTICS • PLANT MAINTENANCE • MANAGEMENT OF TECHNICAL OBJECTS • SERIAL NUMBERS • DISPLAY.

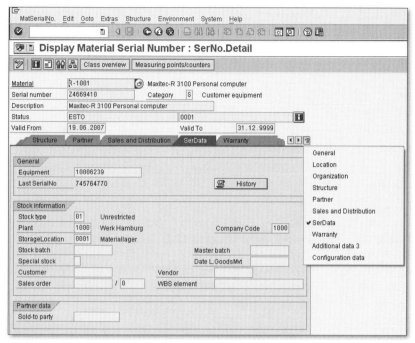

Figure 6.1 Serial Number Record Display in SAP ERP

There are different tabs in the serial number record that contain specific information regarding location, organization, structure, serialization data, warranty, and configuration data as shown in Figure 6.1.

One of the important fields in the serial number record is the serial number Status field. The two types of serial number statuses in the SAP ERP system are the system status and the user status. The system status is set when a function in SAP ERP is executed. For example, when you ship a product to a customer, the ECUS status is set to show that the part is at the customer site. Following are some of the system statuses and their definitions:

▶ **ASEQ: Allocated to superior equipment**
Means this serial number is allocated to other equipment or is a subcomponent of a superior equipment item. For example, if we consider a bicycle to be an assembly or equipment item, the serial number of the wheels will be the serial number of a subcomponent (wheels) of a superior component (bicycle). To view all of the subequipment items linked to a serial number/equipment, you can choose Structure – Subequipment from the menu in the serial number

display. This will show all of the subequipment items linked to the superior equipment being displayed.

▸ **AVLB: Available**
Means this serial number is available for all other functions.

▸ **ECUS: At customer site**
Means this serial number is at the customer site. This status prevents a few functions but allows the serial number to be allocated to a delivery for returns.

▸ **EDEL: Assigned to a delivery note**
Means this serial number is assigned to a delivery note in transit and can't be used in many other business functions until the status is changed from EDEL.

▸ **ESTO: In the warehouse**
Means the material/serial number is in inventory, and the stock in the warehouse is available for outbound functions such as shipping.

The purpose of the serial number status is to limit changes to the serial number master done via a goods movement. For example, system status EDEL (assigned to a delivery note) prevents the user from assigning the serial number to another delivery note to ship the product to the customer.

The other status that is present in the serial number master is the user status, which enables you to further limit the functions allowed for a serial number on the basis of a system status. For example, if you want to prevent the serial numbers in status ESTO from being allowed in certain functions that the SAP ERP system allows, you can use the user statuses to achieve this.

6.1.1 Serial Number Profile

A serial number profile defines for which business processes serialization is active. Serial number profiles are configured in SAP ERP, and the serial number profile is attached to the material master. So, a material is considered serialized if a serial number profile is assigned to the material master.

The serial number profile consists of a group of data summarized by a four-digit identification code that defines the conditions and business processes involved when assigning serial numbers to items of material. The serial number profile is maintained in the material master at the plant level to identify the business process for which the material will be serialized in that plant.

Even though a serial number profile is assigned to the material master, the material doesn't require serial number processing during all business processes; this is defined in the serial number profile.

A bicycle manufacturer procures wheels from an external vendor that provides a warranty on the wheels. The bicycle manufacturing company captures the serial number data of the wheels as it receives them into inventory. The bicycle manufacturer then assembles the cycle and uses the wheels as one of the components. Because the company ships the bicycle and doesn't sell the wheels as a product to the customers, the company only needs to track the serial number of the bicycle, not the wheels. To achieve this, you can define a serial number profile that needs serial numbers tracked only at the goods receipt process and not the shipping process and then assign this to the material master data of the wheels.

All serial number configurations are defined under Plant Maintenance and Customer Service in the IMG, as shown in Figure 6.2.

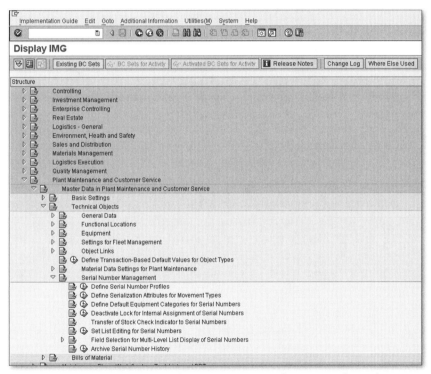

Figure 6.2 Serialization/Serial Number Management Configuration in the Implementation Guide

The serial number profile is defined in the configuration by going to Plant Maintenance and Customer Service • Serial Number Management • Define Serial Number Profiles.

SAP ERP provides some standard serial number profiles, such as 0001, 0002, 0003, and 0004, with preconfigured data, as shown in Figure 6.3.

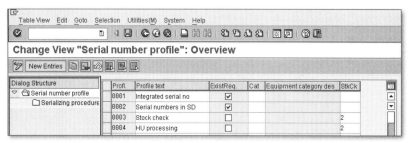

Figure 6.3 Preconfigured Serial Number Profiles in the Standard SAP ERP System

The following settings are defined in the serial number profile configuration:

▶ **Serial number existence requirement (ExistReq.):** If this indicator is selected, the serial number can only be used if the serial number record already exists in the system for some functions as defined by the serial number profile For example, during the delivery creation, packing, or goods issue, serial number existence can be a requirement if this field is selected in the configuration of the serial number profile. This prevents users from trying to use serial numbers in the shipping process that don't exist in the SAP ERP system. This also ensures any human error, such as mistyping the serial number during the shipping process, is identified and prevented. If this indicator isn't set, the system can potentially accept an incorrect serial number as a legitimate serial number, and instead of stopping the user from further processing, the SAP ERP system will create a new serial number record for the material with an incorrect serial number. This will result in a serial number status inconsistency because the incorrect serial number was assigned during the shipping process resulting in a new serial number record showing a status of being shipped, and the correct serial number will show a status of in stock when it has actually already physically left the warehouse.

Although this feature offers advantages in terms of preventing user errors, there are times when this indicator should not be selected for specific reasons. For example, when doing an initial conversion of materials from an external system to SAP ERP, your company might prefer not to identify serial numbers of existing inventory in the legacy system if serialization wasn't activated in the legacy system. Instead, your company may choose to convert the inventory into the new SAP ERP system and then track serial numbers because the materials are being used in different business processes.

▶ **Equipment Category:** The Equipment Category field determines screens and fields that are displayed in the serial number record. The equipment master will be discussed in Section 6.2, Equipment Master, later in this chapter.

▶ **Stock check for Serial numbers (StkCk):** This field determines whether a stock check is done when transactions are performed using the serial number. This is very useful to ensure that the serial number statuses reflect the actual status of the serial number physically. If this field is selected when performing a transaction for this serial number, SAP ERP checks to see if this serial number record is maintained in the plant and storage location used for that transaction. The plant and storage location information is stored in the SerData tab under Stock Information, as show in Figure 6.4.

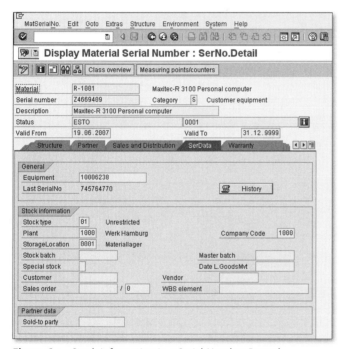

Figure 6.4 Stock Information in a Serial Number Record

If the stock information in the serial number record doesn't match the transaction data, then you can decide if the SAP ERP system should display a warning or error message. This is done by selecting either the value 1 or 2 in the Stock Check for Serial Number field in the Serial Number Profile definition, as shown in Figure 6.5.

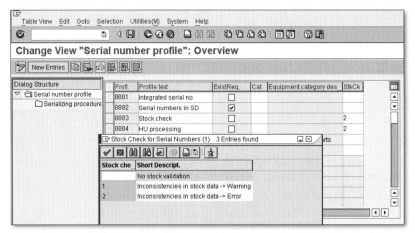

Figure 6.5 Stock Check for Serial Number Options in the Serial Number Profile

After these fields are selected in the serial number profile, the serial number profile is assigned to serialization procedures in the configuration. This is done in the same menu used to configure the serial number profile earlier. To assign serialization procedures, you select the serial number profile and then select the Serialization Procedures folder in the left side of the configuration, as shown in Figure 6.6.

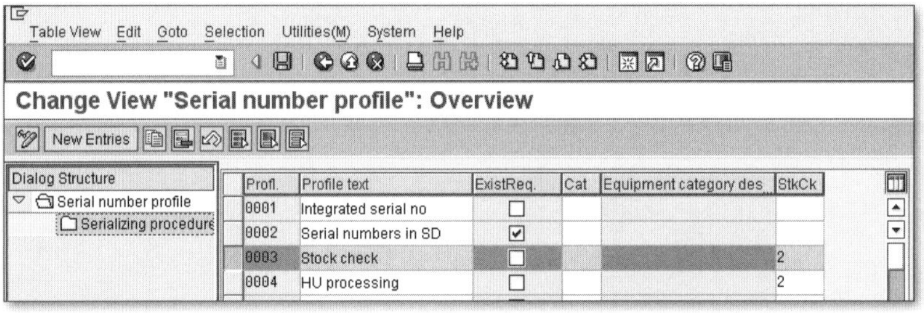

Figure 6.6 Assigning Serialization Procedures to a Serial Number Profile

In the next screen, you assign the applicable business procedures to this serial number profile and also define serial number usage for every business procedure in the serial number profile.

SAP ERP provides standard business procedures that can be configured according to your company's requirements. A list of these provided business procedures for serialization is shown in Figure 6.7.

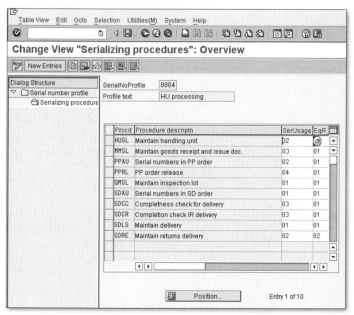

Figure 6.7 SAP ERP Business Procedures for Serialization

You can choose which business procedure you want to activate serialization for every serial number profile. You do that by either adding or removing the business procedures in the serial number configuration shown in Figure 6.7. For example, if you want serialization to be active for the business procedure of maintaining handling units, then you can include the procedure HUSL in the serial number profile.

In addition to configuring the business procedures for a serial number profile, you must decide if serial number usage is optional, obligatory, or automatic. You do so by choosing one of the following values for the Serial Number Usage field in the configuration of serialization procedures for the serial number profile (see Figure 6.8):

▶ **01:** None

▶ **02:** Optional

▶ **03:** Obligatory

▶ **04:** Automatic

Depending on the option you choose, the serial number entry becomes optional or mandatory for that business procedure.

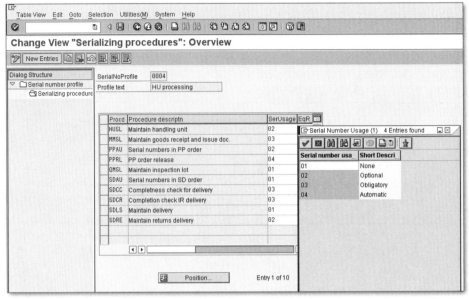

Figure 6.8 Choosing the Serial Number Usage for Business Procedures in a Serial Number Profile

In addition to defining the serial number usage, you can also configure whether an equipment record needs to be created when a serial number record is created in SAP ERP. Serial numbers can be created for different types of materials such as spare parts stored in inventory for sale and machines that are installed. For serial numbers that refer to an equipment item, more information about the equipment can also be obtained from the equipment record. The equipment record information is also available from the serial number record of the equipment in the Ser-Data tab of the serial number record as shown earlier in Figure 6.4. In SAP ERP, you can also view the equipment record by using Transaction IEO3 or by choosing LOGISTICS • PLANT MAINTENANCE • MANAGEMENT OF TECHNICAL OBJECTS • EQUIPMENT • DISPLAY. Equipment records are discussed in detail in this section.

Typically, serial numbers are used to track materials that are stored in inventory, while machines and equipment are tracked using equipment records. Machines/equipment can contain components as a part of their bill of material (BOM), which in turn could be materials that are serialized in SAP ERP. The material/serial number information is stored in the material serial number record that can be viewed via Transaction IQ03. The equipment information can be viewed via Transaction IE03.

The serial number record and equipment number record also provide information about the components under the material/equipment viewed in the serial number/

equipment record. To view components, you can choose Structure – Structure List from the serial number record/equipment number record in SAP ERP. Figure 6.9 shows the BOMs for material T-FP400 displayed from the serial number record using the structure list.

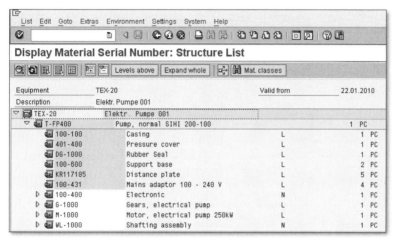

Figure 6.9 The BOM from the Serial Number Record

As we mentioned previously, a serial number profile is assigned to the material master to serialize a material. In SAP ERP, you can also create a serial number record for a material that doesn't contain a serial number profile. This record can be created manually and doesn't get created automatically or get updated automatically by different business processes because it isn't linked to the serial number profile that defines how serialization works for different business processes.

> **Example**
>
> A cell phone manufacturing company in the research and development stage of a new product procures components for testing. The company isn't sure if the product will be serialized when the product is released but wants to capture the serial numbers provided by the vendor during the testing phase. To do this, the company can create serial number records manually for all of the components during receipt. No data are updated on the serial number master record if the component is used or scrapped; however, if the component is unused and needs to be returned, then the company can refer to the serial number record created manually to see if the component is under warranty.

In the material master, the serial number profile is assigned in the Sales: General/ Plant tab in the SerialNoProfile field. The organizational level for setting up serial numbers is Plant. To view the serial number profile in the material master, in the Sales: General/Plant tab, you can enter the Material number and the Plant number using Transaction MM03. You can also use the following menu path to display the material master: MATERIALS MANAGEMENT • MATERIAL MASTER • MATERIAL • DISPLAY. The material master Sales: General/Plant tab with the serial number profile is shown in Figure 6.10.

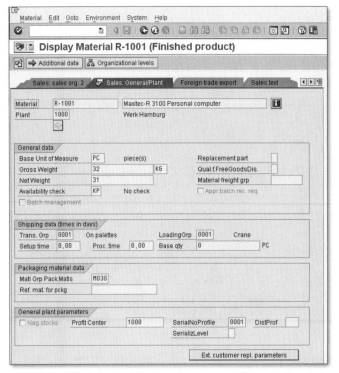

Figure 6.10 Material Master Sales: General/Plant Tab with Serial Number Profile Assignment

Along with the serial number profile assignment, there is also another field specific to serialization in the material master Sales: General/Plant tab — the serialization level (SerializLevel) or the level of explicitness of a serial number.

Maintaining this field in the material master determines whether the combination of material and serial number is unique. The other option is to set up the serial number and the equipment number in sync, so the serial numbers are unique at the client level in the SAP ERP system.

Note

This setup depends on the material that is being configured. If the material master is set up for a material that isn't a machine or equipment item and that will be stored in inventory, procured, and sold, then typically only the material/serial number combination will be unique. If the material is an equipment item, then the preferred option is to make the equipment number unique along with the serial number.

Figure 6.11 shows the configuration options for the serialization level in the material master Sales: General/Plant Data view.

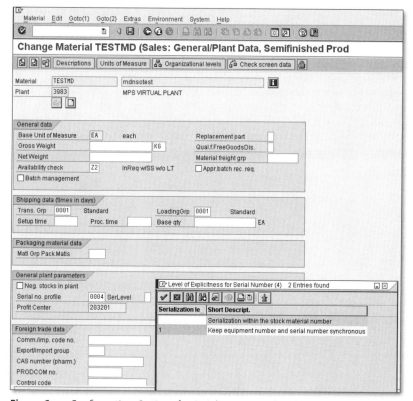

Figure 6.11 Configuration Options for Serialization Level in the Material Master

Materials can be maintained with different serial number profiles for different plants. Typically, this is required only if some plants have business procedures that require serialization and other plants don't require serialization for the same business procedures.

Example

In a semiconductor manufacturing company, in the manufacturing plant, serialization isn't required for components during the shipping process but only during the assembly process. But in a plant where the component is stored for sale as a spare part, the serialization check needs to happen at the delivery level. You can handle this requirement by defining a serial number profile X001, selecting the maintain delivery business procedure (SDLS), setting the serial number usage to 03 (which is obligatory or mandatory), and creating another profile X002 that has serialization usage for SDLS business procedures with no entry, thus making serialization not required. Now you can assign the X001 profile in the material master to the spares sale plant and assign the X002 profile to the manufacturing plant for the same material, thus making serialization a requirement for delivery processing in the spare parts plant and not a requirement in the manufacturing plant

Caution

If you assign different serial number profiles for the same material in two different plants, you'll have issues if you need to ship the materials between these two plants using a stock transport order (STO). SAP ERP checks the serial number profiles for the material master between these two plants at the time of the post goods issue and issues an error message, as shown in Figure 6.12.

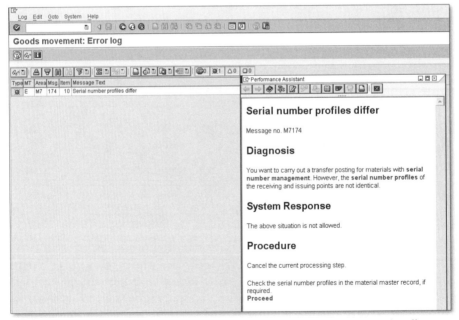

Figure 6.12 Error Message When Shipping Between Two Plants Using an STO with Different Serial Number Profiles

Now that you understand serial numbers, let's discuss equipment masters and their relevance to serialization.

6.2 Equipment Master

The *equipment master* in SAP refers to the master data relevant to an equipment item or a machine. When this machine needs to be managed as a piece of inventory, serialization data needs to be linked to the equipment record. When a serial number is created for an equipment item, the equipment number gets assigned automatically in the serial number record depending on the configuration. But the equipment data isn't activated until the equipment view is activated in the serial number record.

The equipment master in SAP is displayed using Transaction IE03 (LOGISTICS • CUSTOMER SERVICE • MANAGEMENT OF TECHNICAL OBJECTS • EQUIPMENT • DISPLAY), while the equipment record is created using Transaction IE01 (LOGISTICS • CUSTOMER SERVICE • MANAGEMENT OF TECHNICAL OBJECTS • EQUIPMENT • CREATE). When creating an equipment master, you can provide the description and other manufacturing data regarding the equipment in the General tab of the equipment master, as shown in Figure 6.13.

Figure 6.13 Equipment Creation

In addition to general data, more information is included in the Location tab, such as the maintenance plant and work center assigned to the equipment (see Figure 6.14). The maintenance plant (MaintPlant) is the plant where the company's technical objects are installed, where maintenance is performed, and where all required materials and services are obtained and stored to perform service on these equipment items and machines.

The difference between a serial number and an equipment item in terms of master data is the fact that the data maintained for fields in the serial number and equipment will be different, even though the same field names appear in both of the master records.

Figure 6.14 shows the location detail of the equipment master, while Figure 6.15 shows the stock information details from the serial number record.

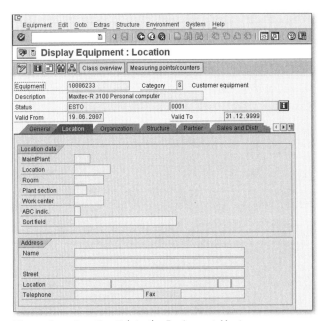

Figure 6.14 Location Tab in the Equipment Master

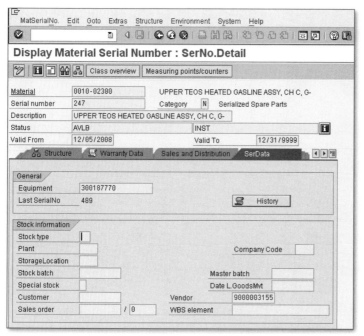

Figure 6.15 Stock Information Data in the Serial Number Master

6.3 Warranty Recovery Using the Serial Number/ Equipment Master

One of the main reasons to use serialization is to provide customers with excellent support in the form of warranties for the products sold. In addition to providing support to the customers, serial numbers also provide valuable information to the company in analyzing the performance of the products in the field.

Vendor warranty also can be captured in the serial number record to provide valuable data regarding products that are under warranty with the vendor. With this information available, returned products or products with bad quality can be checked for warranty from the OEM vendors, and the company can make necessary decisions to recover the warranty.

When serialized materials are received from OEM vendors, the vendor serial number can be captured in the serial number record of the material. This allows the company to provide the serial number information of the product back to the vendor in case of returns or failures.

Capturing vendor warranty information also allows the SAP ERP system to make decisions based on the length of the warranty provided by the vendor. In addition to helping with recovering the vendor warranty, serialization also helps analyze vendor quality.

During vendor evaluation, the quality of the products procured from the vendor plays an important role in considering the vendor. If the serial number analysis shows that the products are being returned often or if there are too many quality issues, then the company might decide not to procure products from the vendor or start finding alternate sources for supply.

Figure 6.16 shows the Warranty tab of the serial number record/equipment master record with data fields to capture both customer and vendor warranty.

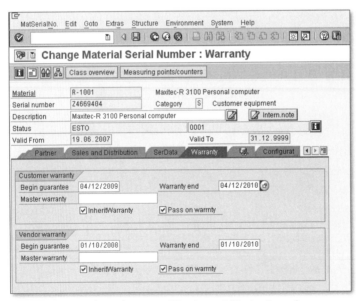

Figure 6.16 Serial Number Record/Equipment Master Record

SAP ERP doesn't update the date of vendor or customer warranty at the time of material receipt or during shipment of the product automatically. Typically, the vendor warranty is updated at the time of goods receipt to indicate the beginning of the vendor warranty date as the date of goods receipt. The end date of the vendor warranty is calculated using an enhancement or custom development in the Inventory Management section of SAP ERP used for performing goods receipt.

The enhancement or custom development is a standalone program that calculates the end warranty date based on the criteria specific to the company.

This becomes a mandatory requirement if the vendor warranty recovery needs to be checked at the time of receipt of returns or repair products. During the returns process, a custom code can be written at the order management level using standard user exits provided by SAP ERP. You can check the vendor warranty on the serial number of the product being returned. The warranty claim document uses this logic and process exclusively to determine subsequent actions upon return of serialized products.

When companies sell products to customers, a standard warranty length is provided for certain serialized parts. When customers return the product, the serial number is checked to identify whether the product is still under warranty and if a return can be accepted.

Even though the serial master record captures the history of all transactions and goods movements, the customer warranty date isn't automatically updated in the serial number record at the time of delivery creation, shipment creation, final goods issue, or goods movement to the customer. The serial number being sent to the customer is provided in the shipping process during delivery creation, picking, or packing, or during the goods issue.

A custom development can be coded to update the customer master warranty information in the serial number based on the shipping transactions and goods movement during shipping.

During the returns processing, while using the warranty claims document, the customer's warranty entitlement can be checked to ensure that the product returned is still under warranty and can be accepted for returns.

Both the vendor and customer warranty in the equipment master can be inherited from a master warranty record.

> **Example**
>
> A furniture manufacturing company is selling a new set of chairs with variations in the color of the chair and the design of the armrest. Every combination of the chair based on color and arm rest design is defined as a unique material number, but the company provides the same warranty for all chairs it sells. So instead of creating individual warranty information in SAP ERP, the company can create a master warranty for the product group chair, and all individual equipment/serial number records for chairs can inherit the warranty from this master warranty record.

To create master warranties in SAP ERP, you can use Transaction BGM1 (LOGISTICS • CUSTOMER SERVICE • SERVICE PROCESSING • ENVIRONMENT • WARRANTIES • MASTER WARRANTY • CREATE) to maintain the different materials included in the master warranty, as shown in Figures 6.17 and 6.18.

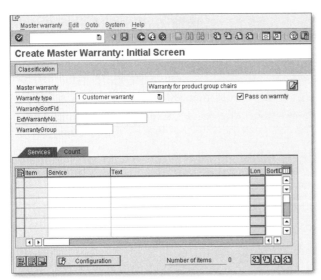

Figure 6.17 Maintaining a Master Warranty

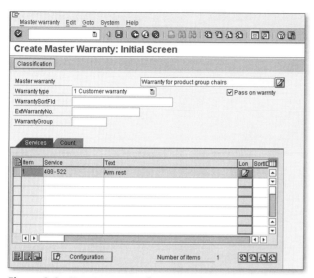

Figure 6.18 Entering Materials to Be Included in the Master Warranty

In addition to specifying the material, the warranty length of every item/service is identified in the Count tab of the master warranty, as shown in Figure 6.19.

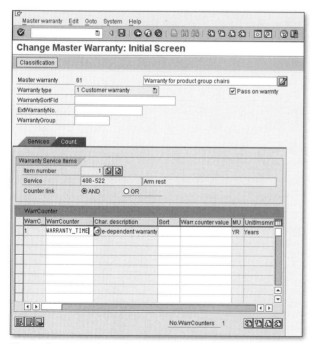

Figure 6.19 Specifying the Warranty Length in the Count. Tab of the Master Warranty

After the master warranty is created, this master warranty number can be specified in the serial number record so that you can copy the master warranty data into the serial number record, as shown in Figure 6.20.

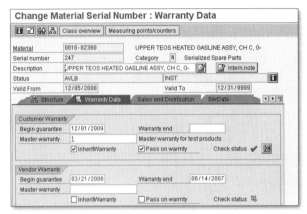

Figure 6.20 Linking the Master Warranty to Inherit Warranty Data from the Master Warranty to the Serial Number Record

After specifying the start date of the customer warranty, SAP ERP calculates the end warranty date based on the counter information. The end warranty date is shown in the subscreen of the serial number record, as shown in Figure 6.21.

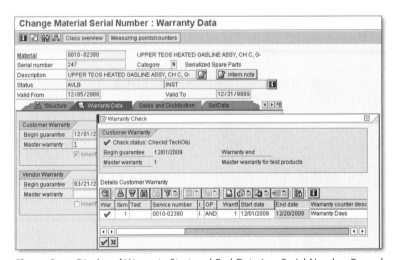

Figure 6.21 Display of Warranty Start and End Date in a Serial Number Record

Now let's move on to inventory data and serial numbers.

6.4   Serial Numbers and Inventory Data

Configuring a stock check in the serial number profile configuration ensures that the serial number data in SAP ERP matches the inventory data for all serialized materials. To ensure that the serial number data always matches the inventory data, all serial number profiles need to have "stock check" selected in their configuration for all business procedures that relate to goods movements. This configuration should be done for all serial number profiles in the company.

Often, not all serial number profiles have stock check selected for business procedures in their profile due to specific reasons such as doing vendor consignment goods movement. For example, if the company stores vendor consignment stocks that contain serialized materials, when the stock is consumed in SAP ERP, a goods movement is used to move the stock from the vendor stock to the company's own stock. This goods movement happens most of the time using a background job because the system calculates the required stock for shipping products out of the company and converts the stock automatically. However because the goods movement happens in the background, it isn't possible for the user to enter the serial number data, so this business process isn't selected for serialization. This means that there are points in the process where the serial number stock status doesn't match the real status of the serialized part. Another example where the serial number status doesn't match the product status is if the serialized part is shipped to customers/internal locations where serialization isn't activated, so that the product is received without a status update in the serial number record in SAP ERP. As you can see from these examples, if you run a report in SAP ERP for the list of serial numbers, the number of serial numbers in SAP ERP may not match the inventory quantity of the same material in SAP ERP due to the lack of stock check in serial number profiles.

Figure 6.22 shows the list of serial numbers of a material in the SAP ERP system.

Display Material Serial Number: Serial Number List

Equipment	S	Material	Serial number	Plant	SLoc	System status	FunctLoc.	Superord. Equipment	PIPI	VenWrtyEnd
300220088		0247-00574	STI_MXP_01	5203	0001	ESTO			5923	
300220089		0247-00574	STI_MXP_02	5203	0001	ESTO			5923	
300220090		0247-00574	STI_MXP_03	5203	0001	ESTO			5923	
300220091		0247-00574	STI_MXP_04	0320	0001	ESTO			5923	
300220092		0247-00574	STI_MXP_05			ASEQ ECUS	55757	600054572	5923	
300220093		0247-00574	STI_MXP_06			ASEQ ECUS	55757	600068310	5923	
300220094		0247-00574	STI_MXP_07	5203	0001	ESTO			5923	
300220095		0247-00574	STI_MXP_08	5203	0001	ESTO			5923	
300220096		0247-00574	STI_MXP_09			ASEQ ECUS	55757	600068327	5923	
300220097		0247-00574	STI_MXP_11	5203	0001	ESTO			5923	
300220098		0247-00574	STI_MXP_12	5203	0001	ESTO			5923	
300220099		0247-00574	STI_MXP_13	5203	0001	ESTO			5923	
300220100		0247-00574	STI_MXP_14			ASEQ ECUS	55757	600054604	5923	

Figure 6.22   Serial Number List of a Material

Figure 6.23 shows the Stock Overview screen of the same material in SAP ERP. As you can see, the Stock Overview screen shows no stock available of this material, while the serial number report in Figure 6.22 shows a couple of serial numbers, STI_MXP_01 and STI_MXP_02, with status ESTO in the system. Status ESTO means the inventory linked to the serial number is in stock.

> **Note**
>
> As we've discussed, the serial number list and inventory list might not match each other. This essentially proves the serial number isn't directly linked to the inventory because the serial number refers to one piece of the material in the inventory. Also, because the serial number status isn't always traced through all business processes, chances are the serial number list won't match the inventory list.

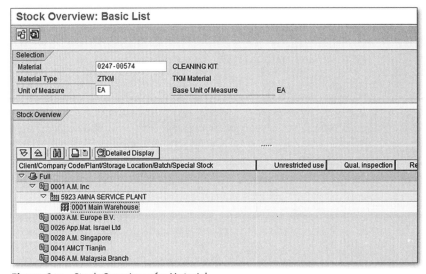

Figure 6.23   Stock Overview of a Material

Next we will discuss serial numbers in warehouse management.

6.5   Serial Number Linking in Warehouse Management

Serial numbers aren't available at the warehouse level at most companies. So, the typical warehouse view of a material inventory in bin stock won't show a serial number. For example, Figure 6.24 shows the bin stock of a serialized material in the warehouse that doesn't contain serial number information.

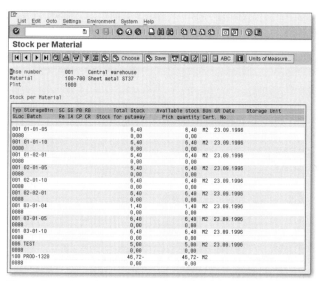

Figure 6.24 Warehouse Bin Stock Display for a Serialized Material

The serial number also isn't available during movements within the warehouse. So, when a serialized part is moved from bin to bin, the serial number entry isn't a requirement. Figure 6.25 shows the movement of a material from one bin to another bin in the warehouse.

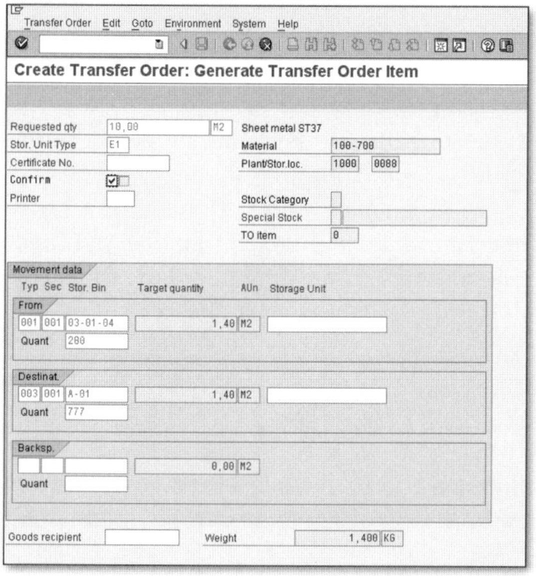

Figure 6.25 Warehouse Bin-to-Bin Movement

Not being able to locate the serial number at the bin level could be problematic for companies using the SAP ERP system and serialization.

> **Example**
>
> In the previously discussed vendor consignment stock scenario, the process for allocating vendor consigned stock to an outbound delivery for shipping is to first create the delivery and then convert the needed vendor consignment stock to the company's own stock so that the serial number of the stock being converted can be recorded.
>
> In SAP ERP, you can convert the vendor consignment stock to a goods movement using movement type 411K and Transaction MIGO. When performing this transaction, the serial number is entered when a serialized material in the vendor consignment stock can be converted to the company's own stock. If the goods movement is performed at a location that is warehouse managed, the same transaction needs to be executed at the warehouse level. To perform this transaction at the warehouse level, you need to know which bins contain the same serial numbers that were converted to the company's own stock in the inventory management level. Because serial numbers aren't stored in the warehouse level, this step can't be executed correctly if the system picks bins that don't store the same serial number. This is one of the main reasons why serialized parts are handled differently when the vendor consignment process is performed in SAP ERP in a plant and storage location that has warehouse management active.

If the company needs to allocate serial numbers at the warehouse management level, one of the solutions is to activate handling unit management at the inventory management level, activate storage unit management at the warehouse management level, and then link storage unit numbers to serial numbers. This is a pretty complex solution to find serial numbers in the warehouse. Based on the complexity of the solution, this isn't recommended. Because this solution isn't easy to implement, the workarounds used in most companies is to turn off serialization for movement type 411, or to perform the goods movement transaction using Transaction MIGO and movement type 411 manually after removing the stock from the warehouse, identifying the serial numbers of the stock pulled out, and using those serial numbers in the 411 goods movement. We'll discuss deactivating serialization at the movement type level in the next section.

6.6 Serializing and Unserializing Processes in SAP ERP

Even though serialization mostly require parts to be serialized through the whole network, there are certain occasions where a serial number isn't provided when transactions or goods movement are performed.

When the company's stock is stored in a customer location and the data regarding transactions are provided after the fact using an interface from the customer or in the form of a file, the serial number isn't provided at the time of performing the transaction.

Another example where serial numbers aren't provided for serialized parts is when a service engineer is responsible for performing a service on the equipment using the company's stock stored at the customer site. He would remove the stock and record the removal, but not the serial number. The customer reports the serial number later in the form of an interface or in a file.

So to perform this transaction without providing a serial number (even though the material number has a serial number profile attached to it), the best solution is to deactivate serialization requirements at the movement type level. You can define this by going to PLANT MAINTENANCE AND CUSTOMER SERVICE • TECHNICAL OBJECTS • SERIAL NUMBER MANAGEMENT • DEFINE SERIALIZATION ATTRIBUTES FOR MOVEMENT TYPES.

In this configuration, there are two options:

▶ Define flow type groups

▶ Assign the movement type group to the movement type

For the define flow type groups, you'll configure movement type groups for a serial number profile and define the serialization usage and equipment master creation requirement with serial numbers.

Even though the same field is defined at the serial number profile configuration, the movement type group setting takes precedence over the serial number profile setting for serial number usage. Figure 6.26 shows the definition of the flow type groups.

After the definition of the flow type group, the movement type group needs to be assigned to individual movement types in the configuration. To assign a movement type group to movement types, use CONFIGURATION • PLANT MAINTENANCE AND CUSTOMER SERVICE • MASTER DATA IN PLANT MAINTENANCE AND CUSTOMER SERVICE • TECHNICAL SETTINGS • SERIAL NUMBER MANAGEMENT • DEFINE SERIALIZATION ATTRIBUTES FOR MOVEMENT TYPES • ASSIGNMENT OF MOVEMENT TYPE GROUP TO MOVEMENT TYPE. Figure 6.27 shows the assignment of movement type 101 to the movement type group SMG1.

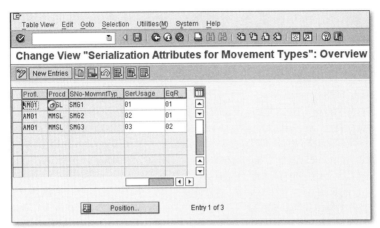

Figure 6.26 Definition of Flow Type Groups for Movement Type Groups in Serialization

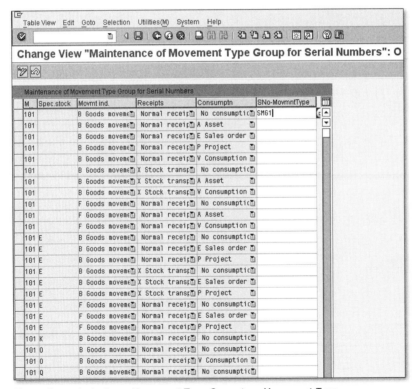

Figure 6.27 Assigning a Movement Type Group to a Movement Type

For every movement type, you assign a movement type group, which makes serialization optional, mandatory, or not applicable. It's important to remember that this configuration overwrites the serial number profile definition requirements for serial number usage.

This configuration helps businesses manage complex serial number requirements.

Example

When your company ships a product to be refurbished, it typically uses a subcontract purchase order. In the subcontract purchase order, the material that is being refurbished is sent to the vendor as a *component*. Because the same part number comes back as a finished product, the parent item in the purchase order also contains the same material number. In SAP ERP, if you ship a component in a subcontract purchase order and provide a serial number in that transaction, you'll receive the "Serial number recursiveness" error message if you try to receive the same material number back with the same serial number after the completion of the subcontracting service.

To avoid this, you can turn off serialization for the movement type that ships the product to the vendor so that when the product is being received back, you can use the same serial number. Because SAP ERP didn't track the part/serial number combination being sent as a component of a subcontract purchase order, this receipt will be allowed.

As you can see, there are several complex serial number requirements that can be easily handled by a combination of configuration options available for serial number management in SAP ERP.

Some companies have requirements on certain locations or plants where they don't want to have serialization. For example, there are some customer-managed locations where companies store products for the customer to use. In some cases, the serial numbers aren't tracked in these locations, so they require that serial number tracking be turned off. This can be easily handled by not maintaining the serial number profile for materials in these plants. This eliminates the need for serialization in this location. But this also causes issues when products are being shipped to this location from some other internal location using an STO. As we discussed earlier in this chapter, if the material serial number profile doesn't match, then SAP ERP won't allow the users to ship products between these two plants on an STO. To handle this requirement, the solution is to maintain a serial number profile for both plants but turn off serialization at the movement type level. To do this, you create a new movement type copied from the existing movement type and assign it to a new schedule line category, which is assigned to a new delivery item category used on the STO.

The new delivery item category is then assigned to the combination of these two plants so SAP ERP will allow shipments between them without serialization requirements. Similarly, the receiving plant can also use a new movement type that doesn't require serialization to receive products.

You can set up different delivery types for stock transfer between two plants by going to MATERIALS MANAGEMENT • PURCHASING • PURCHASE ORDER • SETUP STOCK TRANSPORT ORDER • ASSIGN DELIVERY TYPE AND CHECKING RULE. This configuration is illustrated in Figure 6.28, where the delivery type is assigned for every supplying plant.

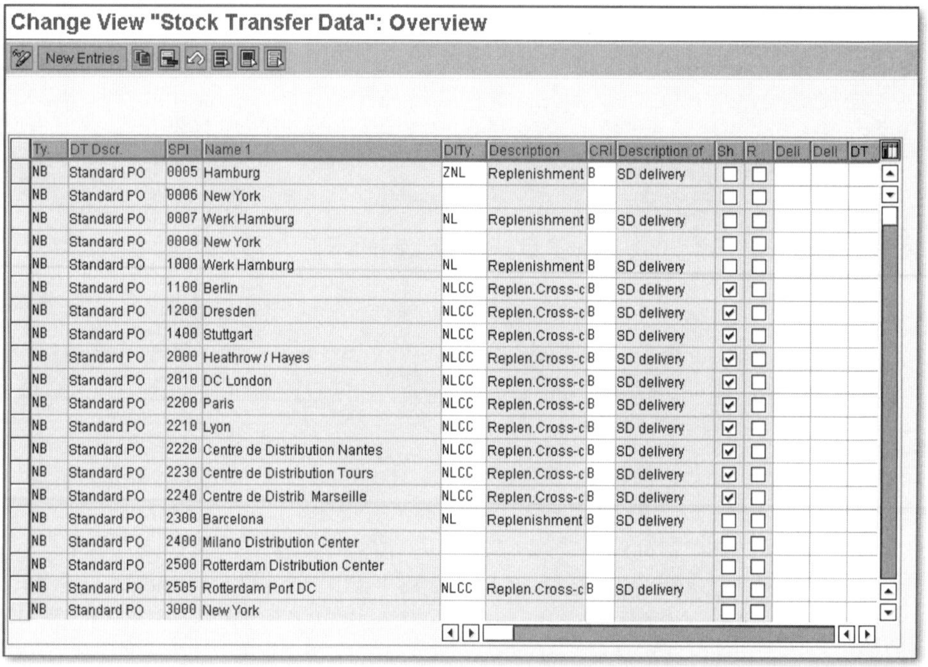

Change View "Stock Transfer Data": Overview

Ty.	DT Dscr.	SPl	Name 1	DITy.	Description	CRl	Description of	Sh	R	Dell	Dell	DT
NB	Standard PO	0005	Hamburg	ZNL	Replenishment	B	SD delivery	☐	☐			
NB	Standard PO	0006	New York					☐	☐			
NB	Standard PO	0007	Werk Hamburg	NL	Replenishment	B	SD delivery	☐	☐			
NB	Standard PO	0008	New York					☐	☐			
NB	Standard PO	1000	Werk Hamburg	NL	Replenishment	B	SD delivery	☐	☐			
NB	Standard PO	1100	Berlin	NLCC	Replen.Cross-c	B	SD delivery	☑	☐			
NB	Standard PO	1200	Dresden	NLCC	Replen.Cross-c	B	SD delivery	☑	☐			
NB	Standard PO	1400	Stuttgart	NLCC	Replen.Cross-c	B	SD delivery	☑	☐			
NB	Standard PO	2000	Heathrow / Hayes	NLCC	Replen.Cross-c	B	SD delivery	☑	☐			
NB	Standard PO	2010	DC London	NLCC	Replen.Cross-c	B	SD delivery	☑	☐			
NB	Standard PO	2200	Paris	NLCC	Replen.Cross-c	B	SD delivery	☑	☐			
NB	Standard PO	2210	Lyon	NLCC	Replen.Cross-c	B	SD delivery	☑	☐			
NB	Standard PO	2220	Centre de Distribution Nantes	NLCC	Replen.Cross-c	B	SD delivery	☑	☐			
NB	Standard PO	2230	Centre de Distribution Tours	NLCC	Replen.Cross-c	B	SD delivery	☑	☐			
NB	Standard PO	2240	Centre de Distrib Marseille	NLCC	Replen.Cross-c	B	SD delivery	☑	☐			
NB	Standard PO	2300	Barcelona	NL	Replenishment	B	SD delivery	☐	☐			
NB	Standard PO	2400	Milano Distribution Center					☐	☐			
NB	Standard PO	2500	Rotterdam Distribution Center					☐	☐			
NB	Standard PO	2505	Rotterdam Port DC	NLCC	Replen.Cross-c	B	SD delivery	☐	☐			
NB	Standard PO	3000	New York					☐	☐			

Figure 6.28 Assigning Delivery Types to a Supplying Plant in Purchasing

> **Note**
>
> This configuration is done for the supplying plant. So if a custom delivery type that doesn't require serialization is configured for a plant, all shipments out of that plant would not require serialization.

Now you should understand how to serialize and unserialize some important processes in SAP ERP, so let's move on to the history in a serial number record.

6.7   History in the Serial Number Record

Serial number records provide valuable information regarding all of the processes and transactions that a material/serial number went through in the network. By default, SAP ERP records all transactions associated with a serial number. You can access the history of the serial number by displaying the serial number record using Transaction IQ03. In this transaction, you can input the material and serial number to display the details, and the history can be viewed by selecting the History button, as shown in Figure 6.29. The History button is available in the General tab along with the equipment number.

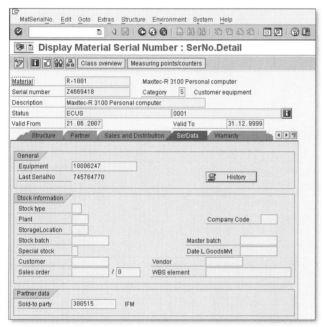

Figure 6.29 Accessing the History of a Serial Number Record

The serial number history can be used as an effective tool for resolving discrepancies, such as the following:

▶ Incorrect serial number status

▶ Discrepancy between the serial number records and the inventory in the system

The serial number history also identifies when the serial number statuses were changed and whether the material number associated with the serial number was changed.

Figure 6.30 shows the serial number history detail showing the serial number being processed through different goods movement and business transactions.

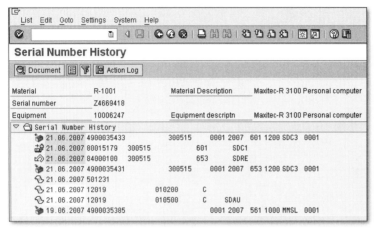

Figure 6.30 Goods Movement in the History of the Serial Number

In the serial number history, different processes are highlighted in different colors. The filter (funnel) icon shows the different processes and colors that are used for the business process. Figure 6.31 shows the filter details of all business processes used in the serial number history in SAP ERP.

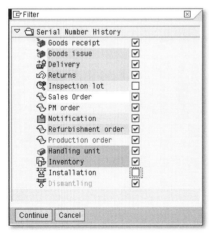

Figure 6.31 Filters Used in Displaying the Serial Number History

You can choose which processes you want to display by selecting the process in the filter. In Figure 6.31, the Goods Receipt and the Goods Issue processes are selected, and the Inspection Lot process is disabled, so the serial number history won't display the inspection lot process history.

6.8   Special Serial Number Functions

SAP ERP provides special functions in the serial number record that allow you to change the material number in the serial number, change the serial number of the serial number record, and change the system status of the serial number record. Although these functions are available in the standard SAP ERP system, these options shouldn't be used often because changing the status of the serial number could cause inconsistencies between the serial number information and the inventory information of the material.

Examples Where Special Serial Number Functions Can Be Used

When a company decides to represent defective material and a material is returned back from a customer, the returns order is created with a different material number than the forward order. If the forward order was created with material number M1 and serial number S1, then on the return order, the material number M2 is used to represent the defective material and the serial number used is still S1. In standard SAP ERP, if you process the return order and bring material M2 into the inventory, a new serial number record with material M2 and serial number S1 is created. This results in losing serial number history because there are two serial number records for the same physical part. To avoid this, you could use the special serial number function, change the material number in the serial number record of M1/S1, and change the record to reflect M2/S1. By doing this, there is only one serial number record in SAP ERP, and also the serial number history reflects the fact that material M1 was changed to M2 for the same serial number S1. One more important advantage of doing this is that if the vendor warranty information was captured in the serial number record of S1, the vendor warranty information would be lost if a new serial number record were created. This would result in the company losing money due to an unclaimed warranty from the vendor for a defective part.

To use the special serial number function, you'll need to use Transaction IQ02 to change the serial number record. You can use the menu LOGISTICS • PLANT MAINTENANCE • MANAGEMENT OF TECHNICAL OBJECTS • SERIAL NUMBERS • CHANGE. In the transaction to change the serial number record, you choose EDIT • SPECIAL SERIAL NO FUNCTIONS. You then have three options: Change Serial Number, Change Material Number, and Manual Transaction.

Note

The special serial number functions might not work for certain situations based on the serial number status. For example, you can't change the material number in the serial number record if the status of the serial number record is ESTO (in stock). You can also change the status of the serial number record by using the manual transaction. When you choose the Manual Transaction option, you can change the status of the serial number record with the options provided there, such as To Stock, From Stock, To Customer, From Customer, Delete, Assign to HU, and Delete Inv Assignment. Figure 6.32 shows changing the serial number status of a serial number using the Manual Transaction option.

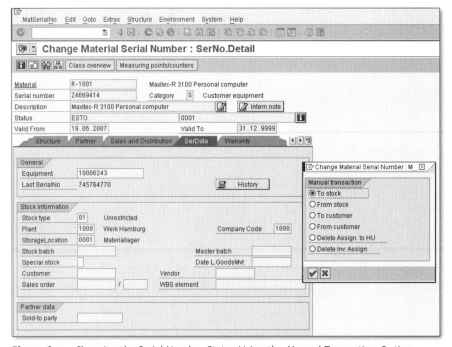

Figure 6.32 Changing the Serial Number Status Using the Manual Transaction Option

As we mentioned before, special serial number functions allow you to change the status, but you should limit using this transaction as much as possible because changing status could cause inconsistencies in the system between the serial number data and the inventory data. If you need to use this often to avoid human error, create a custom program or enhancement that changes the status of the serial number record using standard SAP function modules.

6.9   Batch Management

Batch management is often confused with serial number management in SAP ERP. *Batch management* is used to manage materials in lots or groups, and batches can be grouped by characteristics of a group of material quantities. The basic difference between batch management and serial number management is that a serial number refers to a single piece of material or equipment, whereas a batch can refer to a single piece or multiple pieces or quantities of a material.

Example

A drug manufacturer producing medications on any day classifies quantities of materials out of every machine with the date and time as a batch. WC10101910 means materials produced in machine WC10 on 10/19/2010. Batches allow materials to be classified in groups with similar characteristics and enables monitoring the product sale and recall. In addition, batches allow the company to monitor changing characteristics of the group of materials. A film manufacturing company classifies films based on the characteristic of the film on the date of production. But sometimes as the film is stored for longer periods of time, the characteristics of the film change, making it very difficult to track all of the quantities of the materials if they aren't batch managed. If they are batch managed, the changed characteristics of the batch are automatically reflected on all quantities of the material across the company.

Batch management can also be used to classify materials as broken and refurbished. This is another solution that can be used to identify materials such as a new material number or material group as discussed in Chapter 1, Reverse Logistics. If batch management is used to differentiate broken parts from base or new parts, then the batch determination using batch search procedures can be used to pick materials for business processes such as picking and other goods movements. This ensures that the broken parts aren't picked for a sale to a customer.

If batch management is used to identify broken materials and refurbished materials, then in addition to batch search procedures, some custom programs and outputs might be needed to ensure broken parts aren't included in materials requirement planning (MRP) and other functions.

Batch management is also used to manage materials that expire after the shelf life has been reached. SAP ERP provides standard reports to identify parts with shelf life and also the shelf life data.

During returns, if the material is batch managed and has a shelf life, the expiration date of the material is checked to ensure the product still has enough shelf life remaining before the product is bought back into inventory. This check can be included in the custom actions defined for the warranty claim document that is discussed in Chapter 5, Warranty Claim Processing.

All configurations for batch management are done in the IMG, which can be accessed via Transaction SPRO and going to LOGISTICS GENERAL • BATCH MANAGEMENT.

The critical configuration for batch management relevant for reverse logistics includes the following:

1. Specify the batch level, and activate batch status management.
2. Create new batches.
3. Perform batch valuation.
4. Perform batch determination and batch check.

Now let's discuss these configuration options in detail.

6.9.1 Specifying the Batch Level and Activating Batch Status Management

This configuration is done by choosing LOGISTICS GENERAL • BATCH MANAGEMENT • SPECIFY BATCH LEVEL AND ACTIVATE STATUS MANAGEMENT. You define at which level the batches are unique. The options are Batch Unique at Plant Level, Batch Unique at Material Level, and Batch Unique at Client Level for a Material. If batch management is going to be used in all locations and business processes of the company, then you can choose Batch Unique at the Client Level or Batch Unique at the Client Level for a Material. But if the batch management processes are going to be followed only in certain locations, then batch management should be activated only at the plant level.

Batch management activation should be done only if the company will benefit from it. Deactivating batch management for a material is very difficult and needs all stocks of the material to be removed from the system and also any open document deleted before deactivating batch management for a material that was batch managed for awhile in the system. Also the reverse of the preceding statement is also applicable: If a material wasn't batch managed in the system for awhile, all of the stocks and open documents should be removed before activating batch management for that material. Serial numbers can be activated or deactivated easily compared to batch management because only the serial number records for that material need to be archived. Figure 6.33 shows the batch level activation in the configuration with different options available.

Figure 6.33 Batch Level Activation

In addition to defining the batch levels the batch status management can also be defined in the same configuration menu. Batches can be defined with two statuses – unrestricted and restricted. Unrestricted allows the batches to be available for all processes and functions whereas restricted batches aren't available for all processes. The configuration for batch status management and the options available is shown in Figure 6.34.

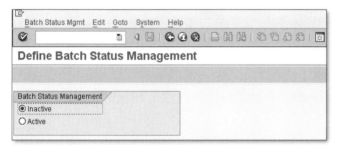

Figure 6.34 Batch Status Definition in SAP ERP

If batch status management is activated then batch status management can be activated at the plant level also in the same configuration menu. This allows batch status to be active only for certain plants.

6.9.2 Creating New Batches

Using this configuration, you can define for each movement type whether a new batch is created with this movement type and how it's created — automatic or manually. Figure 6.35 shows this configuration and the options for creating the batches for every movement type.

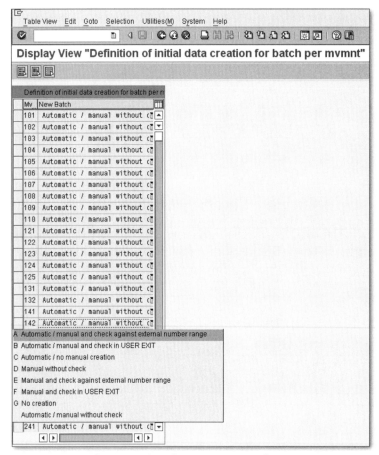

Figure 6.35 Configuration of Batch Creation Settings for Movement Types

6.9.3 Performing Batch Valuation

Batches can be valuated differently, which can be used to valuate broken or defective material inventory against new or base material inventory. To use this functionality, you need to activate split valuation by choosing MATERIALS MANAGEMENT • VALUATION AND ACCOUNT ASSIGNMENT • SPLIT VALUATION • ACTIVATE SPLIT VALUATION.

Here you can activate split valuation at the client level. There are two options available: Split Material Valuation Active and Split Material Valuation Not Active. You need to choose the first button to activate split valuation as shown in Figure 6.36.

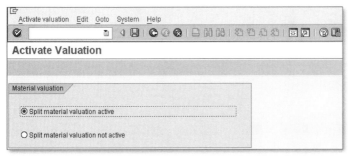

Figure 6.36 Activating Split Valuation

After activating split valuation, you need to define the valuation types and valuation categories for split valuation in the same configuration menu. Valuation categories are the criteria according to which split valuation is carried out. For example, you can have valuation categories based on procurement so that you valuate the material bought from external vendors differently from the material produced in house. You can also use valuation categories as origin or status. Origin can be local or international, and status is relevant for reverse logistics. For status, you can valuate the material depending on whether it's new, used, repaired, or defective. Valuation type specifies the individual characteristic of the valuation category. For example, for the status valuation category, the valuation types can be new, broken, and repaired. You can define the different valuation categories as well as the valuation types in the configuration. You assign the valuation category and define which valuation types are allowed for the material in the material master. To define the valuation type and category, use the same menu path that you used to configure split valuation: MATERIALS MANAGEMENT • VALUATION AND ACCOUNT ASSIGNMENT • SPLIT VALUATION • CONFIGURE SPLIT VALUATION. In this configuration, you can define global types, global categories, and local definitions. Global definitions (types and categories) are applicable to all locations of the company and local definitions (types and categories) are applicable to only some plants in the company.

We'll now look at an example of valuation category and type assignment for plant 1000 that will use batches as a valuation category for split valuation. In the configuration for split valuation described above, choose the Local Definitions option. The SAP ERP system will display all plants available for configuration, as shown in Figure 6.37.

You need to select Plant 1000 and then the Cats – OU (allocate valuation categories) button to show the categories allocated to plant 1000 (see Figure 6.38).

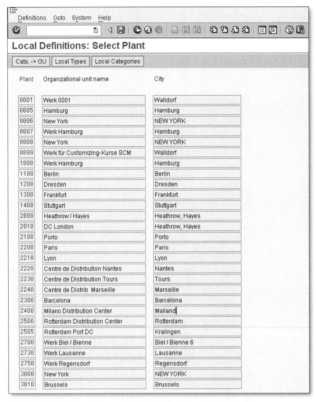

Figure 6.37 Plants Listed for Configuring Local Valuation Categories and Types

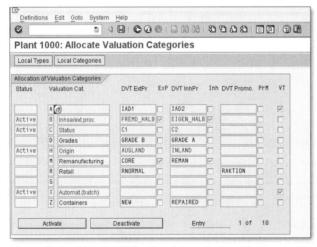

Figure 6.38 Allocating Valuation Categories to a Plant

You need to activate all valuation categories that you want for this plant by selecting the category and selecting the Activate button at the bottom of the screen shown in Figure 6.38. To activate batches for split valuation, you must activate the valuation category X – Automatic (Batch). After this activation is done, then all of the valuation types assigned for valuation category X become available for plant 1000. To view all valuation types assigned to valuation category X, use the same configuration menu, and choose Global Categories. In that screen, choose the valuation category X, and choose the Types – Cat. button to see all of the valuation types assigned to the valuation category X as shown in Figure 6.39. In this screen, you can activate the valuation types that you want to be active for the valuation category by choosing the Activate button at the bottom of the screen. In the example shown in Figure 6.39, the valuation types NEW and REPAIRED are activated for valuation category X that is used for batches.

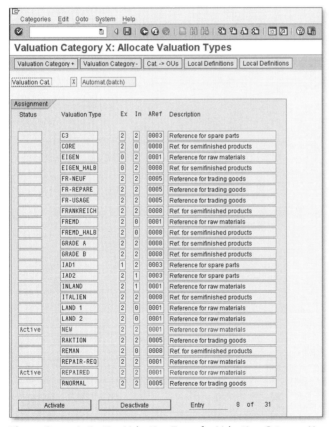

Figure 6.39 Activating Valuation Types for Valuation Category X

After the entire preceding configuration is done, the materials can be valuated differently using batches, and you can use batch management to differentiate materials based on their conditions if you choose to do so. You can also use the same configuration to valuate materials based on the status, such as new, repaired, or broken, by using Status – C as the valuation category as shown earlier in Figure 6.38 and then using the Valuation Types NEW and REPAIRED. You can use this approach if you choose to use the Material status. In the definition of the valuation category C, you can assign the default valuation types used when the material is procured externally using purchase orders (C1) and also when the material is procured internally using production orders (C2) as shown in Figure 6.40. You then define the cost of the material when procured using both valuation types in the material master. Using that information, the materials are valuated differently when procured against a purchase order versus when they are received into inventory against a production order.

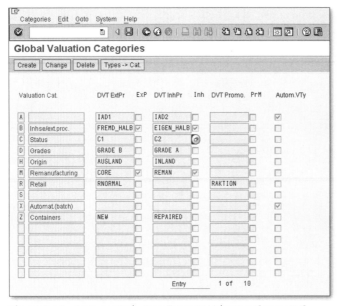

Figure 6.40 Assigning Valuation Types to Valuation Category C

You assign the valuation type during the creation of the accounting view of the material master. You can create a material master using Transaction MM01. You create the accounting view after you create the other views of the material master. When you enter the data for the accounting view, you enter the valuation type C1 or C2 as shown in Figure 6.41.

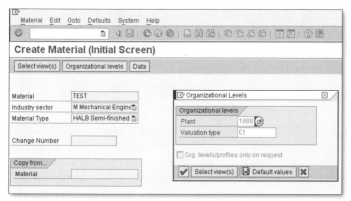

Figure 6.41 Creating an Accounting View for the Material Master with Valuation Type C1

In the accounting view, you define the cost and the valuation category of the material. Work with your SAP finance team to configure the split valuation configuration and also set up the material master with the right valuation types and categories.

6.9.4 Batch Determination and Batch Check

The batch determination process defines how the system selects batches for different functions in SAP ERP. For example, if there are three different batches (A, B, and C) for a material M1, then the batch determination procedure defines which one of these three batches will be picked to meet the requirements for different processes in inventory management, production order, process order, sales and distribution, and warehouse management.

Batch determination is defined in the configuration by going to SAP ERP • LOGISTICS GENERAL • BATCH MANAGEMENT • BATCH DETERMINATION AND BATCH CHECK. In this menu you can configure different elements, such as like condition tables, access sequences, strategy types, batch search procedure definition, batch search procedure allocation, and check activation. Let's proceed to look at this configuration elements in detail.

Condition tables define the different combination of fields that are used to determine which batches will be selected. The condition tables are defined for different areas of SAP, such as Inventory Management and Sales and Distribution. To define a new condition table with the desired required field, go to SAP ERP • LOGISTICS GENERAL • BATCH MANAGEMENT • BATCH DETERMINATION AND BATCH CHECK •

CONDITION TABLES • DEFINE INVENTORY MANAGEMENT CONDITION TABLES • CREATE CONDITION TABLE FOR BATCH DETERMINATION.

Before you create the condition table, first you need to select the required fields that you need and add it to the field catalog if they don't already exist. A field catalog is the list of fields available to use in the condition tables. Field catalogs can contain only fields from the two SAP tables: KOMPH (Batch determination – Communication record for item) or KOMKH (Batch determination – communication block header). To select fields from these two tables and add them to the field catalog, you can use the same configuration menu for creating condition tables, but instead of choosing CREATE CONDITION TABLE, you should choose CONDITIONS: ALLOWED FIELDS (INVENTORY MANAGEMENT). Here you can view the fields in the field catalog provided in the standard SAP ERP system, including movement type, customer, storage location, vendor, and material, as shown in Figure 6.42.

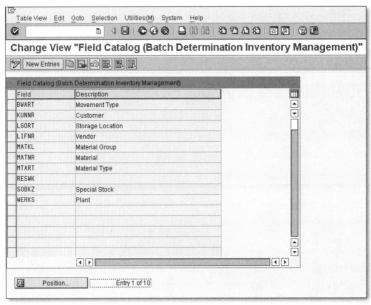

Figure 6.42 Fields Available in the Field Catalog for Batch Determination in Inventory Management

If you want to add more fields in the field catalog, choose New Entries in the field catalog configuration shown in Figure 6.42, and select the fields you want to add by using the pull down menu on the field. SAP ERP will show you all the possible fields available to add in the field catalog, as shown in Figure 6.43.

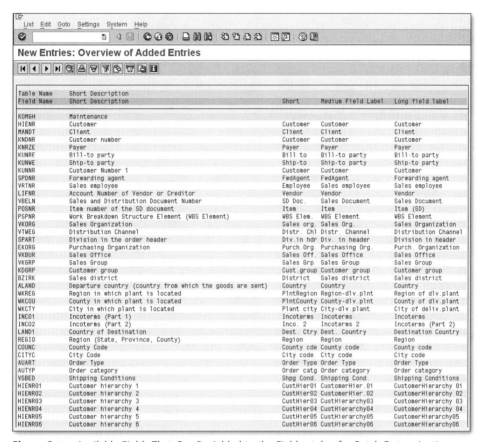

| Table Name | Short Description | | | |
Field Name	Short Description	Short	Medium Field Label	Long field label
KOMGH	Maintenance			
HIENR	Customer	Customer	Customer	Customer
MANDT	Client	Client	Client	Client
KNDNR	Customer number	Customer	Customer	Customer
KNRZE	Payer	Payer	Payer	Payer
KUNRE	Bill-to party	Bill to	Bill-to party	Bill-to party
KUNWE	Ship-to party	Ship-to	Ship-to party	Ship-to party
KUNNR	Customer Number 1	Customer	Customer	Customer
SPDNR	Forwarding agent	FwdAgent	FwdAgent	Forwarding agent
VRTNR	Sales employee	Employee	Sales employee	Sales employee
LIFNR	Account Number of Vendor or Creditor	Vendor	Vendor	Vendor
VBELN	Sales and Distribution Document Number	SD Doc.	Sales Document	Sales Document
POSNR	Item number of the SD document	Item	Item	Item (SD)
PSPNR	Work Breakdown Structure Element (WBS Element)	WBS Elem.	WBS Element	WBS Element
VKORG	Sales Organization	Sales org.	Sales Org.	Sales Organization
VTWEG	Distribution Channel	Distr. Chl	Distr. Channel	Distribution Channel
SPART	Division in the order header	Div.in hdr	Div. in header	Division in header
EKORG	Purchasing Organization	Purch.Org.	Purchasing Org.	Purch. Organization
VKBUR	Sales Office	Sales Off.	Sales Office	Sales Office
VKGRP	Sales Group	Sales Grp	Sales Group	Sales Group
KDGRP	Customer group	Cust.group	Customer group	Customer group
BZIRK	Sales district	District	Sales district	Sales district
ALAND	Departure country (country from which the goods are sent)	Country	Country	Country
WKREG	Region in which plant is located	PlntRegion	Region-dlv.plnt	Region of dlv.plant
WKCOU	County in which plant is located	PlntCounty	County-dlv.plnt	County of dlv.plant
WKCTY	City in which plant is located	Plant city	City-dlv.plnt	City of deliv.plant
INCO1	Incoterms (Part 1)	Incoterms	Incoterms	Incoterms
INCO2	Incoterms (Part 2)	Inco. 2	Incoterms 2	Incoterms (Part 2)
LAND1	Country of Destination	Dest. Ctry	Dest. Country	Destination Country
REGIO	Region (State, Province, County)	Region	Region	Region
COUNC	County Code	County cde	County code	County code
CITYC	City Code	City code	City code	City code
AUART	Order Type	Order Type	Order Type	Order Type
AUTYP	Order category	Order catg	Order category	Order category
VSBED	Shipping Conditions	Shpg Cond.	Shipping Cond.	Shipping Conditions
HIENR01	Customer hierarchy 1	CustHier01	CustomerHier.01	CustomerHierarchy 01
HIENR02	Customer hierarchy 2	CustHier02	CustomerHier.02	CustomerHierarchy 02
HIENR03	Customer hierarchy 3	CustHier03	CustHierarchy03	CustomerHierarchy 03
HIENR04	Customer hierarchy 4	CustHier04	CustHierarchy04	CustomerHierarchy 04
HIENR05	Customer hierarchy 5	CustHier05	CustHierarchy05	CustomerHierarchy05
HIENR06	Customer hierarchy 6	CustHier06	CustHierarchy06	CustomerHierarchy06

Figure 6.43 Available Fields That Can Be Added to the Field catalog for Batch Determination

Once all the required fields are selected, you can create the condition table. To do so, use the configuration menu SAP ERP • LOGISTICS GENERAL • BATCH MANAGEMENT • BATCH DETERMINATION AND BATCH CHECK • CONDITION TABLES • DEFINE INVENTORY MANAGEMENT CONDITION TABLES • CREATE CONDITION TABLE FOR BATCH DETERMINATION. During the creation of the condition table, you will need to enter the new condition table number or name, and in the details screen you can choose the fields you want in the condition table from the field catalog fields that you defined earlier. The field catalog fields are shown in the right side during the condition table creation. Select the fields you want and click Select Field icon on the top of the screen to move the field to the left side, adding it to the condition table selected fields. In the example shown in Figure 6.44, the field plant is selected to be added to the selected fields of the condition table 924.

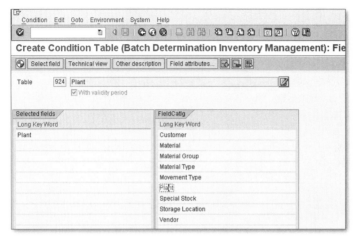

Figure 6.44 Adding Fields to the Condition Table from the Field Catalog for Batch Determination

Once the condition table is created, you need to create an access sequence where the condition table is assigned. The access sequence provides the sequence of condition tables whose field values will be checked to determine whether a strategy type is applicable during batch determination. Access sequence definition is done by going to the menu path LOGISTICS GENERAL • BATCH MANAGEMENT • BATCH DETERMINATION AND BATCH CHECK • ACCESS SEQUENCES • DEFINE INVENTORY MANAGEMENT ACCESS SEQUENCES. In this configuration you can define the access sequence and give the sequence of condition tables that you want to be considered in order to do batch determination. Figure 6.45 shows the different access sequences available, such as ME01, ME02, and ME03.

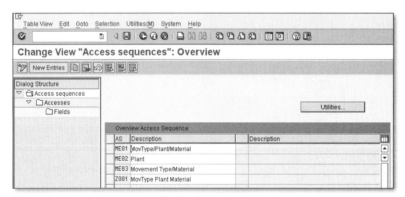

Figure 6.45 Access Sequences for Batch Determination

To define a new access sequence, you can select the New Entries icon on the top of the screen. To view the condition tables defined within the access sequence, you can select the access sequence and click on Accesses on the left side. The condition tables for access sequence ME01 is shown in Figure 6.46.

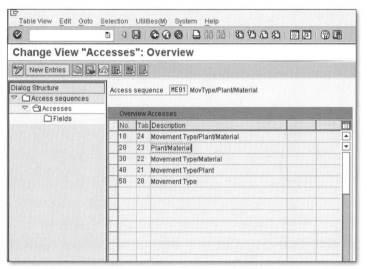

Figure 6.46 Condition Table List for Access Sequence in Batch Determination

To view the fields available within the condition table, select the condition table and choose the fields on the left side of the screen. After the definition of the access sequence, the batch search strategy type is defined. The configuration menu path for defining strategy type is LOGISTICS GENERAL • BATCH MANAGEMENT • BATCH DETERMINATION AND BATCH CHECK • STRATEGY TYPES • DEFINE INVENTORY MANAGEMENT STRATEGY TYPES. Here you can define the strategy types. In the details of the definition, you should specify the class type and the class for batch selection. In the example shown in Figure 6.47, you can define a strategy type ME02 that uses a plant as the field that is used for batch selection, while the batch class used is shelf life and the sort sequence used is to sort the batches by shelf life.

Here you select the class and in the case of batch search, you will select the class – batches and the class type specifies the criteria for selecting batches. To view the details of the class type, you can choose Maintain Next to the Class field, as shown in the Figure 6.47. In the details of the class, you will find the Characteristics tab where you can define the characteristics used for determining batches. In the example shown in Figure 6.48, the characteristic Expiration Date or Shelf Life is used.

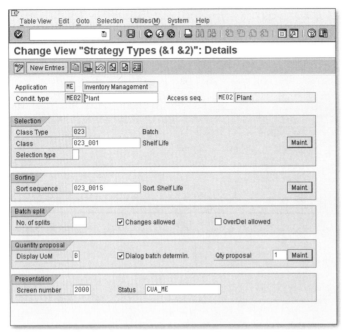

Figure 6.47 Batch Search Strategy Type Definition in SAP ERP

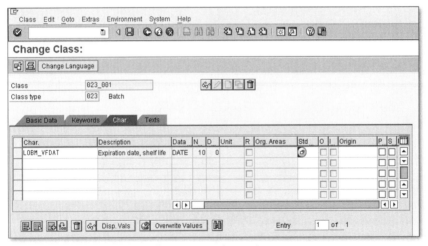

Figure 6.48 Characteristics Definition in Batch Search Strategy

In the maintenance of the Sort Sequence characteristics, which you can view by selecting the Maintenance button next to the Sort Sequence in Figure 6.47, you can see the Order of Sort, as shown in Figure 6.49.

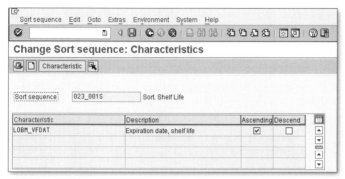

Figure 6.49 Characteristics of the Sort Sequence in the Batch Search Strategy Definition

After the definition of the strategy type, the search procedure is defined under the configuration menu LOGISTICS GENERAL • BATCH MANAGEMENT • BATCH DETERMINATION AND BATCH CHECK • BATCH SEARCH PROCEDURE DEFINITION • DEFINE INVENTORY MANAGEMENT SEARCH PROCEDURE. Here you can define the search procedure and in the definition, you can view the details of the Strategy Types and their sequence by specifying the steps and strategy types (also referred to as condition types) for every step, as shown in Figure 6.50.

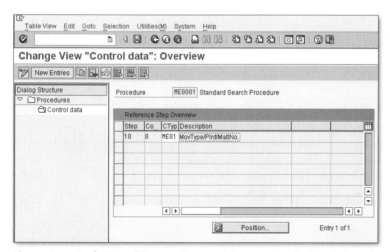

Figure 6.50 Definition of Strategy Types and Sequence in the Search Procedure Definition

Finally, the batch search procedure is assigned to different applications using the configuration menu path LOGISTICS GENERAL • BATCH MANAGEMENT • BATCH DETERMINATION AND BATCH CHECK • BATCH SEARCH PROCEDURE ALLOCATION AND CHECK

ACTIVATION • ALLOCATE IN SEARCH PROCEDURE/ACTIVE CHECK. Here you will assign the batch search procedure to different configuration elements, depending on the area that the procedure is being assigned to. For example, if you are assigning the search procedure for Inventory Management (as described in Figure 6.51), you will assign the search procedure to a movement type whereas if you assign it to the Sales and Distribution area, you will assign it to a combination of Sales Organization, Distribution Channel, Division, and Sales Document type. The Check Batch icon in the assignment of the search procedure specifies if batches were manually entered in the application if the batches are checked against the selection criteria stored for batch determination.

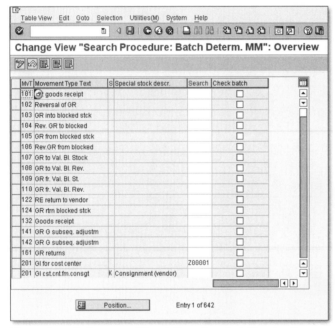

Figure 6.51 Assignment of Search Procedure Definition to Movement Type in Batch Determination

Now, reverse logistics, typically you would store materials that are returned or brought in for repair. If these materials are identified by a different material number or some other field, then this field or material number can be used as criteria to eliminate these batches for certain applications. In short, batch search procedures are assigned to functionalities like Inventory Management, and strategy types are defined in the search procedure. The sort sequence and selection criteria for searching batches are defined in the search procedure. The actual fields for batch search are described in the condition tables, which are in turn assigned to the access sequence that is assigned to the batch search strategy. As mentioned earlier, batch management and serial number management serve different purposes: Serial numbers are used to track warranty and for storing equipment information, whereas batch management is used for shelf-life management and to group material quantities based on other criteria. In reverse logistics, if you configure both of these to meet your needs, they can provide excellent benefits such as ensuring that only products under warranty and still within shelf life are brought back into the supply chain network of the company.

6.10 Summary

Serialization provides a variety of benefits for companies that implement this functionality in SAP ERP. Serialization enables companies to track warranties both to and from the customer and provides an effective method to track the lifecycle of a part, as well as the history of all transactions and goods movements. Serialization implementation increases operational and transactional cost because of the additional requirements of capturing serial numbers in different processes. So, care should be taken to consider the requirements for serialization and weigh it against the benefits it provides to make the decision.

In this chapter, you learned the importance of serialization and how to configure serialization in SAP. We also discussed the equipment master and the difference between the equipment information and the serial number data. We looked at using serialization to recover warranty from the vendor and also to provide warranty to the customers. We also discussed how to configure serialization for only certain processes of the company. You also learned about batch management and how this differs from serial number management. Finally, we discussed split valuation and how to valuate materials differently based on material status and batches. Using serialization should enable companies to recover warranties effectively, and the SAP ERP configuration should help you configure the system to meet your company's specific requirements effectively.

The next chapter looks at how reverse logistics can be configured to meet finance requirements.

Finance ties all of the reverse logistics processes together by ensuring that the reverse logistics transactions are posted to the correct accounts and that the processes are profitable to the company. Proper accounting also enables the company to calculate the costs associated with reverse logistics.

7 Finance in Reverse Logistics

Several departments work together to enable successful reverse logistics processes in a company, but the most important department in a company is the finance department. There are several components in SAP ERP that the finance team can use to cost, price, valuate, credit, debit, and report for reverse logistics. In this chapter, we'll review these finance processes in detail and discuss how they impact different reverse logistics SAP objects. In the first section, we'll discuss the credit and debit memos that are used to credit the customer for returns and debit the vendors for returning a defective product to the vendor.

7.1 Credit and Debit Memos

Credit and debit memos are sales document that precede the customer credit or debit notes. They can be considered as approval requests prior to actually creating the credit or debit notes to the customer. They are also used effectively as a request for approval for credit to the customer. A credit memo is triggered following the processing of a return delivery, if it was created with reference to a sales order. If you have created it with reference to the customer invoice, then the credit memo can be saved with a billing block, and following the approval of the credit memo, the billing block can be removed. You can use the default settings code of 08 (Check Credit Memo) in the billing block parameter of the billing section in the configuration of the credit and debit memo type configuration. Figure 7.1 illustrates the standard delivery credit and debit memo request document types configuration in SAP ERP. This configuration can be accessed by using Transaction VOV8 or using SALES AND DISTRIBUTION • SALES • SALES DOCUMENTS • SALES DOCU- MENT HEADER • DEFINE SALES DOCUMENT TYPES.

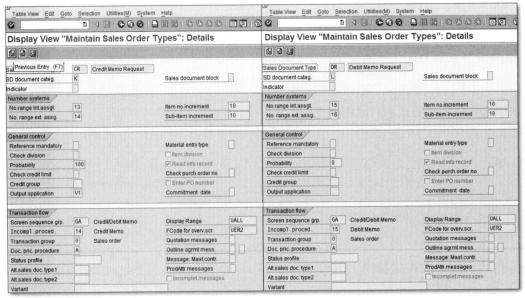

Figure 7.1 Credit Memo and Debit Memo Sales Order Type Configuration

The key difference for this configuration compared to the other sales documents is the SD (Sales and Distribution) Document Categ. field and the Incompl. Proced. field for these two document types. The SD Document Categ. for a credit memo is K, which indicates the credit memo request, and L, which indicates the debit memo request. The Incompl. Proced. for credit memo request is 14 indicating a credit memo, and 15 indicating a debit memo request. Figure 7.2 shows the billing block section in the configuration of the credit memo request.

As you notice in Figure 7.2, the default billing block for a standard credit memo request document type is 08, indicating a billing block for a credit memo.

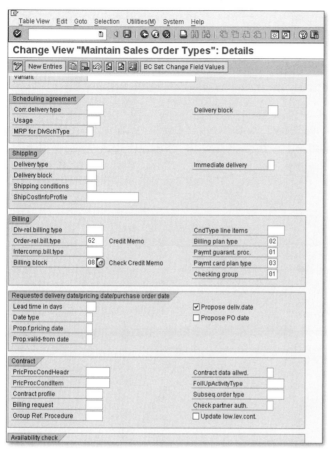

Figure 7.2 Billing Block Definition in the Configuration of a Credit Memo Request Document Type

7.1.1 Sales Process – Credit and Debit

The credit memo can be initiated through a credit memo request (document type CR) or through the invoice correction (document type RK). For the credit memo process, an accounting document is automatically created, which posts to the revenues and deferred revenues accrual accounts. For the debit memo process, an accounting document is automatically created that posts to the unbilled receivables accruals account and the revenue account. The standard delivery billing type for a credit memo is G2 and for a debit memo is L2. Credit memos can be canceled using billing type S2.

When the invoice is created and released to accounting, another accounting document is created that balances (or reduces) the accruals account and posts to the receivables account. As a result, opposite accrual accounts will be used for the credit memo process than are used for the debit memo process (invoices and debit memos have the same posting logic in accounting).

Figure 7.3 displays the process steps using the credit and debit memo process with a sales order directly, while Figure 7.4 displays the credit memo with the return order involved. You can create credit and debit memo either with reference to the credit or debit memo request (sales documents), or, if your company doesn't require a release procedure in case complaints, you can create the memo directly with reference to the billing document.

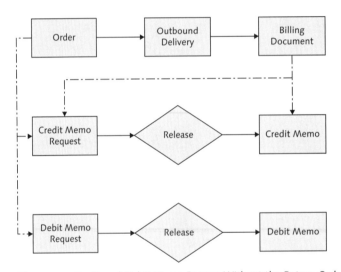

Figure 7.3 Credit and Debit Memo Process Without the Return Order Involved

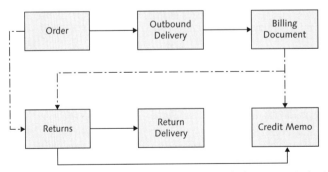

Figure 7.4 Credit and Debit Memo Process with the Return Order Involved

> **Note**
>
> You can use the rejection code to reject a credit or debit memo request line, similar to the application we saw with the return orders.

You can create a debit or credit memo request in SAP ERP using Transaction VA01.

7.1.2 Invoice Correction

The invoice correction request represents a combination of credit and debit memo requests. On one side, credit is granted fully for the incorrect billing item while it's simultaneously debited (automatically created as a debit memo item). The difference represents the final full amount that will be credited to the customer. The invoice correction request must be created with reference to the corresponding billing document (no reference to order or inquiry). When creating an invoice correction request, the items are automatically duplicated; this means that for every item in the billing document, a second item is created. The resulting item categories must have opposite positive and negative values.

First, all credit items are listed, followed by the debit memo items. The reference to the corresponding billing document is created when you specify the preceding document and the preceding item. The credit memo can't be changed. The corresponding debit memo item, however, can be updated according to new characteristics, for example, new pricing, and change in quantity. You can delete the credit and debit memos in pairs, and unchanged pairs of items can be deleted all at once in this way.

> **Note**
>
> The quantity difference is used when a customer complaint is being processed due to a certain amount of damaged or substandard goods. The system corrects the quantity to be billed via the debit memo request.

As shown in Table 7.1, the invoice correction request is used for quantity difference to indicate the difference of 2 pieces with the actual quantity being 8 and the original quantity 10 pieces. The invoice correction request is also used to manage price differences as shown in Table 7.2. In this example, debit memo items are created for $10 and $8. But the net value in both examples for Tables 7.1 and 7.2 is $20.

Billing Document	Invoice Correction Request
Item A: 10 EA $100	Item A Credit Memo Item 10 pieces @ $10 Debit Memo Item 10 pieces @ $10 8 pieces @ $10 Net Value $20

Table 7.1 Quantity Difference

Billing Document	Invoice Correction Request
Item A: 10 EA $100	Item A Credit Memo Item 10 pieces @ $10 Debit Memo Item 10 pieces @ $10 10 pieces @ $8 Net Value $20

Table 7.2 Price Difference

Returns and reversal sales transaction transition from return delivery to inventory and also from return delivery to finance through a movement type. In this section, we've looked at the sales as a return process initiator and capture of the information to start the returns process. The return delivery configuration helps determine the logistics movement of the goods and the inventory management transition. The sales document, credit memo, and debit memo can be used as an approval vehicle or workflow prior to the issue of credit or debit financial transaction.

In the next section, we'll discuss the impact of bringing goods into the inventory using the goods movement and the corresponding financial posting.

7.1.3   Inventory Movement

The sales return or reversal allows you to acknowledge the return, and return delivery allows you to bring the goods back into the inventory, in terms of directing where the goods needs to be received. The following steps show you how to bring the part into inventory:

▶ The returned material/goods are received into inventory by post goods issue (PGI), return delivery, or goods receipt (GR). The PGI or GR reflects the returned goods in the inventory movement or allocates it on a movement type in the system. Movement types are configured through MATERIALS MANAGEMENT •

INVENTORY MANAGEMENT AND PHYSICAL INVENTORY • MOVEMENT TYPE (as shown in Figure 7.5).

▶ Configure the control reason for the movement of the returned goods through Transaction OMBS. Here you configure the reason for movement for the return delivery.

▶ Setting up a movement type involves the following three-step configurations:

   ▶ Recording reason for goods movements

   ▶ Definition of movement type

   ▶ Set up of subscreen for account assignment

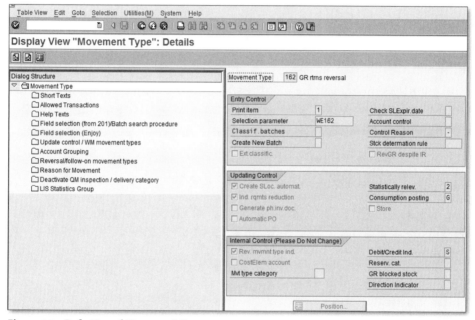

Figure 7.5 Definition of Movement Type

Figure 7.5 displays the different folders for the definition of movement types, including Short Texts, Allowed Transactions, Help Texts, and so on. Within the Short Text folder, you can maintain the short description to represent the purpose of the movement type. Within the movement type details, check the Rev. Mvmnt Type Ind. for the reverse movement type ,and enter S (Debit) in the Debit/Credit Ind. as shown in Figure 7.5

Figure 7.6 displays the transactions allowed with the movement type. This helps set up the system so you can restrict the use of transactions specific to the movement type.

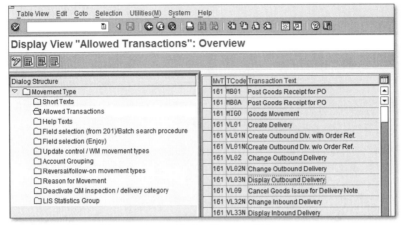

Figure 7.6 Allowed Transactions with the Movement Type

This helps your define the fields that are optional or required for a particular transaction, as shown in Figure 7.7. The CUSTNAME field represents the name of the customer that is returning the goods, while the WEMPF field represents the return reason code.

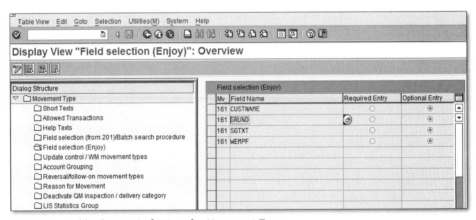

Figure 7.7 Field Selection Definitions for Movement Types

Figure 7.8 shows the update control with the inventory movement. By checking the Quantity checkbox, you indicate that the movement type updates the quantity into the material master stock, and within the Mvt indicator column, you can select the select the value L for goods movement with delivery (return delivery) and B for purchase orders (vendor returns). The movement indicator indicates the reference document used for movement.

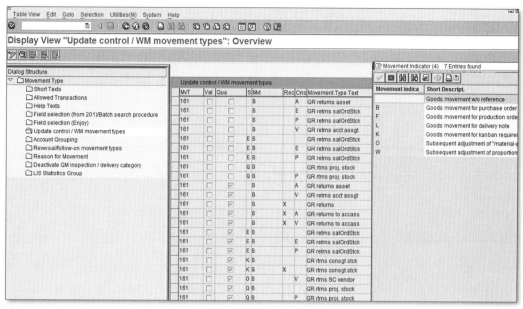

Figure 7.8 Update Control with Inventory Movement

Figure 7.9 displays the configuration settings for Account Grouping. This configuration is also done in the movement type definition. To configure the details for the account grouping, select the account grouping information on the left side of the movement type definition as shown earlier in Figure 7.5. The Val. String column (Valuation String) shown in Figure 7.9 refers to a posting string that is used for automatic account determination. Through the allocation of a posting string or valuation string to a movement type, the SAP ERP system automatically determines the general ledger accounts to be updated in the event of a goods movement. The TEKey (Transaction Event) key is also used in combination with the posting key to determine the general ledger account to be posted to during goods movement. The Check Acct. Assignment checkbox shown in Figure 7.9 indicates that the account assignment information should be used for account determination if account assignment is provided at the item level during goods movement. If this checkbox isn't selected, then the account assignment at the line item level in the goods movement is ignored, and only automatic account determination data is used to determine general ledger accounts during goods movement.

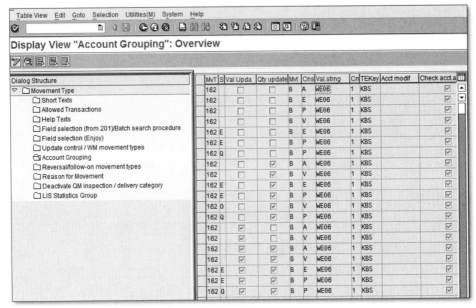

Figure 7.9 Configuration Settings for Account Grouping

Figure 7.10 illustrates mapping the reversal transaction for the original movement type. In other words, if you want to correct the return movement type, you can use this movement type to correct it. So for movement type 161, you can use 101 and 162.

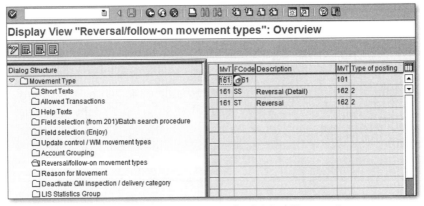

Figure 7.10 Mapping of Reversal Movement to the Original Movement

The movement type enables the system to find predefined posting rules that help the system determine the account postings (stock and consumption) and the stock fields in the master data records. A goods movement can be a goods receipt, goods issue, or transfer posting of materials. You can set up the debit or credit indicator with the movement type definition. This configuration step can be accessed using Transaction OMJJ. Based on the material moving out or into the inventory, the movement type is configured as credit (H) or debit (S), respectively. In the same transaction, you also map the transaction codes that are allowed for the movement type.

The last step in the configuration for the movement type is recording the reason for goods movement. This is again subdivided into two configuration steps:

▶ Control reason

▶ Reason for movement

To define the reason for movement, you can use MATERIALS MANAGEMENT • INVENTORY MANAGEMENT AND PHYSICAL INVENTORY • MOVEMENT TYPES • RECORD REASON FOR GOODS MOVEMENTS.

In the control reason, you define whether the field for reason for movement is optional, suppressed, or required. This is defined for every movement type as shown in Figure 7.11.

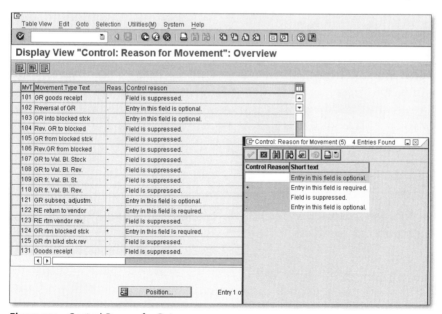

Figure 7.11 Control Reason for Return

After the reason for movement is defined as required or optional, you can define the possible reasons for movement in the next subsection called Reason for Movement. Here you define all possible reason for movements for every movement type as shown in Figure 7.12.

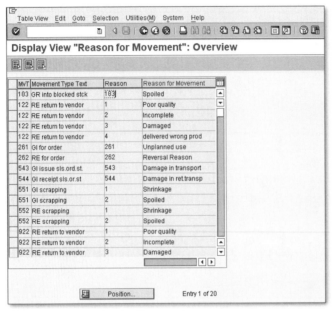

Figure 7.12 Reason for the Movement

Figure 7.12 shows the Reason for Movement screen, which captures the movement type for returns. The reasons for movement types include Incomplete, Damaged, Poor Quality, Damaged in Transport, and so on. The reason for movement is used in inventory reporting for goods movements. So the company can run reports to identify goods movements, for example, those goods damaged in transport for a particular month.

7.1.4 Inventory Posting and Accounting

In this section, we'll discuss the accounts posted for inventory recording and their importance to reverse logistics.

The return or reversal transaction has the following two effects for accounting and goods movement in SAP ERP:

▶ The reverse document increases the transaction credit figures by the same amount because it was debited early with the forward movement or sale.

▶ After posting the document, the SAP system reverses the previous forward movement document generated.

These transactions have both sales and inventory account postings. Let's discuss these postings in detail.

Let's use the example of the material document that was created against a return delivery that brought material into the unrestricted stock of the company. Figure 7.13 shows the material document for inventory movement type 653. As you see in this figure, an account assignment was used to indicate posting to general ledger account 893015.

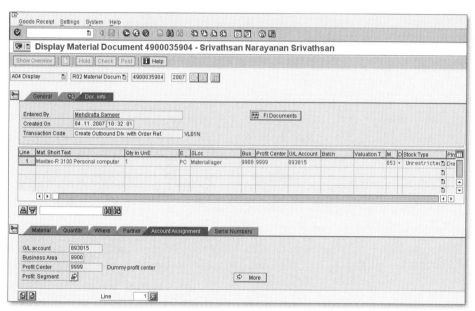

Figure 7.13 Account Assignment Information in a Material Document for Movement Type 653 to Bring Returns Stock into the Company

The material document displayed in Figure 7.13 is attached to an accounting document that can be viewed by clicking on the FI Documents button at the top of the screen. After you click the button, you'll get a popup that shows all of the relevant financial documents for the transaction. You then select the accounting document and display it to view the general ledger accounts that were used for this transaction. The accounting document details with the account information are shown in Figure 7.14.

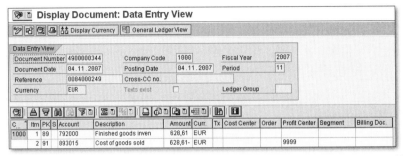

Figure 7.14 Accounting Document Details for Goods Movement Using Movement Type 653

Now let's look at how the SAP ERP system determined the two general ledger accounts displayed in the accounting document. The first account is 792000, which was determined using the following steps:

▶ The valuation class is determined from the material master accounting view. The valuation class for the material used in this example is 7920, as shown in Figure 7.15. The accounting view of the material master can be displayed using Transaction MM03 and selecting the accounting view.

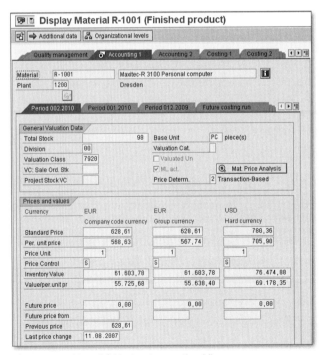

Figure 7.15 Material Master Accounting View

▶ SAP determines the general ledger accounts for posting in the accounting document based on the configuration in Transaction OMWB. This can be accessed using MATERIALS MANAGEMENT • VALUATION AND ACCOUNT ASSIGNMENT • ACCOUNT DETERMINATION • ACCOUNT DETERMINATION WITHOUT WIZARD • CONFIGURE AUTOMATIC POSTINGS. Here you can select the Account Assignment button to view details of the accounts. In the next screen, SAP ERP shows the list of all accounting procedures for which account determination is setup. The procedure used for inventory posting is BSX. If you select the procedure and double-click on the procedure in the next screen, you need to enter the chart of accounts. After you enter that detail, SAP displays all of the accounts relevant for all valuation classes as shown in Figure 7.16. The account used for the valuation class 7920 is 792000.

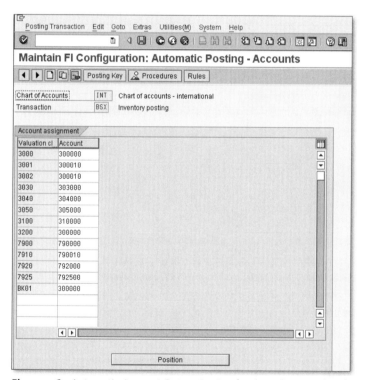

Figure 7.16 Automatic Account Determination for the Valuation Class for Inventory Posting

▶ The other account that was determined in the accounting document was 893015, which was determined based on the account assignment details at the item level of the inventory posting as discussed before. The SAP ERP system used this information, even though there were accounts set up in the account determination procedure, because the Check Account Assignment checkbox was selected in the account grouping section for movement type 653 of procedure GBB, which is used for offsetting the entry for inventory posting, as shown in Figure 7.17. This indicates that SAP ERP should use the information from the account assignment in the transaction and not the account determination.

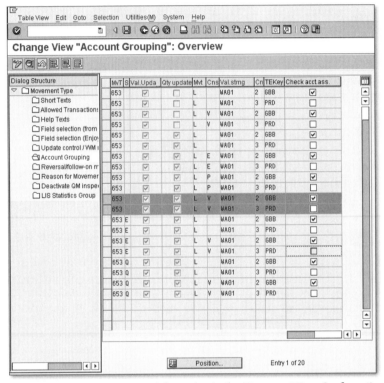

Figure 7.17 Account Grouping Information in the Movement Type Configuration

Now that we understand how the general ledger accounts are determined in goods movements let's review how pricing works in SAP ERP.

7.1.5 Returns: Pricing

Pricing is critical to all sales documents, such as sales orders, because pricing is used to determine the selling price to a customer. There are several other conditions such as discounts and taxes that are taken into account before the final price is determined. Of course, customer pricing is calculated based on the cost of the material. The standard cost of the material is carried forward through the pricing condition into the pricing procedure of the sales document and then to the financial documents, for example, invoices, credit documents, and debit documents.

From the sales point of view, when you issue a credit memo request or credit for return, accounting needs to be set up to capture the value transacted in the revenue account and customer account. The typical financial postings during invoice creation for returns are credit customer account and debit revenue.

Figure 7.18 shows the typical pricing procedure (SAP standard delivered with all conditional value listed). The revenue account is determined automatically through the account key mapped for each condition type in the pricing procedure. You can configure this by going to SALES AND DISTRIBUTION • BASIC FUNCTION • PRICING • PRICING CONTROL SUB MENU to configure the pricing for returns. Figure 7.18 displays the typical pricing procedure, which can be accessed through Transaction V/08. The account key is part of the revenue account determination. Figure 7.19 displays the configuration step for the account key along with other conditions for determining the general ledger account.

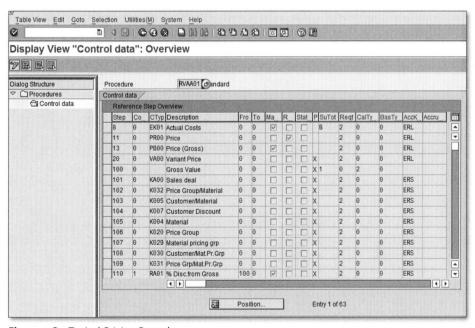

Figure 7.18 Typical Pricing Procedure

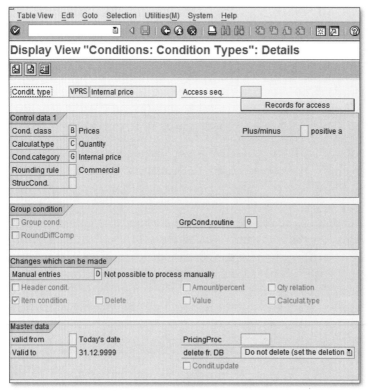

Figure 7.19 Display of Condition Type VPRS

The material cost is carried over to the sales document through the pricing procedure condition value. The pricing procedure has other condition values that capture the sales value, for example, the List Price, Discount, Freight, and so on.

Accounts Posting

The reconciliation account for the customer is defined under the customer master record. To update this field, you can use SAP AREA MENU • LOGISTICS • SALES AND DISTRIBUTION • MASTER DATA • BUSINESS PARTNER. Figure 7.20 displays the customer master maintenance screen. Select the appropriate partner (sold to or payer), click Create or Change, select the Accounting Information view from the company code data, and press Enter. This takes you to the accounting information for updating the reconciliation account (general ledger) for the customer.

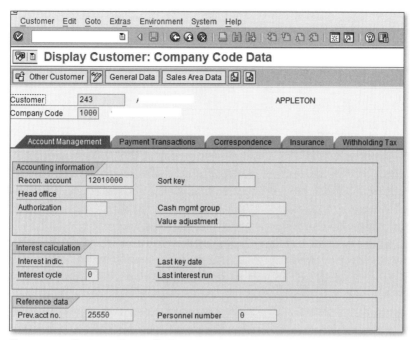

Figure 7.20 Customer Reconciliation Account

So, to summarize the inventory to accounting and finance touch point:

▶ The material valuation links to the possible account.

▶ The material cost is carried over through the pricing condition.

▶ The account key links the general ledger to revenue recognition.

▶ The customer account ties to the reconciliation account.

The revenue account is determined automatically through the account key mapped to each condition type in the pricing procedure you saw in the previous section. The account key (ERL, ERS) is part of the revenue account determination. The account key and the other conditions are mapped for determining the general ledger account.

Following the return delivery note creation, the goods are available for goods receipt. When the return delivery notes are post goods issued, they trigger a material document for goods receipt. You can also choose to manually receive the returned goods, but you lose the tracking capability. The material document creates an accounting entry for the inventory posting. The inventory posting is determined based on the movement type, and this is tallied with the sales reversal for the customer account and the selling pricing condition. The standard cost of the material is carried forward through the condition, and sales prices are posted to the appropriate account.

7.2   Summary

In this chapter, you've developed a good understanding of the accounting impact of the inventory movement returned goods and the credit issue to the customer. We discussed how the goods movements are linked to the general ledger accounts using account determination, as well as the configuration of the movement types and their importance for reverse logistics. We also discussed pricing in SAP ERP and how pricing conditions are created and maintained. Ensuring proper accounts are posted for goods movements and also sales documents is key to recapturing value in reverse logistics so be sure to configure your accounts and postings carefully.

7.3   Contributor

Rajen Iyer is a business- and technology-focused professional, with demonstrated success in systems implementation, support, product development, and leading successful teams. He is a thought leader in system solutions and author of two SAP PRESS books: *Effective SAP SD* and *Implementing SAP BusinessObjects Global Trade Services.* He has also authored several in-depth papers and best practices articles, and is a regular speaker in conferences.

8   Conclusion

Reverse logistics improves the bottom line of a company by providing additional sources of supply and revenue. In this chapter, we'll summarize the different aspects of reverse logistics and the implementation of SAP software to enable reverse logistics.

8.1   What You've Learned

The goal of this book has been to provide insight into reverse logistics processes and describe how the corresponding tools and processes are configured or implemented in SAP ERP. Having read this book, you should have a solid understanding of reverse logistics processes and be able to configure and use it in a supply chain process, providing enormous benefits. Just like all of the other processes, SAP ERP software can be used either in the configuration, technical development, or enhancement to improve your experience as a user and ultimately enable faster and more efficient processes. This book has also provided you with knowledge that will enable you to optimize your company's reverse logistics processes by reviewing your SAP ERP system's configuration and objects and modifying them to meet your requirements better. This book also provides a strong foundation for implementing SAP ERP transactions in your company's reverse logistics processes.

To improve the reverse logistics performance, focus should be on the following areas of reverse logistics:

- Cycle time of every process in reverse logistics
- Transaction cost of performing reverse logistics processes
- Elimination of waste in resources (materials, labor, and system resources)
- Improving user experience in the system when executing transactions for reverse logistics processes
- Clear identification and segregation of materials for storing and processing in reverse logistics
- Proper accounting and different pricing for materials that are not in new condition

In the following sections, we'll visit each of these bullet items and discuss how to improve these areas in more detail with the system objects and process details provided in each chapter of the book.

8.1.1 Cycle Time

Cycle time is the time it takes to complete one cycle of any process. For example, the order cycle time provides the time it takes from the returning entity's initial contact to completion of the order creation, including providing the return authorization to the returning entity. Reverse logistics refers not just to the return of the physical materials but also to the return of services for credit. Order cycle time is applicable to the return of services as well.

To improve cycle time of the reverse logistics processes, you need to break down the processes into smaller subprocesses and analyze how they are executed and recorded in the system. Improvements can eliminate transactions that don't add value or combine multiple transactions into one if possible.

> **Example**
>
> In the SAP system, you can issue the goods in a source plant and automatically perform the receipt in the destination location. Doing this eliminates the need to perform the receipt transaction, which saves time, money, and transaction costs as long as there is a scenario in the reverse logistics chain in the company. Similarly, you can locate transactions where the data is copied from previous transactions or from documents created as a result of previous processes and copy them to the subsequent document, thereby eliminating the need to enter the data again. This also saves time, money, and transaction costs.

> **Example**
>
> In another example, a semiconductor company provides credit to its customers and accepts all returns from the customer. The company provides credit to the customers before the inspection in the warehouse. The company receives the returns in its local depots that are closer to the customer and then moves the returned stock in a consolidated shipment later to a central processing center. One of the improvements done to their receiving and processing of returns is to change their SAP ERP configuration to allow the returns movement type to post the returned inventory into the unrestricted inventory instead of returns stock. To do this, the company created a custom movement type that posted the stock into unrestricted stock and also posted the corresponding accounting entries as needed. This improved the returns receipt process by eliminating the returns stock to unrestricted stock movement that is performed in SAP ERP typically after inspection. Movement type configuration is discussed in detail in Chapter 2, Returns.

Major improvement is executed in the initial order entry area, where all information for returns and repair is obtained from the returning entity. By streamlining or automating the initial order entry process, the company can establish an excellent base for reverse logistics, which will ensure success in returns and refurbishment.

Another area where cycle time can be dramatically improved is the warranty claim processing in reverse logistics, which was discussed in Chapter 5, Warranty Claim Processing. Using the validation/substitution rule (VSR) to validate the entitlement of the customer and also to check the warranty provided by the vendor during the warranty claim document processing allows return or no return decisions to be made much earlier than if the decision had to be made manually. Using the warranty claim document with the VSR can provide companies with a dream reverse logistics solution that is completely automated with the customer service representative asking the customer questions that provide answers to all organizations involved in reverse logistics. Based on the answers provided by the customer, the SAP ERP system can make decisions such as the return-to location and can provide a return document to be emailed to the customer automatically by the system based on the information stored in the customer master in SAP ERP. This functionality also can be extended to customers by providing a website that they can use to enter the details of the return that, in turn, interacts with the SAP ERP system and provides the customer the output needed to ship the returned product immediately.

8.1.2 Cost of Performing Reverse Logistics

The costs of performing reverse logistics include the labor and time. To reduce the cost of processing reverse logistics, you can automate processes and enable the system to make automatic decisions wherever applicable. For example, you could use the warranty claim document and VSR as described in Chapter 4, Customer Paid Repair, to automate the returns process. Even if a material is accepted for returns and is going to be refurbished, the system can identify a suitable vendor to create a subcontracting purchase order for and return the material to.

Another area where you can reduce cost in the system is in identifying a return that needs to be scrapped. You can either scrap at the returning entity or at a location close to the returning entity that has scrap capability. Being close to the returning entity eliminates additional transportation costs, thereby reducing the cost of the overall reverse logistics process. Using the rules engine in combination with the VSR checks allows you to perform the return location determination automatically.

The logic for identifying the ideal scrapping location can be incorporated into the VSR checks, which eliminates transportation costs. Chapter 4 discussed the use of the rules engine and the VSR checks in detail.

Reducing touch points in the network before the product reaches the final location also saves on transaction and transportation costs. Creating a custom returns delivery type and a custom shipment type might help in consolidating the returns stock to be shipped between locations in the company. The configuration of the returns delivery type and shipment type was discussed in Chapter 2, Returns. Reducing data input in transactions also reduces the cost and time for reverse logistics. For example, using copy controls to pass data from the source documents to the subsequent documents, such as from the returns sales order to the returns delivery to the returns shipment, eliminates the need to enter the data manually, which may result in human errors and loss of time and money. As described in Chapter 2, the use of the copy control configuration effectively helps lower the cost of transactions and reduces transaction errors. The goal of the company should be to obtain the necessary information for a return from the returning entity and find the fastest, most cost efficient way to enable the subsequent processes.

8.1.3   Elimination of Waste and Automation

When you automate transactions, you prevent wasted system resources and labor time. Although automation costs money, automating high-volume transactions that are performed often, such as order entry or return delivery creation, saves money. In SAP ERP, there are ways to automate transactions, such as the return delivery creation, by creating a batch job that can run in preset intervals and create deliveries as needed. This eliminates the need to create the deliveries manually, and in so doing, you eliminate wasting time and resources on this activity. Similarly, batch jobs can be used to automate shipment creation and also post goods issuing of a delivery to bring the returns stock into the company.

Automation capabilities are available in all reverse logistics processes and are discussed for return order and delivery in Chapter 2, for subcontracting purchase orders in Chapter 3, and also for warranty claims and the rules engine in Chapter 5.

8.1.4   User Experience

User experience is enhanced by providing system screens that require minimum data entry and screens that are sequenced correctly to minimize confusion for the user as he enters data. Throughout this book, we've discussed SAP ERP tools that can either eliminate complex transactions or minimize data entry, enabling a better user experience when performing transactions for reverse logistics. Enabling RF (Radio Frequency) programs or transactions can also help the users perform transactions faster and more smoothly in the warehouse.

Example

Extending reverse logistics transactions and providing them on a portal on the web allows users to enter the data in a much more user-friendly screen than entering the data in SAP ERP directly. For example, you can extend the return order capability into a web and provide the customer service representative or the end customer with questions that are much more meaningful, such as "Was the material being returned ever opened from the package?" or "Was the material being returned ever used?" This is better than providing a SAP ERP field name, such as Material Status, and expecting the customer service representative or the customer to enter the data by viewing all possible data options for this field. To optimize reverse logistics processes for users, identify configurations that will help make transactions easier and provide screens and data that users can understand easily. Work with your SAP portal team to help convert transactions in the initial reverse logistics process or transactions that are used by the vendors or the customers directly such as sending ASNs (advance shipping notifications) or entering a returns order.

8.1.5 Identification and Segregation of Material for Reverse Logistics

One of the important requirements to perform reverse logistics efficiently in a company is to identify returns, repairs, and refurbished material throughout the process. Failing to properly identify these materials along the process could cause serious issues such as mixing the defective material with new material. To identify materials, you can use different stock types such as blocked stock and returns in SAP ERP, and you can configure your movement types to identify the returns stock type upon receipt into the company. Chapter 2 discusses the movement type configuration in detail and how it can be changed to meet your company's needs. This configuration also helps in accounting to ensure that proper accounts are credited and debited when a return is posted, which is discussed in the next section. Physical identification using material identifiers and segregation within the warehouse is also a requirement that needs to be met to ensure effective reverse logistics. How you identify a defective material in the SAP ERP system as well as physically using a material identifier is a decision that forms the backbone of the SAP ERP system design for reverse logistics. As discussed extensively in Chapter

1, Reverse Logistics, you can use a copy of the new material number and include a suffix, you can create a new material number, you can use different fields in the material master such as material groups and material statuses, and you can use batch management to identify the defective material. Depending on the decision you choose, you'll need to align your warehouse processes and all of the outputs that are printed/emailed for the defective material in all reverse logistics processes. Custom development is needed in an amount determined based on the decision made previously. For simplicity, a lot of the discussion in this book assumes that you chose to use a material number with a suffix or a new material number to identify the defective material, but you can also use the information in this book for your reverse logistics even if you chose batch management or material status to identify defective material.

8.1.6 Accounting in Reverse Logistics

Proper valuation of defective, repaired, and refurbished material is crucial for the success of reverse logistics processes in every company. In SAP ERP, you have several options to valuate these materials that depend on how the defective material is represented in the SAP ERP system as discussed in the previous section. If you chose a new material number or a material number with suffix to identify defective, repaired, or refurbished material, then you can use the material master cost to clearly indicate that the cost of the material isn't the same as new material. You can also use split valuation to classify materials based on status or batches to valuate materials differently. Split valuation was discussed in detail along with batch management in Chapter 6, Serial Number Management in Reverse Logistics.

Pricing the returns order and the order to sell refurbished products also requires accounting that is a little bit different from selling new material. We discussed pricing in Chapter 7, Finance in Reverse Logistics, in detail.

Customer paid repair processes discussed in Chapter 4 describe how to set up repair orders that can handle the complete repair from a customer, including receiving the return material, identifying the repair stock, and capturing the costs of the service order and the purchase order used for repairing the product. Materials sent by the customer are generally classified as nonvaluated materials because the materials are owned by the customer and the customer pays only for the service of repairing the product. Capturing all of the repair costs associated with the repair order is important to provide the accurate quote and bill the customer for the repair.

8.2   Organizational Impact on Reverse Logistics

As we touched on in Chapter 1, there are several organizations in a company, and all of them are responsible for performing their actions or functions to ensure that reverse logistics is smoothly executed.

8.2.1   Order Management

The configuration of order type, item category, and schedule line category are important to ensure return orders can be processed effectively. In addition, the movement type assignment to the schedule line category plays an important part in determining how the subsequent processes in SAP ERP are going to be handled in processing the returns. In addition to processing returns using a returns order, the order management users are process repair orders that need configuration enabled to perform internal and external repair. An important aspect of reverse logistics that makes it complex is the fact that there are many data needs at several points of the process that need to be provided by the returning entity. The data collected from the returning entity needs to be stored in SAP ERP in different documents, such as warranty claim, return order, repair order, and return delivery. There are several enhancements that can be activated or developed to improve the order entry efficiency, including activating the workflow to approve or reject a return order. In addition, using a warranty claim to check for the validity of the returned product's warranty, either by checking against the serial number or the reference order, ensures that the customer is credited only for the parts under warranty.

To monitor the efficiency of the reverse logistics process and to control the returns, the following reports help in the order-management processes:

- Cycle time of returns from order to credit
- Return for replacement versus return for credit
- Returns to refurbishment

Order-management processes need to integrate with other processes, such as finance for crediting the customer and calculating pricing for repairs, and also integrate with logistics for receiving and processing returns. For repairs, the order-management processes integrate with procurement to quote a price for repair based on the cost or repair quoted by external vendors for a subcontracting situation. For internal repairs, production orders need to be created and integrated with repair orders to roll up the costs to quote the correct price to the customer. This was discussed in detail in Chapter 4.

8.2.2 Planning

The planning team impacts reverse logistics by providing input to the most important decision in reverse logistics: whether to accept the return. Planning makes this decision based on the current inventory in addition to other factors such as version of the material, capability of the vendor to repair the product, and so on. Key enhancements in SAP ERP that can help the planning process to increase the efficiency of reverse logistics include automatically determining the inventory levels and deciding whether to return or scrap the part based on a set level of inventory of the material. These automatic decisions can be handled by the rules engine using the VSR checks in combination with some custom development that can make decisions based on inventory data stored in SAP ERP. This was discussed in Chapter 5 in detail with examples from customer cases. The planning data relevant for every material gets stored in the material master in one of the many available fields to store the preset stock level manually, or the calculation for the stock level can be done based on a percentage of the inventory available automatically. In addition to this, data planning also stores the repair capability of the material based on the input from the vendor in one of the material status fields that allow the custom enhancement to make decisions automatically at the time of the product return. The material master input from planning was discussed in Chapter 1.

8.2.3 Logistics

Key responsibilities of logistics include receiving and processing the returns, shipping the products for repair to the vendor, and shipping components of the products on a need basis. Automatic processing for logistics in the reverse logistics area includes determination of the return location (based on the repair or scrap capability of the return location) and the proximity to the returning entity. Proximity is important to save on transportation costs, which is of prime importance for the logistics team. Enhancements in this area include automatic determination of the return location using either the Global Available to Promise (GATP) interface with SAP SCM and SAP ERP, or using the rules engine VSR capabilities in combination with custom development. The rules engine and VSRs were discussed in Chapter 5 along with the warranty claim. Proximity to the returning plant is determined by classifying all of the plants in the network based on their reverse logistics capabilities. These capabilities include but are not limited to the internal repair process and equipment available, scrap capability, cleaning capability, and assembly and disassembly capability. If maintained in the plant master, this information can help identify the destination location by obtaining the information of the returning entity and comparing that data to the locations available in SAP ERP to find a suitable location that can perform the necessary operation based on the type of return.

Example of Return Location Determination Automatically

In a car manufacturing company, the network contains several plants with different capabilities, such as a depot storing spare parts inventory, a repair plant capable of rework and repair of the front assembly, a scrap plant capable of handling hazardous materials, and so on. When a customer in Germany returns a steering wheel that didn't perform at the expected level, the planning team in the company determines that the wheel can be repaired and sold again. So, the company initiates a return and expects the customer to return the part back to a plant in the network. The customer sends it back to Switzerland because that is the closest location capable of performing this activity. This is determined automatically by a SAP ERP enhancement and the VSRs setup in SAP ERP discussed in Chapter 4. After the destination plant is determined, the order-management team creates a return sales order with Switzerland as the location, so all documentation for the return is provided to the customer with the information of the Switzerland plant in the return-to address.

In addition to the repair and rework capability, logistics also needs incoming inspection capability to process returns and repairs. Logistics makes the determination of the receipt and subsequent process, so it makes the important decisions regarding the system capability and the configuration of the correct movement type needed at the time of return. The movement type configuration determines the type of stock the returns will be posted into, so it ultimately determines how the consequent warehouse processes will be performed.

To price the returned product correctly, the pricing procedures have to be defined when configuring reverse logistics, and they can't be different from the forward logistics pricing. Reverse logistics pricing is based on the condition of the part, and often the returned part (if not in good condition) is valuated at a lower amount compared to the original part cost. Pricing also needs to be controlled via a workflow that gets the necessary approvals from the company managers and allows the reverse logistics process to flow without any stops or gaps.

Determining how a returned part will be identified in the system requires all of the organizations to work together, as discussed in Chapter 1. After a procedure has been identified and has been followed, it can't be changed later easily.

Foreign trade restricts the kinds of products that can be transported between countries, so a good system such as SAP BusinessObjects Global Trade Services or a custom built compliance check system is necessary. If needed, the export and import duties need to be calculated and paid to the governing entity, so the foreign trade system needs to interface with SAP ERP to determine the return part condition and obtain the destination location information.

Service management is another critical process that you need to configure properly to ensure the engineers can return their products back into the network and get accurate credit to pass the credit back to the customer if needed. In terms of interfacing with other processes, service management interacts with almost all of the processes in the company at different points of the internal return. Although the product is returned internally, the subsequent processes need to be executed similarly to external returns to enable returns to be processed and the credit to be given back.

8.3   Additional Resources

There are several resources to learn more about reverse logistics in general and the future of reverse logistics, including information from the Reverse Logistics Association (*www.reverelogisticstrends.com*) and *Reverse Logistics Magazine* (*www.rlmagazine.com*). APICS, which is the Association for Operations Management, also provides updates regarding reverse logistics and the new trends in reverse logistics.

SCM Expert online (*www.scmexpertonline.com*) is also a valuable resource for SAP professionals interested in reverse logistics and has a variety of articles on the topic.

8.4   Reverse Logistics with SAP in the Future

As SAP offers more new products that provide more capabilities in the reverse logistics area, companies can look forward to more functionality within the reverse logistics subprocesses, including repair, entitlement management, and scrap and recycling management.

SAP offers the following capabilities for reverse logistics within its service parts management software:

▶ Warranty management
▶ Claims processing

- Entitlement management
- Returns logistics
- In-house and outsourced repair
- Remanufacturing and refurbishment
- Scrap and recycling management

All of these capabilities are available with the following enterprise applications in SAP:

- SAP Customer Relationship Management
- SAP ERP Operations
- SAP Supply Chain Management
- SAP BusinessObjects intelligence platform
- Combining this with modern SAP SCM technologies, such as RFID, the future of reverse logistics in SAP is bright and continues to expand. This book provides the baseline for implementing and optimizing reverse logistics in SAP, and you can continue to expand these capabilities based on the tools listed above. As more capabilities arrive, it's even more important to have a strong baseline design for reverse logistics that works for all organizations in the company and also serves as a good starting point to implement advance software solutions in SAP.

This book is intended to improve your reverse logistics processes and provide you insights in the world of reverse logistics in SAP ERP. Please contact us if you have any questions or comments. Thank you.

The Author

A native of India, **Srivathsan Narayanan** worked as a manufacturing system engineer after his graduation as a mechanical engineer from Annamalai University in 1994. He began working in SAP R/3 in 1997 in the Materials Management module in India. In 1998, he migrated to the United States and began working as a SAP R/3 consultant. Since then, he has been implementing logistics execution functionalities, including shipping, transportation, and warehouse management. He has worked in projects in different roles such as an implementation team member, functional consultant, and a project manager in different industries such as consumer goods and high tech manufacturing. Srivathsan currently consults through GNAN Corporation, Dreamweavers LLC, and Krypt Inc.

Srivathsan has published papers in SCMExpert online and has presented in the SAP Reporting and Analytics conference in 2007, as well as the SAP Supply Chain Management conference in 2009. His topics included serialization and its impact on reverse logistics, shipping and transportation configuration, and warehouse reporting. Srivathsan lives with his wife and daughter in Milpitas, California.

Index

Substitution, 207
Supplying plant, 135

T

Tasks, 157
Third-party logistics providers (3PL), 38, 124
Transaction, 81, 277, 281
Transaction costs, 151
Transfer order, 105, 106
Transfer requirement, 105

U

Update control, 272
Usage decision, 109
User exits, 231
User experience, 285

V

Validation, 208
Valuation, 151
Valuation string, 273
Vendor consignment, 235
Vendor master, 179
VSR, 114

W

Warehouse Management, 151, 152, 255
Warranty, 213
Warranty claim, 177
    document, 133
Work center, 56, 118
Workflow, 270

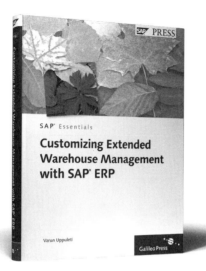

Discover how to customize the Extended Warehouse Management functions of Yard Management, Task and Resource Management, and Value Added Services

Learn how each function integrates with SAP WM

Learn from examples and screenshots detailing EWM configuration, transaction execution, and mobile data entry

Varun Uppuleti

Customizing Extended Warehouse Management with SAP ERP

SAP PRESS Essentials #69

This book will teach users all about the EWM tools in WM. It explains what they are and how and when to use them in your company. The book begins by introducing the EWM tools and explaining how they are structured. From there it moves to the real heart of the book -- how to configure and customize TRM, YM, and VAS. The book also covers possible YM and TRM enhancements, and details the functionality for SCM EWM.

The book is written in a straightforward style with many screen shots and example business cases learned from the author's consulting projects. This is the one resource you need to really understand what is involved in EWM and how you customize it to meet your own business requirements.

226 pp., 2009, 69,95 Euro / US$ 84.95
ISBN 978-1-59229-286-8

>> www.sap-press.com

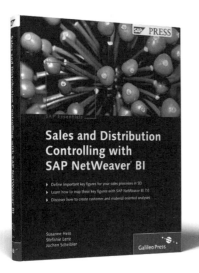

Teaches how to identify and assess key figures for your sales processes in SD

Provides step-by-step instructions for creating customer and material oriented analysis

Contains practical tips on how to create effective, useful data and analysis

Susanne Hess, Stefanie Lenz, Jochen Scheibler

Sales and Distribution Controlling with SAP NetWeaver BI

This book teaches users how to define, evaluate, and report key figures for sales and distribution controlling in SD (SAP ERP 6.0) using SAP NetWeaver BI 7.0. It starts with an overview of essential key figures in SD controlling and explains their business background. From there, it details the sales processes, and provides an overview of how raw data is created. Users learn how to map key figures for business controlling in a business warehouse, and how to use key figures in various analysis tools.

250 pp., 2009, 68,– Euro / US$ 85
ISBN 978-1-59229-266-0

>> www.sap-press.com

Master CTM tools and techniques

Learn advanced planning methods and special modeling techniques

Find valuable tips and best practices from real-life projects

Balaji Gaddam

Capable to Match (CTM) with SAP APO

This is the first book that explains and teaches all of the core functions of SAP's Capable-to-Match (CTM) functionality. This step-by-step guide for configuring CTM, including CTM Master Data selection, Order Selection, CTM Profile maintenance, and CTM configuration, educates readers on the basic aspects of CTM, such as Demand Prioritization, Supply Categorization, Multilevel Inventory, and Production Planning, as well as several advanced topics including CTM planning for Safety Stock, Safety Days of Supply, and Maximum Earliness.

273 pp., 2009, 68,– Euro / US$ 85
ISBN 978-1-59229-244-8

>> www.sap-press.com

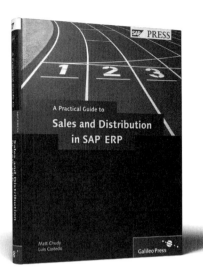

Provides a comprehensive guide to key sales and distribution functions

Teaches how to use Sales and Distribution in SAP ERP in daily processes, including sales, pricing, delivery, transportation, and billing

Includes support and troubleshooting information for common problems and pitfalls

Matt Chudy, Luis Castedo

Practical Guide to Sales and Distribution in SAP ERP

If you use SAP ERP for sales and distribution, this book is a must-have resource that uses a process-driven approach to teach you how to use key sales and distribution functions effectively in your day-to-day processes.
You'll learn how to perform transactions with fewer steps and less effort, and you'll discover how to troubleshoot minor problems and system issues. In addition to the core areas of sales and distribution, you'll also find coverage of more advanced topics such as billing and reporting. And there are several appendices dedicated to quick-reference materials, such as lists of transaction codes and menu paths. If you work with sales and distribution on a daily basis, this guide can help you master the system and work more efficiently.

approx. 425 pp., 69,95 Euro / US$ 69.95
ISBN 978-1-59229-347-6, July 2010

>> www.sap-press.com

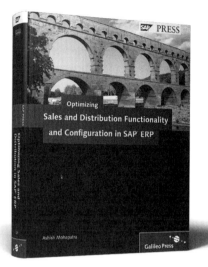

Get the most out of your SAP SD implementation using the step-by-step instructions provided throughout

Discover tips and tricks for using SAP SD to maximize your daily operations

Find useful details about SD-FI integration and reporting/analysis

Up to date for SAP ERP 6.0

Ashish Mohapatra

Optimizing Sales and Distribution Functionality and Configuration in SAP

Whether you're a consultant or project lead, this is the book you need to learn how to configure and use SAP SD to optimize your sales and distribution processes, so you can streamline your business. You'll be able to use SAP SD to fulfill orders and deliver your products and services more effectively, improving performance of the system and getting a better return on investment for your SAP SD implementation. Throughout this book, you'll find tips, step-by-step instructions, and real-world examples to help you understand and optimize your SAP SD implementation.

approx. 500 pp., 69,95 Euro / US$ 69.95
ISBN 978-1-59229-329-2, May 2010

>> www.sap-press.com